Willy Russell
Plays

GW00361386

Blood Brothers; Our Day Out – The Musical; Shirley Valentine; John, Paul, George, Ringo . . . and Bert

'Willy Russell is a dramatist of exceptional warmth and humanity.' *Evening Standard*

Blood Brothers: 'Undoubtedly the most exciting thing to have happened to the English musical theatre in years.' Sheridan Morley, in *Punch*

Our Day Out – The Musical: 'The skill and zest of the show . . . derive from its success in following the adult argument through while preserving all the fun of a story for and mainly played by children . . . I have rarely seen a show that combined such warmth and such bleakness.' Irving Wardle, in *The Times*

Shirley Valentine: 'A simple and brilliant idea . . . the profound and perennial point of the comedy is the problem we seem to have contemplating the idea of a woman alone – in a pub, on a beach, in a restaurant. This is what Shirley learns to combat as she unravels her own sexual and social identity.' *Financial Times*

John, Paul, George, Ringo . . . and Bert: 'The complement of mood and music is perfect, ironic, unsentimentally accurate . . . *John, Paul, George, Ringo . . . and Bert*, the adventurous biographical play about the Beatles at Liverpool's Everyman Theatre, bursts with incisive moments . . . It is a fine piece of work . . . And can Mr Russell write dialogue!' *The Sunday Times*

Willy Russell was born in Whiston, near Liverpool. Leaving school at fifteen, he worked variously as a ladies' hairdresser, warehouseman and girder cleaner until, at the age of twenty one, he returned to education. It was while training to become a teacher that he wrote his first plays for both stage and television. Playground, Keep Your Eyes Down and Sam O'Shanker were premiered at St Katherine's College in 1972. Under the collective title Blind Scouse these were presented later the same year at the Edinburgh Festival Fringe, where they were seen by playwright John McGrath and led to Russell writing *When the Reds*, adapted from an original script by Alan Plater, for the Everyman Theatre, Liverpool (1973). Subsequently he has written *John Paul George Ringo . . . and Bert* (Everyman and Lyric, London, 1974; winner of the *Evening Standard* and London Theatre Critics' Awards for Best Musical), *Breezeblock Park* (Everyman, 1975; Mermaid and Whitehall, London, 1977), *One for the Road* (Contact Theatre, Manchester, 1976; Lyric, London, 1987), *Stags and Hens* (Everyman, 1978; Young Vic, 1983; revised and presented as *Stags and Hens – The Remix*, Royal Court, Liverpool, 2008), *Educating Rita* (RSC Warehouse and Piccadilly, London, 1980, winner of SWET Best Comedy Award), *Blood Brothers* (play version, Merseyside Young People's Theatre Company, 1981), *Blood Brothers* (musical version, Liverpool Playhouse and Lyric, London, 1983; Albery and Phoenix, London, 1988; Music Box, New York, 1993), *Our Day Out* (play version, Everyman and Young Vic, 1983; musical version, Royal Court, Liverpool, 2009), *Shirley Valentine* (Everyman, 1986; Vaudeville, London, 1988, winner of Olivier Award for Best Comedy; Booth Theatre, New York, 1989).

For television he has written *King of the Castle* (BBC, 1973), *Break-In* (BBC, 1974), *Death of a Young Young Man* (BBC, 1974), *Our Day Out* (BBC, 1976), *Lies* (BBC, 1978), *The Daughters of Albion* (ITV, 1979), *Politics and Terror* (ITV, 1980), *The Boy with the Transistor Radio* (ITV, 1980), the *One Summer* series (Channel 4, 1983), *Terraces* (BBC, 1993). Feature films and screenplays include *Educating Rita* (winner of *Evening Standard* Award for Best Screenplay, 1983), *Shirley Valentine* (1989),

Dancin' Thru the Dark (1990), *Blood Brothers* (with Alan Parker, 2006). As a composer Russell has written for the TV series *Connie* and the feature film *Mr Love*, as well as for his own films, *Shirley Valentine* and *Dancin' Thru the Dark*. He wrote music and lyrics for *Blood Brothers* and (with Bob Eaton and Chris Mellor) music and lyrics for *Our Day Out*. With the poets Adrian Henri, Brian Patten and Roger McGough, he wrote and performed *Words on the Run* (1995–97), and with playwright Tim Firth he wrote and performed *In Other Words* (2004) and *The Singing Playwrights* (2004). In 2003 he wrote and recorded the CD *Hoovering the Moon*. His novel *The Wrong Boy* was published by Doubleday in 2000.

Willy Russell
Plays: 2

Blood Brothers

Our Day Out – The Musical

Shirley Valentine

John, Paul, George, Ringo . . . and Bert

Bloomsbury Methuen Drama
An imprint of Bloomsbury Publishing Plc

B L O O M S B U R Y
LONDON · OXFORD · NEW YORK · NEW DELHI · SYDNEY

Bloomsbury Methuen Drama

An imprint of Bloomsbury Publishing Plc

50 Bedford Square	1385 Broadway
London	New York
WC1B 3DP	NY 10018
UK	USA

www.bloomsbury.com

Bloomsbury is a registered trade mark of Bloomsbury Publishing Plc

This collection first published by Bloomsbury Methuen Drama 2016

Blood Brothers book © 1985 by Willy Russell
Lyrics © 1983 Timeact Ltd t/a Willy Russell Music

Our Day Out – The Musical First published in 2011 by Methuen Drama. Reprinted by Bloomsbury Methuen Drama 2015. © Willy Russell 2011. Lyrics copyright © Willy Russell and Bob Eaton 2011

Shirley Valentine © 1988 Willy Russell

John, Paul, George, Ringo . . . and Bert © 2016 Willy Russell

Collection copyright © Willy Russell 2016

Willy Russell has asserted his right under the Copyright, Designs and Patents Act, 1988, to be identified as author of this work.

British Library Cataloguing-in-Publication Data
A catalogue record for this book is available from the British Library.

ISBN:	PB:	978-1-4742-3004-9
	ePub:	978-1-4742-3006-3
	ePDF:	978-1-4742-3005-6

Library of Congress Cataloging-in-Publication Data
A catalog record for this book is available from the Library of Congress.

Series: Contemporary Dramatists

Typeset by RefineCatch Limited, Bungay, Suffolk
Printed and bound in India

Contents

Chronology

1947   Born in Whiston, near Liverpool.

1962   Left school to become a ladies' hairdresser.

1969   Returned to education as a mature student.

1972   *Blind Scouse* premièred at the Edinburgh Festival.
Tam Lin (for children) produced in Liverpool.

1973   *When the Reds*, an adaptation of Alan Plater's play *The Tigers Are Coming – OK?*, produced in Liverpool.
King of the Castle shown on BBC1.

1974   *John Paul George Ringo . . . and Bert* premièred at the Everyman Theatre, Liverpool, transferred to the Lyric Theatre, London; wins the *Evening Standard*'s and London Theatre Critics' Award for Best Musical.
Break-In shown on BBC1.

1975   *Breezeblock Park* premièred at the Everyman Theatre, Liverpool, transferred to the Mermaid Theatre, London (1977) and then to the Whitehall Theatre.
Death of a Young Young Man shown on BBC2.

1976   *One for the Road* premièred (as *Painted Veg and Parkinson*) at the Contact Theatre, Manchester.

1977   *Our Day Out* shown on BBC1.

1978   *The Daughters of Albion* shown on ITV.
Stags and Hens, originally a student piece for Manchester Polytechnic, opens at the Everyman Theatre, Liverpool.
Politics and Terror shown on television.

1979   *Lies* shown on BBC1.

1980   *Educating Rita* commissioned by the Royal Shakespeare Company; wins London's SWET Award for Best Comedy.
The Boy with the Transistor Radio commissioned and shown by ITV.

1983   Film of *Educating Rita*, directed by Lewis Gilbert, starring Michael Caine and Julie Walters; screenplay by Willy Russell nominated for an Academy Award.

Blood Brothers (for which Willy Russell also wrote the music) premièred in Liverpool and transferred to Lyric Theatre, London.

Our Day Out (revised for the stage) produced at the Everyman Theatre, Liverpool, and subsequently the Young Vic Theatre, London.

Awarded an Honorary MA by the Open University.

One Summer shown on Channel 4.

1984   *Stags and Hens* produced at the Young Vic, London.

1986   *Shirley Valentine* first produced at the Everyman Theatre, Liverpool.

1987   *One for the Road* produced at the Lyric Theatre, London.

1988   New West End production of *Blood Brothers*.
Shirley Valentine produced at the Vaudeville Theatre, London.

1989   *Shirley Valentine* nominated for the Tony Award and Drama Desk Award for Best Play and wins the Olivier Award for Best Comedy of the Year.

1990   Screenplay of *Dancing Thru' the Dark*, based on *Stags and Hens*.
Screenplay of *Shirley Valentine*; film directed by Lewis Gilbert, starring Pauline Collins.
Awarded a D.Litt. by Liverpool University.

1993   *Terraces*, in series Scene Drama, shown on BBC1.
Blood Brothers opens on Broadway.

1995   Willy Russell is made a Fellow of Liverpool John Moores University.
Words on the Run, an evening of prose, poetry, song and music, curated with poets Adrian Henri, Brian Patten, Roger McGough and musician Andy Roberts, premieres ahead of a tour of Great Britain.

1996   *Our Day Out* opens at Belgrade Theatre Coventry in a revised stage version.

1997   *Terraces* is broadcast by BBC Schools Television.

1998   Begins work on two novels, one of which would later become *The Wrong Boy*.

2000   *The Wrong Boy* is published by Doubleday to positive reviews and is subsequently translated into fifteen languages.

2001   *Willy Russell and Friends*, an event also featuring Paul McCartney and Adrian Mitchell, is staged at the Everyman Theatre.

2003   *Hoovering the Moon*, an album of fourteen original songs is recorded.
For One Night Only, an evening of comedy, readings and song featuring Willy Russell and Alan Bleasdale, is staged at the Liverpool Playhouse.

2004   *Hoovering the Moon* CD released.
The Singing Playwrights, created in association with Tim Firth, premieres at the Edinburgh Festival.
Willy is made a Companion of Honour at Liverpool Institute of Performing Arts, receiving his award from Sir Paul McCartney.

2007   With Sir Alan Parker, writes the screenplay for the feature-length movie of *Blood Brothers*.

2008   *Stags and Hens: The Remix*, a reworking of the 1978 play, is staged at the Royal Court Theatre, Liverpool, during the city's year as European Capital of Culture.

2009   A new version of *Our Day Out: The Musical* is staged at the Royal Court Theatre, Liverpool, in a production directed by Bob Eaton.

2010   The Menier Chocolate Factory revives *Educating Rita* and *Shirley Valentine*; both productions subsequently transfer to Trafalgar Studios.
The 2009 production of *Our Day Out: The Musical* is revived at the Royal Court Theatre, Liverpool.

2012   *Dancin' Thru the Dark* is released on DVD.

2013   Willy Russell's personal archive is donated to Liverpool John Moores University.

2014   A neon artwork sign, 'Words', commissioned by BBC Radio 4 Front Row, is unveiled in Salford.

2015   The Liverpool Playhouse revival of *Educating Rita* starring Leanne Best and Con O'Neill is the first of many significant productions staged in Britain and abroad on the 35th anniversary of the play's premier.

Willy Russell: Behind the Scenes, an exhibition of materials from the Russell archive housed at Liverpool John Moores University, opens at the Kirkby Gallery.

Introduction

Since their original creation, these plays have had to survive many knocks and much buffeting to make their way in the world. Along with the knocks, they have had to weather well-intentioned 'interpretations', ranging from the bizarre to the bonkers to the downright demented. Very occasionally the works have been the subject of what can only be termed theatrical butchery. Although the law of copyright seeks to protect the author and his play, there are still those who are quite prepared to test just how much elasticity there is in that rule of copyright – hence, the Korean production of *Blood Brothers* in which the action was 'reconceived', re-set in the 1950s and given a military setting against the backdrop of the Korean war. Closer to home, was the German production of *Blood Brothers* in which the inspired producers elected simply to abandon my score and lyrics and to fill the gaps instead with tracks by The Rolling Stones! The first of my plays to be translated and performed abroad was *John, Paul, George, Ringo . . . and Bert* or as it had somehow become by the time it had opened in Mexico, *John, Paul, George and Ringo*. Having been deemed superfluous by the producer, Bert and his side of the narrative was simply dumped and dropped from the Mexican proceedings!

Thankfully, even this kind of cavalier mangling and casual vandalism did not cause any lasting damage and, I'm delighted to say, the plays/musicals continue to be widely produced.

Nevertheless, these works are undoubtedly the product of the age in which they were written, an age in which, for example, it was still possible (and many even thought it likely) that the men who had once been The Beatles would eventually put their differences behind them, regroup and astound us even further with the breathtaking audacity of their combined genius.

In days such as those, days when songs were distributed in the form of vinyl discs, books were not yet electronic, telephones were still bolted to walls, when setting down lines such as these involved ink, ribbon and the bash and clatter of metal typewriter keys, when lattes and pilates were a gobbledygook yet to be foisted, Apple was just a record label, tablets were things you took for ailments and a bank was a place where you put your money to keep it safe, in those days, the world of theatre into which I was fortunate enough to step was, for a young writer, a very different world than it is today.

Let us not be golden-ageist here and fall prey to the soft sentimental clutch and warm hug of nostalgia in which the nowadays are a celebrity-plagued, dumbed-down, morally bankrupt, X-Factored hell while the past becomes a soft-focus pioneering, shawl-wearing, all-caring sugar-swapping, neighbour-helping lost Eden. The different age of which I write also had its fair share of social horrors – slum housing (both old and new), the stigma of illegitimacy, routine racism, sexism, homophobia, production-line monotony, spiralling inflation, cultural imperialism, economic decline . . . the Osmonds!

In the mid-1970s the area of Liverpool known as the Dingle was probably still best known for being the birthplace and home to Richard Starkey – one of the many Starkeys who came from the Dingle but the only one to metamorphose into Ringo Starr, the only drummer with whom Paul McCartney, John Lennon and George Harrison were able to forge any kind of lasting musical relationship.

By the 1980s, with riots on the streets of Merseyside and memories of Ringo beginning to fade, the Dingle and its well-defined neighbouring areas of Warwick Street, Wellie Road, Granby, Lodge Lane and Upper Parly became collectively known as Toxteth.

Myth has it that, dispatched to film the kick-off in the streets, a hapless southern TV reporter, knowing nothing of the true local topography, took his cue from the official road sign, referring in his bulletin that night and identifying the scene of the riots as being Toxteth. Other broadcasters and newspapers followed suit, dubbing the Liverpool unrest the 'Toxteth Riots' and thereby establishing a place name that up to that time, locals had rarely, if ever, used but subsequently have never been able to shake off.

In 1973, when the Dingle was still the Dingle, I was a young teacher at the newly formed Shorefields School. At the stroke of a pen, someone in Whitehall had decreed that four very disparate schools, spread over three very tribally separate sites should coalesce into one single comprehensive school. Thus, Dingle Vale Boys (amongst whose alumni was one Richard Starkey) joined Dingle Vale Girls, Tocky Tech and Wellington Road to become the singular Shorefields Comprehensive.

Someone at Whitehall must have been having a laugh; that same year a similar stroke of a pen had instigated ROSLA, the raising of the school leaving age whereby children who had been led to believe that they would be free to quit school on attaining the age of fifteen, would now have to endure their education until reaching the age of sixteen.

Unsurprisingly, this led to a significant number of kids being somewhat pissed off – especially those who had already deemed it a pointless waste of time to be forced to attend school at all, yet alone to have to stay on until virtual adulthood!

For reasons that were never explained I, a mere probationary teacher, was given responsibility for a number of the classes in which these disgruntled victims of the system were expected to do little more than kill the extra time they'd been given. I had some sympathy with the plight of these unfortunate ROSLA souls. Having myself been a reluctant, rebellious, truculent and often truanting pupil, I recognized the deadening mix of frustration and apathy that now greeted me daily as a teacher, while I was expected to teach a humanities curriculum and somehow engage and stimulate these reluctant minds with distant geographies, ancient histories and all kinds of global phenomena that would, even had I been graced with the gifts of David Attenborough, still have been met with glazed-eyed, gob-gaping disinterest.

In the staff room I tried to raise with the more senior staff, who bore the responsibility for designing and instituting this curriculum, how best we were supposed to ignite the vital spark of interest in these kids if what we were starting out with was so culturally remote; might it not be a better idea, I ventured, if we were to begin with *their* lives, *their* culture, sparking interest and engagement via the specificity of *their* lives and then broadening out, opening up to the rest of the world, to wider history? I was brusquely reminded that as a probationary teacher my job was to teach what I was told to teach and to stick to the curriculum which had been assembled by minds much more experienced, attuned and qualified than mine.

And I tried. I went back to one of my classes and, as the curriculum prescribed, told everyone to open their books and pay attention to the passage dealing with the staple diet of the Bora Indian of the Amazon Basin. And then, faced with the prospect of another double period of passive hostility and a shared sense of just having to doggedly crawl against the clock and get through it all, I closed the book, sat down at my desk, put my feet up, stared out towards the window and in the same voice, with the same accent and words that the kids used amongst themselves, I started to speak the story of Billy and Icky . . .

'*Two little fifteen year old scals from the Dingle who hadn't been near no school for three months now la an' they weren't gonna go neither cos school was just like shit an' who'd wanna waste his time with the dickheads divs an homos? But then Billy said, "We've gotta go back in – today!" Icky looked up, disgusted, "What?" Billy nodded, "If we wanna go to Sugarloaf Mountain, we'll have to go in". Icky laughed, "Sugarloaf what?" Billy frowned. There are some things you don't laugh about. He turned and fixed Icky with his gaze, daring him to risk laughing again as he repeated, "Sugarloaf Mountain." Icky just nodded this time, pretending he knew what Billy was talking about. Icky did a lot of that with Billy. "Oh. Okay then", was all that Icky said*'.

I carried on in a similar vein, busking most of it but encouraged, even inspired by the level of attention and concentration on the faces of kids whose usual mask of surly resentment had fallen away, replaced now by a rapt and eager alertness as they soaked up Billy and Icky's antics and mounting dilemma. Even though I was making up the tale on the hoof I instinctively knew that I was now responsible both to the kids in the tale and the kids to whom the tale was being told. I knew I had to treat these lives seriously. The same instinct understood that seriousness of purpose is no reason to close the door on comic possibility and I exploited to the full both the intentional and unintentional comic strain in the character of Icky, a willing performing Fool to Billy's sombre feral Lear. The kids in the class loved it. And oh how I loved it that they loved it and was thrilled as they laughed joyously and fretted openly for the fate of the characters in this story that came directly from their world, from them – flawed and even doomed they may be but these all too recognizable characters were, for them, heroes.

We never got back to the curriculum. I serialized the story of Billy and Icky for all my ROSLA classes, some of which had now swelled to include notorious serial truants who, like the characters in the story, hadn't been inside school for months but had now been persuaded back by their mates' re-telling passages of this saga of Billy and Icky. I later learnt that some of the kids selectively creeping back to the classes weren't even on the Shorefields register!

Despite the kids' enthusiasm for these storytelling sessions I found myself starting to question what I was up to, agonizing as to whether what I was really doing was denying them education and, instead, merely entertaining them. It was to be some years yet before I was to learn that there is nothing 'mere' about entertainment and that the tendency to apply that pejorative prefix is largely the preserve of those who are singularly incapable of ever entertaining anything or anyone.

Concluding that on balance and despite my own misgivings, the storytelling sessions were at least ones in which the ROSLA classes were engaged, I carried on with the tale of the two Dingle scallies forced to flee the city and to try and live in the alien environment of wildest Wales where the parenting that each of them has been denied is belatedly given to them. That Kidder, their potestial saviour is ultimately revealed to be the one type of human being that Billy and Icky most profess to hate – a male homosexual – is one of those twists of storytelling fate that never failed to shock and stun those classroom listeners every bit as much as it stunned the story's central pair. Kidder? They'd come to love Kidder . . . and now he was a . . . he was . . . was . . . a . . .

Watching these kids, many of whom undoubtedly shared with Billy and Icky this deep, ingrained, knee-jerk prejudice, listening to them in the classroom, wrestling with the dilemma that the story had now thrown them, seeing them try to square their previous benign, loving and admiring view of Kidder with what they now had to think of him, I started to get the beginning of a sense that if this was what 'merely' entertaining the kids meant, then perhaps

we weren't doing too bad after all. Years after I'd left teaching it
was not uncommon for me to be confronted in a pub or street or
restaurant by some strapping and sometimes fearsome looking
thirty-something who would turn out to be one of the ex-kids
from those ROSLA classes, addressing me still as 'Sir' and
eagerly recalling those classes which featured the exploits of
Billy and Icky. No ex-pupil ever stopped me to recall and
remember the dietary preference of the Bora Indian of the Amazon
basin.

Each term the ROSLA kids became less and less as each of their
birthdays finally rolled around, freeing them from further schooling
and allowing them to go out into the world, get a job, make some
money. This could still be done in this different age, when the
factories and the foundries and the car plants and the docks still had
some life left in them along with capacity to absorb fresh-from-
school youngsters whose only qualification, a willingness to work,
was the only one required.

I still had other classes to teach, younger classes made up of kids
who seemed to see the purpose of school and education and who
would happily get on with their work while I sat at my desk quietly
getting on with marking.

Or not. Because as well as being a teacher I was on my way to
becoming a writer. And in the old Dingle Vale Boys building, at the
teacher's desk in a classroom where former pupil Richard Starkey
had also sat, I was busy writing, apparently marking pupils' work
but in truth, quickly scribbling, trying to set down, before the bell,
the latest scene in the work I'd been commissioned to write for the
Liverpool Everyman Theatre.

I'd already had the great good fortune of seeing some work
professionally produced – a half hour play for the BBC, an
adaptation of an Alan Plater play for the Everyman and a one-act
pub show for Vanload, the Everyman's five-piece guerilla group of
actors charged with the splendidly well-intentioned but potentially
life-shortening mission of taking theatre out of the theatre and
presenting it instead in some of the toughest, roughest, Merseyside
pubs and clubs in which hardened and dedicated drinkers had
miraculously managed to survive, flourish and happily live their

lives thus far without any concern whatsoever for the complete lack
of theatre in those lives.

Having paid my own community-commitment dues with the play
I'd written for Vanload, I'd now been asked by the Everyman's
director (and brilliant de facto producer), Alan Dossor, to write a
new, full-length musical play, scheduled for a four-week run at the
Everyman. In terms of the theatrical then and now could there be a
more revealing half sentence than those last few lines? A young,
semi-experienced, part-time writer/full-time teacher was being
offered a four-week run of a new play at one of Britain's principle
regional theatres.

Such was the theatrical landscape at that time that this situation
was not unique to Liverpool or the Everyman. Throughout Britain
theatres were, to a greater or lesser extent, embracing the notion
that including new plays in the repertoire did not necessarily create
mass audience-desertion and certain death at the box office. Indeed,
some of those theatres had already begun to discover that by
presenting new plays they were beginning to attract a wider, younger,
non-traditional   theatregoing   audience   without   significantly
alienating their existing loyal patrons. The opportunity and
possibility that had come about for me in Liverpool was being
replicated up and down the country with writers being
commissioned and produced in Devon and Scotland, the North
East, in Hull and Stoke and Nottingham and Leeds, in Wales and
Leicester, Scarborough, Sheffield, Lancaster, Manchester, in just
about every British large town and city, all of this happening and,
in large part made possible, because theatre was the beneficiary
of a much more benign political attitude towards the arts in
general.

The Arts Council of the time was happy to invest faith and finance
and to put it as directly as possible into the hands of those who
practised rather than the hands of those later appointed (it seemed)
to create layer upon layer of mediation, bureaucracy and
administration between the funders and the funded. In this now
long-gone age there was, simply, an atmosphere of greater trust, of
collaboration even. And a marked result of this was that theatres and
directors were at much greater liberty to take the kind of risk that the
Everyman and Alan Dossor took when they commissioned a part-

time, barely-proven playwright to write a show about the four most famous sons of Merseyside.

Today's aspirant young playwright might reasonably assume that given the paucity of the theatrical dues I'd paid up to that time this as yet to be written new work of mine would be premiering in the theatre's studio where, as is so often the practice today, the young playwright could have the opportunity of seeing his or her work tried out and tested in a safer smaller space than the main stage. But in the very different theatrical landscape of which I write, the Liverpool Everyman and indeed, almost every comparable theatre in the country could make no distinction between 'main' and 'studio' because there was, simply, gloriously, terrifyingly, just 'the stage' – the one big, gaping stage where nothing can be hidden, no bets hedged, no quarter given, where faults and flaws are instantly and ruthlessly exposed for the sham and the fudge, the fatal over-reaching or failure of nerve that they undoubtedly are. On the page, in the rehearsal room, in the bijou intimacy of the studio theatre the small deceits, fledgling errors of the playwright and his play can be overlooked, go undetected, be generously disguised by the wisdom, skill and talent of his or her collaborators. So too, in the confines of a studio space, can this work be generously indulged by an audience that in its very compactness and intimacy seems always to become a much more benign, tolerant and forgiving beast than it would ever be when watching the same work played out in the unforgiving auditorium upstairs.

When Alan Dossor gave me the responsibility for what would be on the Everyman stage between May and June 1974 he offered no safety net, not for me, not for himself. There was no literary department at the theatre, no dramaturge, literary manager or script editor. There was no process in which I had to consult, pitch, be mentored, developed, group-critiqued, supported, mediated, nurtured; between the man whose task was to write the play and the man whose task was to direct it there was nothing. Although the creation and presentation of new work was at the core of the Everyman's operation, it would be many years still before the business of coming up with new plays would become the 'new writing' fetish of today in which, with no doubt the very best of intentions, layer upon layer of advice and help has been wedged between the one who writes the play and the one who stages it.

In the days when I was still half-teacher, half-playwright my longing, my dream was that I would somehow find a way to become not just a semi-dramatist but a fully fledged, full-time playwright. I didn't hate teaching. Rather than see it as some restrictive yoke, I appreciated that my teacher's salary paid the bills and for a young married man with his first child on the way there was no way that I could give that up and expect our small family to be entirely dependent upon the unpredictable, intermittent rewards that had thus far flowed from my pen. I continued to teach with, I thought, good grace and humour. To anyone who cared to look more deeply, however, it must have been obvious that my heart was not involved in the way it should be if you're going to be the kind of teacher that the kids at Shorefields deserved. Mrs King was one such teacher. One who cared to look more deeply. And one day in the staff room, she looked at me and said:

'*You're not enjoying it any more are you?*'
'*What?*' I countered, defensive.
'*Teaching*', she smiled.

Dorothy King and her Progress Class was something of an institution at Shorefields. Many of Dorothy's fellow staff openly attested to the belief that she should be *in* an institution! Progress Class was the euphemistic gossamer draped across the shoulders of what had formerly been known as the remedial unit, providing classes and individual tuition to kids who, for whatever reason, were having difficulty keeping up in those regular classes where the Bora Indian, on their diet of maize, continued to flourish. Along with those who needed to catch up on, say, lessons missed because of illness, the Progress Class became the repository for every don't-know-what-to-do-with kid in the school, those who today would be identified as dyslexic, hyperactive, dyspraxic, attention-deficient etc. Mrs King welcomed them all without distinction; disturbed, dyslexic, delinquent, it didn't matter, she just saw kids who needed a certain kind of mothering calm and gave them that in spades. In return the kids would do anything for her. Having heard her talking to a fellow member of staff one spring morning, lamenting how no one had thought to bring in flowers to brighten up the classroom a group of the kids, out at lunchtime, found themselves in nearby Princes Park. And seeing the display of spring flowers newly planted by the council ground staff, all of whom had now gone off to lunch. . . .

When Mrs King got back from her own lunch and opened the Progress Class door she was met with a clutch of proud and smiling faces barely visible beyond the mounds of lilies, pansies, snapdragon and gladioli that now festooned the classroom.

The day that she confronted me in the staff room and persuaded me to acknowledge that I wasn't overjoyed to be doing the kind of teaching I was, Dorothy King suggested that I go and work in her department. Having heard of the work I'd done with the ROSLA kids she rightly believed that I'd be a much more effective teacher and find far more reward if I worked in the less curriculum-controlled world of the Progress Class. I accepted and within days was working alongside a woman guided not by an educational orthodoxy or rigid philosophy but by the innate goodness that dictated that every child no matter how difficult or damaged was worthy of her care and attention.

She was also, it must be said, one tube stop short of barking – a fact that only seemed to endear her more to the kids in her charge, all of whom probably recognized in her apparent eccentricity, the kind of whizz-bang, stoned nuttiness that is so often the state of childhood and which Dorothy King, despite her years, still seemed to possess.

Sometimes this was manifested in sudden and wild enthusiasms that resulted in sketchily planned and barely organized events – one such being the Progress Class day out. The events of that day inspired what would eventually become the film and then stage play *Our Day Out* (the latest version included here in the form of *Our Day Out: The Musical*). In the fictional version I chose to portray the trip as involving just one school coach but on the actual day, Mrs King had commissioned three double-decker buses, destined to transport and deposit almost two hundred excited inner city Liverpool kids on the unsuspecting coastal towns of North Wales. It was no surprise when the school's top brass hastily deputed one of their number to join the trip in the hope that his presence might curb some of the potential excess and anarchy that might be unleashed in the absence of such a counterbalance. The putting together of these two archetypal opposing forces meant that for an alert, fledgling playwright the day itself offered up the arc of a story that was just begging to be made into a play.

It was while I was still working in the Progress Class that *John Paul George Ringo . . . and Bert* opened at the Everyman. My ambition for the play had been that it would find an audience and be deemed to have been worthy of its place in that season's programme. It mattered to me that the work would also be considered worthy of the stunning talent that was brought to the production by the extraordinary group of young actors and musicians that was then the permanent company.

Amongst that company there was, to my ears anyway, never any talk of things such as the West End, transfers or awards; such talk would undoubtedly have been regarded then as some kind of betrayal of the radical, politically challenging, theatrically subversive ethos that the theatre embodied. Nobody involved in the production approached the opening night with thoughts beyond the four-week run on Hope Street. If we thought about the future at all, I suppose the actors looked to the start of the next season's work, beginning in September under the directorship of Jonathan Pryce, who was taking over while Alan Dossor spent a year with the BBC learning to develop and make films. Barbara Dickson, Terry Canning and Bobby Ash, the show's musicians, were no doubt thinking of resuming their regular club gigs, one-night stands and recording. As I got into a taxi the night of the show's opening, I was thinking less about the night itself and whether the now very overdue woman sat beside me would make it to the end of the show without going into labour. Having just narrowly been turned down by the BBC for a Fellowship which would have secured me the full-time writer status I so craved, perhaps I was also thinking that like it or not, I'd just have to plough on and continue in the dual role of half-teacher/half-playwright for the foreseeable future.

Then the house lights began to fade, the stage lights came up, the straggle of musicians who'd been busking Beatles songs outside the theatre now made their way along the aisles, clambered up and took their places onstage as the band; a single spot picked out George Costigan as Bert, the evening's narrator, and Bernard Hill, Trevor Eve, Philip Joseph and Anthony Sher walked on as John Lennon, Paul McCartney, George Harrison and Ringo Starr. Nothing was ever quite the same again.

Willy Russell
December 2015

Blood Brothers

Blood Brothers was first performed at the Liverpool Playhouse on 8 January, 1983, with the following cast:

Mrs Johnstone (*Mother*)	Barbara Dickson
Mickey	George Costigan
Eddie	Andrew C. Wadsworth
Sammy	Peter Christian
Linda	Amanda York
Mrs Lyons	Wendy Murray
Mr Lyons	Alan Leith
Narrator	Andrew Schofield
Chorus	Hazel Ellerby
	Eithne Brown
	David Edge

Directed by Chris Bond
Designed by Andy Greenfield
Musical Director Peter Filleul
(Presented by arrangement with Bob Swash)

Blood Brothers was subsequently presented by Bob Swash, by arrangement with Liverpool Playhouse, at the Lyric Theatre, London, on 11 April 1983, with the following cast:

Mrs Johnstone (*Mother*)	Barbara Dickson
Mickey	George Costigan
Eddie	Andrew C. Wadsworth
Sammy	Peter Christian
Linda	Kate Fitzgerald
Mrs Lyons	Wendy Murray
Mr Lyons	Alan Leith
Narrator	Andrew Schofield
Chorus	Hazel Ellerby
	David Edge
	Ian Burns
	Oliver Beamish

Directed by Chris Bond and Danny Hiller
Designed by Andy Greenfield
Musical Director Richard Spanswick

The setting for *Blood Brothers* is an open stage, with the different settings and time spans being indicated by lighting changes, with the minimum of properties and furniture. The whole play should flow along easily and smoothly, with no cumbersome scene changes. Two areas are semi-permanent – the Lyons' house and the Johnstone house. We see the interior of the Lyons' comfortable home but usually only the exterior front door of the Johnstone house, with the 'interior' scenes taking place outside the door. The area between the two houses acts as communal ground for street scenes, park scenes, etc.

Act One

The Overture comes to a close.

Mrs Johnstone (*singing*)   Tell me it's not true, Say it's just a story.

The **Narrator** *steps forward.*

Narrator (*speaking*)   So did y' hear the story of the Johnstone twins?
    As like each other as two new pins,
    Of one womb born, on the self same day,
    How one was kept and one given away?
    An' did you never hear how the Johnstones died,
    Never knowing that they shared one name,
    Till the day they died, when a mother cried
    My own dear sons lie slain.

The Lights come up to show a re-enactment of the final moments of the play – the deaths of **Mickey** *and* **Edward**. *The scene fades.*

Mrs Johnstone *enters with her back to the audience.*
    An' did y' never hear of the mother, so cruel,
    There's a stone in place of her heart?
    Then bring her on and come judge for yourselves
    How she came to play this part.

The **Narrator** *exits.*

Music is heard as **Mrs Johnstone** *turns and walks towards us. She is aged thirty but looks more like fifty.*

Mrs Johnstone (*singing*)   Once I had a husband,
    You know the sort of chap,
    I met him at a dance and how he came on with the chat.
    He said my eyes were deep blue pools,
    My skin as soft as snow,
    He told me I was sexier than Marilyn Monroe.

And we went dancing,
We went dancing.
Then, of course, I found
That I was six weeks overdue.
We got married at the registry an' then we had a 'do'.
We all had curly salmon sandwiches,
An' how the ale did flow,
They said the bride was lovelier than Marilyn Monroe.
And we went dancing,
Yes, we went dancing.
Then the baby came along,
We called him Darren Wayne,
Then three months on I found that I was in the club again.
An' though I still fancied dancing,
My husband wouldn't go,
With a wife he said was twice the size of Marilyn Monroe.
No more dancing
No more dancing.
By the time I was twenty-five,
I looked like forty-two,
With seven hungry mouths to feed and one more nearly due.
Me husband, he'd walked out on me,
A month or two ago,
For a girl they say who looks a bit like Marilyn Monroe.
And they go dancing
They go dancing
Yes they go dancing
They go . . .

An irate **Milkman** (*the* **Narrator**) *rushes in to rudely interrupt the song.*

Milkman   Listen love, I'm up to here with hard luck stories; you own me three pounds, seventeen and fourpence an' either you pay up today, like now, or I'll be forced to cut off your deliveries.

Mrs Johnstone   I said, I said, look, next week I'll pay y' . . .

Milkman   Next week, next week! Next week never arrives around here. I'd be a rich man if next week ever came.

Mrs Johnstone   But look, look, I start a job next week. I'll have money comin' in an' I'll be able to pay y'. Y' can't stop the milk. I need the milk. I'm pregnant.

Milkman   Well, don't look at me, love. I might be a milkman but it's got nothin' to do with me. Now you've been told, no money, no milk.

The **Milkman** *exits.*

Mrs Johnstone *stands alone and we hear some of her kids, off.*

Kid One (*off*)   Mam, Mam the baby's cryin'. He wants his bottle. Where's the milk?

Kid Two (*off*)   'Ey Mam, how come I'm on free dinners? All the other kids laugh at me.

Kid Three (*off*)   'Ey Mother, I'm starvin' an' there's nothin' in. There never bloody well is.

Mrs Johnstone (*perfunctorily*)   Don't swear, I've told y'.

Kid Four (*off*)   Mum, I can't sleep, I'm hungry, I'm starvin' . . .

Kids (*off*)   An' me, Mam. An' me. An' me.

Mrs Johnstone (*singing*)   I know it's hard on all you kids,
　　　But try and get some sleep.
　　　Next week I'll be earnin',
　　　We'll have loads of things to eat,
　　　We'll have ham, an' jam, an' spam an'
　　　(*Speaking.*) Roast Beef, Yorkshire Puddin', Battenberg Cake,
　　　Chicken an' Chips, Corned Beef, Sausages, Treacle Tart,
　　　Mince an' Spuds, Milk Shake Mix for the Baby:

There is a chorus of groaning ecstasy from the **Kids**.

Mrs Johnstone *picks up the tune again.*
　　　When I bring home the dough,
　　　We'll live like kings, like bright young things,
　　　Like Marilyn Monroe.
　　　And we'll go dancing . . .

Mrs Johnstone *hums a few bars of the song, and dances a few steps, as she makes her way to her place of work –*

Mrs Lyons' *house. During the dance she acquires a brush, dusters and a mop bucket.*

Mrs Lyons' *house where* **Mrs Johnstone** *is working.*

Mrs Lyons *enters, carrying a parcel.*

Mrs Lyons   Hello, Mrs Johnstone, how are you? Is the job working out all right for you?

Mrs Johnstone   It's, erm, great. Thank you. It's such a lovely house it's a pleasure to clean it.

Mrs Lyons   It's a pretty house isn't it? It's a pity it's so big. I'm finding it rather large at present.

Mrs Johnstone   Oh. Yeh. With Mr Lyons being away an' that? When does he come back, Mrs Lyons?

Mrs Lyons   Oh, it seems such a long time. The Company sent him out there for nine months, so, what's that, he'll be back in about five months' time.

Mrs Johnstone   Ah, you'll be glad when he's back won't you? The house won't feel so empty then, will it?

Mrs Lyons *begins to unwrap her parcel.*

Mrs Lyons   Actually, Mrs J, we bought such a large house for the – for the children – we thought children would come along.

Mrs Johnstone   Well y' might still be able to . . .

Mrs Lyons   No, I'm afraid . . . We've been trying for such a long time now . . . I wanted to adopt but . . . Mr Lyons is . . . well he says he wanted his own son, not someone else's. Myself, I believe that an adopted child can become one's own.

Mrs Johnstone   Ah yeh . . . yeh. Ey, it's weird though, isn't it. Here's you can't have kids, an' me, I can't stop havin' them. Me husband used to say that all we had to do was shake hands and I'd be in the club. He must have shook hands with me before he left. I'm havin' another one y' know.

Mrs Lyons   Oh, I see . . .

Mrs Johnstone   Oh but look, look it's all right, Mrs Lyons, I'll still be able to do me work. Havin' babies, it's like clockwork to me. I'm back on me feet an' workin' the next day y' know. If I have this one at the weekend I won't even need to take one day off. I love this job, y' know. We can just manage to get by now –

She is stopped by **Mrs Lyons** *putting the contents of the package, a pair of new shoes, on to the table.*

Jesus Christ, Mrs Lyons, what are y' trying to do?

Mrs Lyons   My God, what's wrong?

Mrs Johnstone   The shoes . . . the shoes . . .

Mrs Lyons   Pardon?

Mrs Johnstone   New shoes on the table, take them off . . .

Mrs Lyons *does so.*

Mrs Johnstone (*relieved*)   Oh God, Mrs Lyons, never put new shoes on a table . . . You never know what'll happen.

Mrs Lyons (*twigging it; laughing*)   Oh . . . you mean you're superstitious?

Mrs Johnstone   No, but you never put new shoes on the table.

Mrs Lyons   Oh go on with you. Look, if it will make you any happier I'll put them away . . .

Mrs Lyons *exits with the shoes.*

Music is heard as **Mrs Johnstone** *warily approaches the table and the* **Narrator** *enters.*

Narrator   There's shoes upon the table an' a joker in the pack,
The salt's been spilled and a looking glass cracked,
There's one lone magpie overhead.

Mrs Johnstone   I'm not superstitious.

Narrator   The Mother said.

Mrs Johnstone   I'm not superstitious.

Narrator   The Mother said.

The **Narrator** *exits to re-enter as a* **Gynaecologist**.

Mrs Johnstone   What are you doin' here? The milk bill's not due 'till Thursday.

Gynaecologist (*producing a listening funnel*)   Actually I've given up the milk round and gone into medicine. I'm your gynaecologist. (*He begins to examine her.*) OK, Mummy, let's have a little listen to the baby's ticker, shall we?

Mrs Johnstone   I was dead worried about havin' another baby, you know, Doctor. I didn't see how we were gonna manage with another mouth to feed. But now I've got me little job we'll be OK. If I'm careful we can just scrape by, even with another mouth to feed.

The **Gynaecologist** *completes his examination.*

Gynaecologist   Mouths, Mummy.

Mrs Johnstone   What?

Gynaecologist   Plural, Mrs Johnstone. Mouths to feed. You're expecting twins. Congratulations. And the next one please, Nurse.

The **Gynaecologist** *exits.*

Mrs Johnstone, *numbed by the news, moves back to her work, dusting the table upon which the shoes had been placed.*

Mrs Lyons *enters.*

Mrs Lyons   Hello, Mrs. J. How are you?

There is no reply.

(*Registering the silence*) Mrs J? Anything wrong?

Mrs Johnstone   I had it all worked out.

Mrs Lyons   What's the matter?

Mrs Johnstone   We were just getting straight.

Mrs Lyons   Why don't you sit down.

Mrs Johnstone   With one more baby we could have managed. But not with two. The Welfare have already been on to me. They say I'm incapable of controllin' the kids I've already got. They say I should put some of them into care. But I won't. I love the bones of every one of them. I'll even love these two when they come along. But like they say at the Welfare, kids can't live on love alone.

Mrs Lyons   Twins? You're expecting twins?

The **Narrator** *enters.*

Narrator   How quickly an idea, planted, can take root and grow into a plan.
     The thought conceived in this very room
     Grew as surely as a seed, in a mother's womb.

The **Narrator** *exits.*

Mrs Lyons (*almost inaudibly*)   Give one to me.

Mrs Johnstone   What?

Mrs Lyons (*containing her excitement*)   Give one of them to me.

Mrs Johnstone   Give one to you?

Mrs Lyons   Yes . . . yes.

Mrs Johnstone (*taking it almost as a joke*)   But y' can't just . . .

Mrs Lyons   When are you due?

Mrs Johnstone   Erm, well about . . . Oh, but Mrs . . .

Mrs Lyons   Quickly, quickly tell me . . . when are you due?

Mrs Johnstone   July he said, the beginning of . . .

Mrs Lyons   July . . . and my husband doesn't get back until, the middle of July. He need never guess . . .

Mrs Johnstone (*amused*)   Oh, it's mad . . .

Mrs Lyons   I know, it is. It's mad . . . but it's wonderful, it's perfect. Look, look, you're what, four months pregnant, but you're only just beginning to show . . . so, so I'm four months pregnant and I'm only just beginning to show. (*She grabs a cushion and arranges it beneath her dress.*) Look, look. I could have got pregnant just before he went away. But I didn't tell him in case I miscarried, I didn't want to worry him whilst he was away. But when he arrives home I tell him we were wrong, the doctors were wrong. I have a baby, our baby. Mrs Johnstone, it will work, it will if only you'll . . .

Mrs Johnstone   Oh, Mrs Lyons, you can't be serious.

Mrs Lyons   You said yourself, you said you had too many children already.

Mrs Johnstone   Yeh, but I don't know if I wanna give one away.

Mrs Lyons   Already you're being threatened by the Welfare people. Mrs Johnstone, with two more children how can you possibly avoid some of them being put into care? Surely, it's better to give one child to me. Look, at least if the child was with me you'd be able to see him every day, as you came to work.

Mrs Lyons *stares at* **Mrs Johnstone**, *willing her to agree.*

Please, Mrs Johnstone. Please.

Mrs Johnstone   Are y' . . . are y' that desperate to have a baby?

Mrs Lyons (*singing*)   Each day I look out from this window,
I see him with his friends, I hear him call,
I rush down but as I fold my arms around him,
He's gone. Was he ever there at all?
I've dreamed of all the places I would take him,
The games we'd play, the stories I would tell,
The jokes we'd share, the clothing I would make him,
I reach out. But as I do. He fades away.

The melody shifts into that of **Mrs Johnstone** *who is looking at* **Mrs Lyons**, *feeling for her.* **Mrs Lyons** *gives a half smile and a shrug, perhaps slightly embarrassed at what she has revealed.* **Mrs Johnstone** *turns and looks at the room she is in. Looking up in*

*awe at the comparative opulence and ease of the place. Tentatively
and wondering she sings*

Mrs Johnstone   If my child was raised
      In a palace like this one,
      (He) wouldn't have to worry where
      His next meal was comin' from.
      His clothing would be (supplied by)
      George Henry Lee.

Mrs Lyons *sees that* **Mrs Johnstone** *might be persuaded.*

Mrs Lyons (*singing*)   He'd have all his own toys
      And a garden to play in.

Mrs Johnstone   He could make too much noise
      Without the neighbours complainin'.

Mrs Lyons   Silver trays to take meals on.

Mrs Johnstone   A bike with *both* wheels on?

Mrs Lyons *nods enthusiastically.*

Mrs Lyons   And he'd sleep every night
      In a bed of his own.

Mrs Johnstone   He wouldn't get into fights
      He'd leave matches alone.
      And you'd never find him
      Effin' and blindin'.
      And when he grew up
      He could never be told
      To stand and queue up
      For hours on end at the dole
      He'd grow up to be

Mrs Lyons
Mrs Johnstone   } (*together*)   A credit to me

Mrs Johnstone   To you.

Mrs Johnstone   I would still be able to see him every day,
wouldn't I?

Mrs Lyons   Of course.

Mrs Johnstone   An' . . . an' you would look after him, wouldn't y'?

Mrs Lyons (*singing*)   I'd keep him warm in the winter
And cool when it shines.
I'd pull out his splinters
Without making him cry.
I'd always be there
If his dream became a nightmare.
My child.
My child.

There is a pause before **Mrs Johnstone** *nods.* **Mrs Lyons** *goes across and kisses her, hugs her.* **Mrs Johnstone** *is slightly embarrassed.*

Oh. Now you must help me. There's so much . . . I'll have to . . . (*She takes out the cushion.*) We'll do this properly so that it's thoroughly convincing, and I'll need to see you walk, and baby clothes, I'll have to knit and buy bottles and suffer from piles.

Mrs Johnstone   What?

Mrs Lyons   Doesn't one get piles when one's pregnant? And buy a cot and . . . Oh help me with this, Mrs J. Is it in the right place? (*She puts the cushion back again.*) I want it to look right before I go shopping.

Mrs Johnstone (*helping her with the false pregnancy*)   What you goin' the shops for? I do the shopping.

Mrs Lyons   Oh no, from now on I do the shopping. I want everyone to know about my baby. (*She suddenly reaches for the Bible.*)

Music.

Mrs J. We must make this a, erm, a binding agreement.

Mrs Lyons *shows the Bible to* **Mrs Johnstone**, *who is at first reluctant and then lays her hand on it.*

The **Narrator** *enters. A bass note, repeated as a heartbeat.*

Narrator   In the name of Jesus, the thing was done,
    Now there's no going back, for anyone.
    It's too late now, for feeling torn
    There's a pact been sealed, there's a deal been born.

Mrs Lyons *puts the Bible away.* **Mrs Johnstone** *stands and stares as* **Mrs Lyons** *grabs shopping bags and takes a last satisfied glance at herself in the mirror.*

Mrs Johnstone   Why . . . why did we have to do that?

Mrs Lyons   Mrs J, nobody must ever know. Therefore we have to have an agreement.

Mrs Johnstone *nods but is still uncomfortable.*

Mrs Lyons   Right, I shan't be long. Bye.

Mrs Lyons *exits.*

Mrs Johnstone *stands alone, afraid.*

The heartbeat grows in intensity.

Narrator   How swiftly those who've made a pact,
    Can come to overlook the fact.
    Or wish the reckoning to be delayed
    But a debt is a debt, and must be paid.

The **Narrator** *exits.*

As the heartbeat reaches maximum volume it suddenly stops and is replaced by the sound of crying babies.

Two nurses appear, each carrying a bundle. A pram is wheeled on.

The nurses hand the bundles to **Mrs Johnstone** *who places them, smiling, into the pram. Making faces and noises at the babies she stops the crying. The babies settled, she sets off, wheeling the pram towards home.*

Various debt collectors emerge from her house to confront **Mrs Johnstone**.

Catalogue Man   I'm sorry love . . . the kids said you were at the hospital. (*He looks into the pram.*) Ah . . . they're lovely, aren't they? I'm sorry love, especially at a time like this, but, you are twelve weeks behind in your payments. I've got to do this, girl . . .

Finance Man   Y' shouldn't sign for the bloody stuff, missis. If y' know y' can't pay, y' shouldn't bloody well sign.

Catalogue Man   Look, if y' could give me a couple of weeks' money on this I could leave it.

Mrs Johnstone *shakes her head.*

Finance Man   Y' shouldn't have signed for all this stuff, should y'? Y' knew y' wouldn't be able to pay, didn't y'?

Mrs Johnstone (*almost to herself*)   When I got me job, I thought I would be able to pay. When I went in the showroom I only meant to come out with a couple of things. But when you're standing there, it all looks so nice. When y' look in the catalogue an' there's six months to pay, it seems years away, an' y' need a few things so y' sign.

Finance Man   Yeh, well y' bloody well shouldn't.

Mrs Johnstone (*coming out of her trance; angrily*)   I know I shouldn't, you soft get. I've spent all me bleedin' life knowin' I *shouldn't*. But I do. Now, take y' soddin' wireless and get off.

Catalogue Man   Honest love, I'm sorry.

Mrs Johnstone   It's all right lad . . . we're used to it. We were in the middle of our tea one night when they arrived for the table. (*She gives a wry laugh.*)

Catalogue Man   Ah well as long as y' can laugh about it, eh, that's the main thing isn't it?

The **Catalogue Man** *exits.*

Mrs Johnstone (*not laughing*)   Yeh.

Other creditors continue to enter the house and leave with goods.

Mrs Johnstone *watches the creditors. The babies begin to cry and she moves to the pram, rocking it gently as she sings, as if to the babies in the pram.* (*Singing*)

Only mine until
The time comes round
To pay the bill.
Then, I'm afraid,
What can't be paid
Must be returned.
You never, ever learn,
That nothing's yours,
On easy terms.
Only for a time,
I must not learn,
To call you mine.
Familiarize
That face, those eyes
Make future plans
That cannot be confirmed.
On borrowed time,
On easy terms.
Living on the never never,
Constant as the changing weather,
Never sure
Who's at the door
Or the price I'll have to pay.
Should we meet again
I will not recognize your name.
You can be sure
What's gone before
Will be concealed.
Your friends will never learn
That once we were
On easy terms.
Living on the never never,
Constant as the changing weather,
Never sure
Who's at the door
Or the price I'll have to pay . . .

Mrs Lyons *enters, still with the pregnancy padding.*

Mrs Lyons   They're born, you didn't notify me.

Mrs Johnstone   Well I . . . I just . . . it's . . . couldn't I keep them for a few more days, please, please, they're a pair, they go together.

Mrs Lyons   My husband is due back tomorrow, Mrs Johnstone. I must have my baby. We made an agreement, a bargain. You swore on the Bible.

Mrs Johnstone   You'd better . . . you'd better see which one you want.

Mrs Lyons   I'll take . . .

Mrs Johnstone   No. Don't tell me which one. Just take him, take him. (*Singing*)
>   Living on the never never,
>   Constant as the changing weather,
>   Never sure
>   Who's at the door
>   Or the price I'll have to pay,
>   Should we meet again . . .

Mrs Lyons *rapidly pulls out the padding from beneath her dress. Amongst it is a shawl which she uses to wrap around the baby before picking it up from the pram.*

Mrs Lyons   Thank you Mrs Johnstone, thank you. I'll see you next week.

Mrs Johnstone   I'm due back tomorrow.

Mrs Lyons   I know but why don't you . . . why don't you take the week off, on full pay of course.

Mrs Lyons *exits.*

Mrs Johnstone *turns and enters her house with the remaining twin in the pram.*

Kid One (*off*)   What happened to the other twin, Mother?

Kid Two (*off*)   Where's the other twinny, Mam?

Mrs Johnstone   He's gone. He's gone up to heaven, love. He's living with Jesus and the angels.

Kid Three (*off*)   What's it like there Mam, in heaven?

Mrs Johnstone   It's lovely son, he'll be well looked after there. He'll have anything he wants.

Kid One (*off*)   Will he have his own bike?

Mrs Johnstone   Yeh. With both wheels on.

Kid One (*off*)   Why can't I have a bike? Eh?

Mrs Johnstone   I'll . . . I'll have a look in the catalogue next week. We'll see what the bikes are like in there.

Kids (*together, off*)   Mam, I want a Meccano set.
        You said I could have a new dress, Mother.
        Why can't I have an air pistol?
        Let's look in the catalogue now, Mam.
        It's great when we look in the catalogue, Mam.
        Go on, let's all look in the catalogue.

Mrs Johnstone   I've told y', when I get home, I've got to go to work.

Mr and **Mrs Lyons** *enter their house and we see them looking at the child in its cot.*

Mrs Johnstone *enters and immediately goes about her work.*

Mrs Johnstone *stops work for a moment and glances into the cot, beaming and cooing.* **Mr Lyons** *is next to her with* **Mrs Lyons** *in the background, obviously agitated at* **Mrs Johnstone**'s *fussing.*

Aw, he's really comin' on now, isn't he, Mr Lyons? I'll bet y' dead proud of him, aren't y', aren't y', eh?

Mr Lyons (*good naturedly*)   Yes . . . yes I am, aren't I Edward? I'm proud of Jennifer, too.

Mr Lyons *beams at his wife who can hardly raise a smile.*

Mrs Johnstone   Ah . . . he's lovely. (*She coos into the cot.*) Ah look, he wants to be picked up, I'll just . . .

Mrs Lyons   No, no, Mrs Johnstone. He's fine. He doesn't want to be picked up.

Mrs Johnstone   Ah, but look he's gonna cry . . .

Mrs Lyons   If he needs picking up, *I* shall pick him up. All right?

Mrs Johnstone   Well, I just thought, I'm sorry I . . .

Mrs Lyons   Yes. Erm, has the bathroom been done? Time is getting on.

Mrs Johnstone   Oh. Yeh, yeh . . .

Mrs Johnstone *exits.*

Mr Lyons   Darling. Don't be hard on the woman. She only wanted to hold the baby. All women like to hold babies, don't they?

Mrs Lyons   I don't want her to hold the baby, Richard. She's . . . I don't want the baby to catch anything. Babies catch things very easily, Richard.

Mr Lyons   All right, all right, you know best.

Mrs Lyons   You don't see her as much as I do. She's always fussing over him; any opportunity and she's cooing and cuddling as if she were his mother. She's always bothering him, Richard, always. Since the baby arrived she ignores most of her work. (*She is about to cry.*)

Mr Lyons   Come on, come on . . . It's all right Jennifer. You're just a little . . . it's this depression thing that happens after a woman's had a . . .

Mrs Lyons   I'm not depressed Richard; it's just that she makes me feel . . . Richard, I think she should go.

Mr Lyons   And what will you do for help in the house?

Mrs Lyons   I'll find somebody else. I'll find somebody who doesn't spend all day fussing over the baby.

Mr Lyons (*glancing at his watch*)   Oh well, I suppose you know best. The house is your domain. Look, Jen, I've got a board meeting. I really must dash.

Mrs Lyons   Richard, can you let me have some cash?

Mr Lyons   Of course.

Mrs Lyons   I need about fifty pounds.

Mr Lyons   My God, what for?

Mrs Lyons   I've got lots of things to buy for the baby, I've got the nursery to sort out . . .

Mr Lyons   All right, all right, here. (*He hands her the money.*)
Mr Lyons *exits.*

Mrs Lyons *considers what she is about to do and then calls*

Mrs Lyons   Mrs Johnstone. Mrs Johnstone, would you come out here for a moment, please.

Mrs Johnstone *enters.*

Mrs Johnstone   Yes?

Mrs Lyons   Sit down. Richard and I have been talking it over and, well the thing is, we both think it would be better if you left.

Mrs Johnstone   Left where?

Mrs Lyons   It's your work. Your work has deteriorated.

Mrs Johnstone   But, I work the way I've always worked.

Mrs Lyons   Well, I'm sorry, we're not satisfied.

Mrs Johnstone   What will I do? How are we gonna live without my job?

Mrs Lyons   Yes, well we've thought of that. Here, here's . . . (*She pushes the money into* **Mrs Johnstone**'s *hands.*) It's a lot of money . . . but, well . . .

Mrs Johnstone (*thinking, desperate. Trying to get it together.*)   Ok. All right. All right, Mrs Lyons, right. If I'm goin', I'm takin' my son with me, I'm takin' . . .

As **Mrs Johnstone** *moves towards the cot* **Mrs Lyons** *roughly drags her out of the way.*

Mrs Lyons   Oh no, you're not. Edward is my son. Mine.

Mrs Johnstone   I'll tell someone . . . I'll tell the police . . . I'll bring the police in an' . . .

Mrs Lyons   No . . . no you won't. You gave your baby away. Don't you realize what a crime that is. You'll be locked up. You sold your baby.

Mrs Johnstone, *horrified, sees the bundle of notes in her hand, and throws it across the room.*

Mrs Johnstone   I didn't . . . you told me, you said I could see him every day. Well, I'll tell someone, I'm gonna tell . . .

Mrs Johnstone *starts to leave but* **Mrs Lyons** *stops her.*

Mrs Lyons   No. You'll tell nobody.

Music.

Because . . . because if you tell anyone . . . and these children learn of the truth, then you know what will happen, don't you? You do know what they say about twins, secretly parted, don't you?

Mrs Johnstone (*terrified*)   What? What?

Mrs Lyons   They say . . . they say that if either twin learns that he was one of a pair, they shall both immediately die. It means, Mrs Johnstone, that these brothers shall grow up, unaware of the other's existence. They shall be raised apart and never, ever told what was once the truth. You won't tell anyone about this, Mrs Johnstone, because if you do, you will kill them.

Mrs Lyons *picks up the money and thrusts it into* **Mrs Johnstone's** *hands.* **Mrs Lyons** *turns and walks away.*

The **Narrator** *enters.*

Narrator (*singing*)   Shoes upon the table
An' a spider's been killed.
Someone broke the lookin' glass
A full moon shinin'
An' the salt's been spilled.
You're walkin' on the pavement cracks
Don't know what's gonna come to pass.
Now y' know the devil's got your number,
Y' know he's gonna find y',
Y' know he's right behind y',
He's starin' through your windows
He's creepin' down the hall.
Ain't no point in clutching
At your rosary'
You're always gonna know what was done
Even when you shut your eyes you still see
That you sold a son
And you can't tell anyone.
But y' know the devil's got your number,
Y' know he's gonna find y',
Y' know he's right behind y',
He's starin' through your windows
He's creeping down the hall
Yes, y' know the devil's got your number
He's gonna find y',
Y' know he's right behind y',
He's standin' on your step
And he's knocking at your door.
He's knocking at your door,
He's knocking at your door.

The **Narrator** *exits.*

During the song **Mrs Johnstone** *has gone to her house and locked herself in.*

Mickey, *aged 'seven' is knocking incessantly at the door. He is carrying a toy gun.*

Mrs Johnstone (*screaming; off*)   Go away!

Mickey   Mother . . . will y' open the bleedin' door or what?

Mrs Johnstone (*realizing; with relief; off*)   Mickey?

Mrs Johnstone *comes to open the door.*

Mickey   Mam, Mam.

She grabs him and hugs him. He extricates himself.

Why was the door bolted? Did you think it was the rent man?

She laughs and looks at him.

Mam, our Sammy's robbed me other gun an' that was me best one. Why does he rob all me things off me?

Mrs Johnstone   Because you're the youngest Mickey. It used to happen to our Sammy when he was the youngest.

Mickey   Mam, we're playin' mounted police an' Indians. I'm a mountie. Mam, Mam, y' know this mornin', we've wiped out three thousand Indians.

Mrs Johnstone   Good.

Mickey (*aiming the gun at her and firing*)   Mam, Mam, you're dead.

Mrs Johnstone (*staring at him*)   Hmm.

Mickey   What's up, Mam?

Mrs Johnstone   Nothin' son. Go on, you go out an' play, there's a good lad. But, ey, don't you go playin' with those hooligans down at the rough end.

Mickey (*on his way out*)   We're down at the other end, near the big houses in the park.

Mrs Johnstone   Mickey! Come here.

Mickey   What?

Mrs Johnstone   What did you say, where have you been playin'?

Mickey   Mam, I'm sorry, I forgot.

Mrs Johnstone   What have I told you about playin' up near there. Come here. (*She grabs him.*)

Mickey   It wasn't my fault. Honest.

Mrs Johnstone   So whose fault was it then?

Mickey   The Indians. They rode up that way, they were tryin' to escape.

Mrs Johnstone   Don't you ever go up there. Do you hear me?

Mickey   Yeh. You let our Sammy go up there.

Mrs Johnstone   Our Sammy's older than you.

Mickey   But why . . .

Mrs Johnstone   Just shut up. Never mind why. You don't go up near there. Now go on, get out an' play. But you stay outside the front door where I can see y'.

Mickey   Ah but, Mam, the . . .

Mrs Johnstone   Go on!

Mrs Johnstone *exits.*

Mickey *makes his way outside. He is fed up. Desultory. Shoots down a few imaginary Indians but somehow the magic has gone out of genocide.*

Mickey *sits, bored, looking at the ants on the pavement.*

Mickey (*reciting*)   I wish I was our Sammy
    Our Sammy's nearly ten.
    He's got two worms and a catapult
    An' he's built a underground den.
    But I'm not allowed to go in there,
    I have to stay near the gate,
    'Cos me Mam says I'm only seven,
    But I'm not, I'm nearly eight!
    I sometimes hate our Sammy,
    He robbed me toy car y' know,
    Now the wheels are missin' an' the top's broke off,

An' the bleedin' thing won't go.
An' he said when he took it, it was just like that,
But it wasn't, it went dead straight,
But y' can't say nott'n when they think y' seven
An' y' not, y' nearly eight.
I wish I was our Sammy,
Y' wanna see him spit,
Straight in y' eye from twenty yards
An' every time a hit.
He's allowed to play with matches,
And he goes to bed dead late,
And I have to go at seven,
Even though I'm nearly eight.
Y' know our Sammy,
He draws nudey women,
Without arms, or legs, or even heads
In the baths, when he goes swimmin'.
But I'm not allowed to go to the baths,
Me Mam says I have to wait,
'Cos I might get drowned, 'cos I'm only seven,
But I'm not, I'm nearly eight.
Y' know our Sammy,
Y' know what he sometimes does?
He wees straight through the letter box
Of the house next door to us.
I tried to do it one night,
But I had to stand on a crate,
'Cos I couldn't reach the letter box
But I will by the time I'm eight.

Bored and petulant, **Mickey** *sits and shoots an imaginary Sammy.*

Edward, *also aged 'seven' appears. He is bright and forthcoming.*

Edward   Hello.

Mickey (*suspiciously*)   Hello.

Edward   I've seen you before.

Mickey   Where?

Edward   You were playing with some other boys near my house.

Mickey   Do you live up in the park?

Edward   Yes. Are you going to come and play up there again?

Mickey   No. I would do but I'm not allowed.

Edward   Why?

Mickey   'Cos me mam says.

Edward   Well, my mummy doesn't allow me to play down here actually.

Mickey   'Gis a sweet.

Edward   All right. (*He offers a bag from his pocket.*)

Mickey (*shocked*)   What?

Edward   Here.

Mickey (*trying to work out the catch. Suspiciously taking one*)   Can I have another one. For our Sammy?

Edward   Yes, of course. Take as many as you want.

Mickey (*taking a handful*)   Are you soft?

Edward   I don't think so.

Mickey   Round here if y' ask for a sweet, y' have to ask about, about twenty million times. An' y' know what?

Edward (*sitting beside* **Mickey**)   What?

Mickey   They still don't bleedin' give y' one. Sometimes our Sammy does but y' have to be dead careful if our Sammy gives y' a sweet.

Edward   Why?

Mickey   'Cos, if our Sammy gives y' a sweet he's usually weed on it first.

Edward (*exploding in giggles*)   Oh, that sounds like super fun.

Mickey   It is. If y' our Sammy.

Edward   Do you want to come and play?

Mickey   I might do. But I'm not playin' now 'cos I'm pissed off.

Edward (*awed*)   Pissed off. You say smashing things don't you? Do you know any more words like that?

Mickey   Yeh. Yeh, I know loads of words like that. Y' know, like the 'F' word.

Edward (*clueless*)   Pardon?

Mickey   The 'F' word.

Edward *is still puzzled.* **Mickey** *looks round to check that he cannot be overheard, then whispers the word to* **Edward**. *The two of them immediately wriggle and giggle with glee.*

Edward   What does it mean?

Mickey   I don't know. It sounds good though, doesn't it?

Edward   Fantastic. When I get home I'll look it up in the dictionary.

Mickey   In the what?

Edward   The dictionary. Don't you know what a dictionary is?

Mickey   'Course I do . . . It's a, it's a thingy innit?

Edward   A book which explains the meaning of words.

Mickey   The meaning of words, yeh. Our Sammy'll be here soon. I hope he's in a good mood. He's dead mean sometimes.

Edward   Why?

Mickey   It's 'cos he's got a plate in his head.

Edward   A plate. In his head?

Mickey   Yeh. When he was little, me Mam was at work an' our Donna Marie was supposed to be lookin' after him but he fell out the window an' broke his head. So they took him to the hospital an' put a plate in his head.

Edward   A plate. A dinner plate?

Mickey   I don't think so, 'cos our Sammy's head's not really that big. I think it must have been one of them little plates that you have bread off.

Edward   A side plate?

Mickey   No, it's on the top.

Edward   And . . . and can you see the shape of it, in his head?

Mickey   I suppose, I suppose if y' looked under his hair.

Edward (*after a reflective pause*)   You know the most smashing things. Will you be my best friend?

Mickey   Yeh. If y' want.

Edward   What's your name?

Mickey   Michael Johnstone. But everyone calls me Mickey. What's yours?

Edward   Edward Lyons.

Mickey   D' they call y' Eddie?

Edward   No.

Mickey   Well, I will.

Edward   Will you?

Mickey   Yeh. How old are y' Eddie?

Edward   Seven.

Mickey   I'm older than you. I'm nearly eight.

Edward   Well, I'm nearly eight, really.

Mickey   What's your birthday?

Edward   July the eighteenth.

Mickey   So is mine.

Edward   Is it really?

Mickey   Ey, we were born on the same day . . . that means we can be blood brothers. Do you wanna be my blood brother, Eddie?

Edward   Yes, please.

Mickey (*producing a penknife*)   It hurts y' know. (*He puts a nick in his hand.*) Now, give us yours.

Mickey *nicks* **Edward**'s *hand, then they clamp hands together.*

See this means that we're blood brothers, an' that we always have to stand by each other. Now you say after me: 'I will always defend my brother'.

Edward   I will always defend my brother . . .

Mickey   And stand by him.

Edward   And stand by him.

Mickey   An' share all my sweets with him.

Edward   And share . . .

Sammy *leaps in front of them, gun in hand, pointed at them.*

Mickey   Hi ya, Sammy.

Sammy   Give us a sweet.

Mickey   Haven't got any.

Edward   Yes, you have . . .

Mickey *frantically shakes his head, trying to shut* **Edward** *up.*

Yes, I gave you one for Sammy, remember?

Sammy *laughs at* **Edward**'s *voice and* **Mickey**'s *misfortune.*

Sammy   Y' little robbin' get.

Mickey   No, I'm not. (*He hands over a sweet.*) An' anyway, you pinched my best gun.

Mickey *tries to snatch the gun from* **Sammy**, *but* **Sammy** *is too fast.*

Sammy   It's last anyway. It only fires caps. I'm gonna get a real gun soon, I'm gonna get an air gun.

Sammy *goes into a fantasy shoot out. He doesn't notice* **Edward** *who has approached him and is craning to get a close look at his head.* (*Eventually noticing*)   What are you lookin' at?

Edward   Pardon.

Mickey   That's Eddie. He lives up by the park.

Sammy   He's a friggin' poshy.

Mickey   No, he's not. He's my best friend.

Sammy (*snorting, deciding it's not worth the bother*)   You're soft. Y' just soft little kids. (*In quiet disdain he moves away.*)

Mickey   Where y' goin'?

Sammy (*looking at* **Mickey**)   I'm gonna do another burial. Me worms have died again.

Mickey (*excitedly; to* **Edward**)   Oh, y' comin' the funeral?

Our Sammy is having a funeral. Can we come, Sammy? **Sammy** *puts his hand into his pocket and brings forth a handful of soil.*

Sammy   Look, they was alive an wrigglin' this mornin'. But by dinner time they was dead.

Mickey *and* **Edward** *inspect the deceased worms in* **Sammy**'s *hand.*

Mrs Johnstone *enters.*

Mrs Johnstone   Mickey . . . Mickey . . .

Edward   Is that your mummy?

Mickey   Mam . . . Mam, this is my brother.

Mrs Johnstone (*stunned*)   What?

Mickey   My blood brother, Eddie.

Mrs Johnstone   Eddie, Eddie who?

Edward   Edward Lyons, Mrs Johnstone.

Mrs Johnstone *stands still, staring at him.*

Mickey   Eddie's my best friend, Mam. He lives up by the park an' . . .

Mrs Johnstone   Mickey . . . get in the house.

Mickey   What?

Mrs Johnstone   Sammy, you an' all. Both of y' get in.

Sammy   But I'm older than him, I don't have to . . .

Mrs Johnstone   I said get, the pair of y' . . .

Mickey (*going, almost in tears*)   But I haven't done nothin'. I'll see y' Eddie. Ta ra, Eddie . . .

Mickey *exits.*

Mrs Johnstone   Sammy!

Sammy   Ah. (*To* **Edward**.) I'll get you.

Edward   Have I done something wrong, Mrs Johnstone?

Mrs Johnstone   Does your mother know that you're down here?

Edward *shakes his head.*
   An' what would she say if she did know?

Edward   I . . . I think she'd be angry?

Mrs Johnstone   So don't you think you better get home before she finds out?

Edward   Yes.

Mrs Johnstone   Go on, then.

Edward *turns to go, then stops.*

Edward   Could I . . . would it be all right if I came to play with Mickey on another day? Or perhaps he could come to play at my house . . .

Mrs Johnstone   Don't you ever come round here again. Ever.

Edward   But . . .

Mrs Johnstone   Ever! Now go on. Beat it, go home before the bogey man gets y'.

Edward *walks towards his home. As he goes* **Mrs Johnstone** *sings*

> Should we meet again,
> I will not recognize your name,
> You can be sure
> What's gone before
> Will be concealed.
> Your friends will never learn
> That once we were
> On easy terms.

Mr and **Mrs Lyons** *enter their house as* **Edward** *walks home.*

Edward *reaches his home and walks in. His mother hugs him and his father produces a toy gun for him.* **Edward**, *delighted, seizes it and 'shoots' his father, who spiritedly 'dies' to* **Edward**'*s great amusement.* **Edward** *and his father romp on the floor.* **Mrs Lyons** *settles herself in an armchair with a story book, calling* **Edward** *over to her.* **Edward** *goes and sits with her,* **Mr Lyons** *joining them and sitting on the arm of the chair.*

Mrs Johnstone *turns and goes into her house at the end of the song.*

Mr Lyons *gets up and walks towards the door.*

Edward   Daddy . . . we haven't finished the story yet.

Mr Lyons   Mummy will read the story, Edward. I've got to go to work for an hour.

Mrs Lyons *gets up and goes to her husband,* **Edward** *goes to the bookshelf and leafs through a dictionary.*

Mrs Lyons   Richard you didn't say . . .

Mr Lyons   Darling, I'm sorry, but if, if we complete this merger I will, I promise you, have more time. That's why we're doing it,

Jen. If we complete this, the firm will run itself and I'll have plenty of time to spend with you both.

Mrs Lyons   I just – it's not me, it's Edward. You should spend more time with him. I don't want – I don't want him growing away from you.

Edward   Daddy, how do you spell bogey man?

Mr Lyons   Ask Mummy. Darling, I'll see you later now. Must dash.

Mr Lyons *exits*.

Edward   Mummy, how do you spell bogey man?

Mrs Lyons   Mm?

Edward   Bogey man?

Mrs Lyons (*laughing*)   Edward, wherever did you hear such a thing?

Edward   I'm trying to look it up.

Mrs Lyons   There's no such thing as a bogey man. It's a – a superstition. The sort of thing a silly mother might say to her children – 'the bogey man will get you'.

Edward   Will he get me?

Mrs Lyons   Edward, I've told you, there's no such thing. *(A doorbell is heard.)*

Mrs Lyons *goes to answer the door*.

Mickey (*off*)   Does Eddie live here?

Mrs Lyons (*off*)   Pardon?

Mickey (*off*)   Does he? Is he comin' out to play, eh?

Edward (*shouting*)   Mickey!

Mickey *enters, pursued by* **Mrs Lyons**.

Mickey   Hi-ya, Eddie. I've got our Sammy's catapult. Y' comin' out?

Edward   Oh! (*He takes the catapult and trys a practice shot.*)
Isn't Mickey fantastic, Mum?

Mrs Lyons   Do you go to the same school as Edward?

Mickey   No.

Edward   Mickey says smashing things. We're blood brothers,
aren't we, Mickey?

Mickey   Yeh. We were born on the same day.

Edward   Come on Mickey, let's go . . .

Mrs Lyons   Edward . . . Edward, it's time for bed.

Edward   Mummy. It's not.

Mrs Lyons *takes over and ushers* **Mickey** *out.*

Mrs Lyons   I'm very sorry, but it's Edward's bedtime.

Edward   Mummy. Mummy, it's early.

Mrs Lyons *exits with* **Mickey** *to show him out. Then she returns.*

Mummy!

Mrs Lyons   Edward. Edward where did you meet that boy?

Edward   At his house.

Mrs Lyons   And . . . and his second name is Johnstone, isn't it?

Edward   Yes. And I think you're very, very mean.

Mrs Lyons   I've told you never to go where that boy – where
boys like that live.

Edward   But why?

Mrs Lyons   Because, because you're not the same as him. You're
not, do you understand?

Edward   No, I don't understand. And I hate you!

Mrs Lyons (*almost crying*)   Edward, Edward, don't. It's . . . what
I'm doing is only for your own good. It's only because I love you,
Edward.

Edward   You don't, you don't. If you loved me you'd let me go out with Mickey because he's my best friend. I like him more than you.

Mrs Lyons   Edward. Edward don't say that. Don't ever say that.

Edward   Well. Well it's true. And I will say it. I know what you are.

Mrs Lyons   What? What!

Edward   You're . . . you're a fuckoff!

Mrs Lyons *hits* **Edward** *hard and instinctively.*

Mrs Lyons   You see, you see why I don't want you mixing with boys like that! You learn filth from them and behave like this like a, like a horrible little boy, like them. But you are not like them. You are my son, mine, and you won't, you won't ever . . .

She notices the terror in **Edward**'*s face and realizes how heavy she has been. Gently she pulls him to her and cradles him.*

Oh, my son . . . my beautiful, beautiful son.

The scene fades as the next scene begins. We hear cap guns and the sound of children making Indian whoops.

The children rush on into the street playing cowboys and Indians; cops and robbers; goodies and baddies etc.

During the battle **Mrs Lyons** *exits.*

Edward *remains on stage, in the background, as though in his garden, watching, unnoticed by the battling children.*

Mickey *and* **Linda** *are in one gang,* **Sammy** *in another.*

Sammy (*singing acapella, kids' rhyme*)
    I got y'
    I shot y'
    An' y' bloody know I did
    I got y'
    I shot y'

Linda   I stopped it with the bin lid.

There is a mass of derisive jeers from the other side.

Music.

　　　(*Singing*): But you know that if you cross your fingers
　　　And if you count from one to ten
　　　You can get up off the ground again
　　　It doesn't matter
　　　The whole thing's just a game.

The shooting starts all over again. A **Kid** *raps on the door of a house.* **Linda**, *as a 'Moll', appears.*

Kid　　My name is Elliot Ness,
　　　And lady, here's my card,
　　　I'm lookin' for one Al Capone

(*To* **Lackeys**):
　　　Mac, check the back
　　　Sarge, you check the yard!

Linda　　But pal, I've told y'
　　　Al ain't home.

We see 'Al' make a break for it. **Ness** *shoots him like he was eating his breakfast.*

Kid　　So, lady can I use your telephone.

As **Ness** *goes to the phone and orders a hearse we see* AL *get up and sing the chorus with the other children*

　　　But you know that if you cross your fingers,
　　　And if you count from one to ten,
　　　You can get up off the ground again,
　　　It doesn't matter the whole thing's just a game.

The **Kid** *who was playing* AL *becomes a cowboy. He turns to face* **Sammy** *and sings*

Cowboy　　When I say draw,
　　　You'd better grab that gun,
　　　An' maybe say a little prayer
　　　Cos I'm the fastest draw
　　　That man you ever saw.

Call up your woman, say goodbye to her,
Cos y' know you're goin' right down there.

As he draws his gun on **Sammy, Sammy** *produces a bazooka and blows him off the stage.*

All   But you know that if you cross your fingers,
And if you count from one to ten,
You can get up off the ground again,
It doesn't matter,
The whole thing's just a game.

A small group of **Children** *become a brigade of* US *troops.*

Sergeant   OK men, let's get them
With a hand grenade.

Corporal   Let's see them try and get outta this.

Rest   He's a hot shot Sergeant
From the Ninth Brigade
He's never been known to miss

Sergeant (*to grenade*)   C'mon give Daddy a kiss. (*He pulls the pin and lobs it.*)

His **Brigade** *cover their ears and crouch down.* **Linda** *catches the grenade and lobs it back at them. After being blown to pieces they get up singing the chorus, along with the 'enemy'.*

All   But you know that if you cross your fingers,
And if you count from one to ten.
You can get up off the ground again,
It doesn't matter,
The whole thing's just a game.

Sammy *comes forward as* **Professor Howe** *carrying a condom filled with water.*

Professor   My name's Professor Howe,
An' zees bomb I 'old,
Eet can destroy ze 'emisphere,
I've primed it, I've timed it

      To explode,
      Unless you let me out of here (NO?)

They don't.

      Then I suggest you cover your ears.

There is an explosion which tops them all. Out of it come all the
children singing the chorus.

All   But you know that if you cross your fingers,
      And if you count from one to ten,
      you can get up off the ground again,
      It doesn't matter,
      The whole thing's just a game
      The whole thing's just a game
      The whole thing's just a . . .

Sammy (*interrupting; chanting*)
      You're dead
      Y' know y' are
      I got y' standin'
      Near that car.

Linda   But when y' did
      His hand was hid
      Behind his back
      His fingers crossed
      An' so he's not

Mickey   So you fuck off!

All the children, apart from **Mickey** *and* **Linda***, point and chant*
the accusing 'Aah!' **Mickey** *is singled out, accused. The rest, led*
by **Sammy** *suddenly chant at* **Mickey** *and point*

All (*chanting*)   You said the 'F' word
      You're gonna die
      You'll go to hell an' there you'll fry
      Just like a fish in the chip shop fat
      Only twenty five million times hotter than that!

They all laugh at **Mickey***.*

Linda *moves in to protect* **Mickey** *who is visibly shaken.*

Linda   Well, well, all youse lot swear, so you'll all go to hell with him.

Sammy   No, we won't Linda.

Linda   Why?

Sammy   'Cos when we swear . . . we cross our fingers!

Mickey   Well, my fingers were crossed.

Children (*variously*)   No they were't.
      Liar!
      Come off it.
      I seen them.

Linda   Leave him alone!

Sammy   Why? What'll you do about it if we don't?

Linda (*undaunted; approaching* **Sammy**)   I'll tell my mother why all her ciggies always disappear when you're in our house.

Sammy   What?

Linda   An' the half crowns.

Sammy (*suddenly*)   Come on gang, let's go. We don't wanna play with these anyway. They're just kids.

The other children fire a barrage of 'shots' at **Mickey** *and* **Linda** *before they rush off.*

Linda   I hate them!

Linda *notices* **Mickey** *quietly crying.*

What's up?

Mickey   I don't wanna die.

Linda   But y' have to Mickey. Everyone does. (*She starts to dry his tears.*) Like your twinny died, didn't he, when he was a baby. See, look on the bright side of it, Mickey. When you die you'll meet your twinny again, won't y'?

Mickey   Yeh.

Linda   An' listen Mickey, if y' dead, there's no school, is there?

Mickey (*smiling*)   An' I don't care about our Sammy, anyway. Look. (*He produces an air pistol.*) He thinks no one knows he's got it. But I know where he hides it.

Linda (*impressed*)   Ooh . . . gis a go.

Mickey   No . . . come on, let's go get Eddie first.

Linda   Who?

Mickey   Come on, I'll show y'.

They go as if to **Edward***'s garden.*

Mickey (*loud but conspiratorially*)   Eddie . . . Eddie . . . y' comin' out?

Edward   I . . . My mum says I haven't got to play with you.

Mickey   Well, my mum says I haven't got to play with you. But take no notice of mothers. They're soft. Come on, I've got Linda with me. She's a girl but she's all right.

Edward *decides to risk it and creeps out.*

Mickey   Hi-ya.

Edward   Hi-ya, Mickey. Hello, Linda.

Linda   Hi-ya, Eddie. (*She produces the air pistol.*) Look . . . we've got Sammy's air gun.

Mickey   Come on, Eddie. You can have a shot at our target in the park.

Linda   Peter Pan.

Mickey   We always shoot at that, don't we Linda?

Linda   Yeh, we try an' shoot his little thingy off, don't we, Mickey?

They all laugh.

Come on gang, let's go.

Edward (*standing firm*)   But Mickey . . . I mean . . . suppose we get caught . . . by a policeman.

Mickey   Aah . . . take no notice. We've been caught loads of times by a policeman . . . haven't we, Linda?

Linda   Oh, my God, yeh. Hundreds of times. More than that.

Mickey   We say dead funny things to them, don't we, Linda?

Edward   What sort of funny things?

Linda   All sorts, don't we Mickey?

Mickey   Yeh . . . like y' know when they ask what y' name is, we say things like, like 'Adolph Hitler', don't we Linda?

Linda   Yeh, an' hey Eddie, y' know when they say, 'What d' y' think you're doin'?' we always say somethin' like, 'waitin' for the ninety-two bus'.

Mickey *and* **Linda** *crease up with laughter.*

Come on.

Edward (*greatly impressed*)   Do you . . . do you really? Goodness, that's fantastic.

Mickey   Come on, bunk under y' fence, y' Ma won't see y'.

Mickey, Linda *and* **Edward** *exit.*

Mrs Lyons *enters the garden.*

Mrs Lyons (*calling*)   Edward, Edward, Edward . . .

The **Narrator** *enters.*

Music.

Narrator (*singing*)   There's gypsies in the wood,
        An' they've been watchin' you,
        They're gonna take your baby away.
        There's gypsies in the wood,
        An' they've been calling you,

Can Edward please come out and play,
Please can he come with us and play.
You know the devil's got your number,
Y' know he's gonna find y',
Y' know he's right behind y',
He's staring through your windows,
He's creeping down the hall.

Mr Lyons *enters the garden.*

Mrs Lyons   Oh Richard, Richard.

Mr Lyons   For God's sake Jennifer, I told you on the phone, he'll just be out playing somewhere.

Mrs Lyons   But where?

Mr Lyons   Outside somewhere, with friends. Edward . . .

Mrs Lyons   But I don't want him out playing.

Mr Lyons   Jennifer, he's not a baby. Edward . . .

Mrs Lyons   I don't care, I don't care . . .

Mr Lyons   For Christ's sake, you bring me home from work in the middle of the day, just to say you haven't seen him for an hour. Perhaps we should be talking about you getting something for your nerves.

Mrs Lyons   There's nothing wrong with my nerves. It's just . . . just this place . . . I hate it. Richard, I don't want to stay here any more. I want to move.

Mr Lyons   Jennifer! Jennifer, how many times . . . the factory is here, my work is here . . .

Mrs Lyons   It doesn't have to be somewhere far away. But we have got to move, Richard. Because if we stay here I feel that something terrible will happen, something bad.

Mr Lyons *sighs and puts his arm round* **Mrs Lyons**.

Mr Lyons   Look, Jen. What is this thing you keep talking about getting away from? Mm?

Mrs Lyons   It's just . . . it's these people . . . these people that Edward has started mixing with. Can't you see how he's drawn to them? They're . . . they're drawing him away from me.

Mr Lyons, *in despair, turns away from her.*

Mr Lyons   Oh Christ.

He turns to look at her but she looks away. He sighs and absently bends to pick up a pair of children's shoes from the floor.

I really do think you should see a doctor.

Mrs Lyons (*snapping*)   I don't need to see a doctor. I just need to move away from this neighbourhood, because I'm frightened. I'm frightened for Edward.

Mr Lyons *places the shoes on the table before turning on her.*

Mr Lyons   Frightened of what, woman?

Mrs Lyons (*wheeling to face him*)   Frightened of . . . (*She is stopped by the sight of the shoes on the table. She rushes at the table and sweeps the shoes off.*)

Music.

Narrator (*singing*)   There's shoes upon the table
    An' a spider's been killed
    Someone broke the lookin' glass
    There's a full moon shinin'
    An' the salt's been spilled
    You're walkin' on pavement cracks
    Don't know what's gonna come to pass
    Now you know the devil's got your number
    He's gonna find y'
    Y' know he's right beyind y'
    He's starin' through your windows
    He's creeping down the hall.

*The song ends with a percussion build to a sudden full stop and the scene snaps from **Mrs Lyons** to the children.*

Mickey, Eddie and **Linda** *are standing in line, taking it in turns to fire the air pistol.* **Mickey** *takes aim and fires.*

Linda (*with glee*)   Missed.

Edward *loads and fires.*

Missed!

Linda *takes the gun and fires. We hear a metallic ping. She beams a satisfied smile at* **Mickey** *who ignores it and reloads, fires. The routine is repeated with exactly the same outcome until*

Mickey (*taking the gun*)   We're not playin' with the gun no more. (*He puts it away.*)

Linda   Ah, why?

Mickey   It gets broke if y' use it too much.

Edward   What are we going to do now, Mickey?

Mickey   I dunno.

Linda   I do.

Mickey   What?

Linda   Let's throw some stones through them windows.

Mickey (*brightening*)   Ooh, I dare y' Linda, I dare y'.

Linda (*bending for a stone*)   Well, I will. I'm not scared, either. Are you Eddie?

Edward   Erm . . . well . . . erm . . .

Linda   He is look. Eddie's scared.

Mickey   No, he isn't! Are y', Eddie?

Edward (*stoically*)   No . . . I'm not. I'm not scared at all, actually.

Linda   Right, when I count to three we all throw together. One, two, three . . .

Unseen by them a **Policeman** *has approached behind them.*

Policeman   Me mother caught a flea, she put it in the tea pot to make a cup of tea . . . And what do you think you're doing? **Linda**

and **Mickey** *shoot terrified glances at* **Edward***, almost wetting themselves.*

Edward (*mistaking their look for encouragement*)   Waiting for the ninety-two bus. (*He explodes with excited laughter.*)

Linda   He's not with us.

Mickey   Sir.

Linda   Sir.

Policeman   No. He's definitely with us. What's your name, son?

Edward   Adolph Hitler.

Edward *laughs until through the laughter he senses that all is not well. He sees that he alone is laughing. The laughter turns to tears which sets the other two off.*

The three children turn round, crying, bawling, followed by the **Policeman**.

The three children exit.

Mrs Johnstone *enters.*

The **Policeman** *goes to confront* **Mrs Johnstone**.

Policeman   And he was about to commit a serious crime, love. Now, do you understand that? You don't wanna end up in court again, do y'?

Mrs Johnstone *shakes her head.*

Well, that's what's gonna happen if I have any more trouble from one of yours. I warned you last time, didn't I, Mrs Johnstone, about your Sammy?

Mrs Johnstone *nods.*

Well, there'll be no more bloody warnings from now on. Either you keep them in order, Missis, or it'll be the courts for you, or worse, won't it?

Mrs Johnstone *nods.*

Yes, it will.

*As the **Policeman** turns and goe/*
is heard.

Mrs Johnstone (*singing*)
> We'll move away
> And start all over a/
> In some new plac/
> Where they don't kno\
> And nobody's heard of my ı.
> Where we can begin again
> Feel we can win an' then . . .
> Maybe . . .

*The music tails off as we see the **Policeman** confronting
Lyons. The **Policeman** has removed his helmet and holds a g.
of scotch. **Edward** is there.*

Policeman An' er, as I say, it was more of a prank, really, Mr
Lyons. I'd just dock his pocket money if I was you. (*Laughs.*) But,
one thing I would say, if y' don't mind me sayin', is well, I'm not
sure I'd let him mix with the likes of them in the future. Make sure
he keeps with his own kind, Mr Lyons. Well, er, thanks for the
drink, sir. All the best now. He's a good lad, aren't you Adolph?
Goodnight, sir. (*He replaces his helmet.*) *The **Policeman** leaves.*

Mr Lyons Edward . . . how would you like to move to another
house?

Edward Why, Daddy?

Mr Lyons Erm, well, various reasons really. Erm, actually
Mummy's not been too well lately and we thought a move, perhaps
further out towards the country somewhere, might . . . Do you
think you'd like that?

Edward I want to stay here.

Mr Lyons Well, you think about it, old chap.

Edward *leaves his home and goes to the **Johnstones'** door. He
knocks at the door.*

Mrs Johnstone *answers the door.*

Mrs Johnstone. How are you?

e   You what?

'm sorry. Is there something wrong?

nstone   No, I just . . . I don't usually have kids enquiring
iy health. I'm er . . . I'm all right. An' how are you, Master
s?

ward   Very well, thank you.

Mrs Johnstone *looks at* **Edward** *for a moment.*

Mrs Johnstone   Yeh. You look it. Y' look very well. Does your
mother look after you?

Edward   Of course.

Mrs Johnstone   Now listen, Eddie, I told you not to come around
here again.

Edward   I'm sorry but I just wanted to see Mickey.

Mrs Johnstone   No. It's best . . . if . . .

Edward   I won't be coming here again. Ever. We're moving
away. To the country.

Mrs Johnstone   Lucky you.

Edward   But I'd much rather live here.

Mrs Johnstone   Would you? When are y' goin'?

Edward   Tomorrow.

Mrs Johnstone   Oh. So we really won't see you again, eh . . .

Edward *shakes his head and begins to cry.*

What's up?

Edward (*through his tears*)   I don't want to go. I want to stay
here where my friends are . . . where Mickey is.

Mrs Johnstone   Come here.

She takes him, cradling him, letting him cry.

Now listen . . . listen, don't you be soft. You'll probably love it in your new house. You'll meet lots of new friends an' in no time at all you'll forget Mickey ever existed.

Edward   I won't . . . I won't. I'll never forget.

Mrs Johnstone   Shush, shush. Listen, listen Eddie, here's you wantin' to stay here, an' here's me, I've been tryin' to get out for years. We're a right pair, aren't we, you an' me?

Edward   Why don't you Mrs Johnstone? Why don't you buy a new house near us?

Mrs Johnstone   Just like that?

Edward   Yes, yes.

Mrs Johnstone   Would you like a picture of Mickey, to take with you? So's you could remember him?

Edward   Yes, please.

She removes a locket from around her neck.

Mrs Johnstone   See, look . . . there's Mickey, there. He was just a young kid when that was taken.

Edward   And is that you Mrs Johnstone?

She nods.

Can I really have this?

Mrs Johnstone   Yeh. But keep it a secret eh, Eddie? Just our secret, between you an' me.

Edward (*smiling*)   All right, Mrs Johnstone. (*He puts the locket round his neck.*)

He looks at her a moment too long.

Mrs Johnstone   What y' lookin' at?

Edward   I thought you didn't like me. I thought you weren't very nice. But I think you're smashing.

Mrs Johnstone (*looking at him*)   God help the girls when you start dancing.

Edward   Pardon?

Mrs Johnston   Nothing. (*Calling into the house.*) Mickey, say goodbye to Eddie – he's moving.

Mickey *comes out of the house.*

Music is quietly introduced.

Eddie *moves to* **Mickey** *and gives him a small parcel from his pocket.* **Mickey** *unwraps a toy gun. The two boys clasp hands and wave goodbye.* **Mrs Johnstone** *and* **Mickey** *watch as* **Edward** *joins his parents, dressed in outdoor clothes, on their side of the stage.*

Edward   Goodbye.

Mr Lyons   Well, Edward . . . do you like it here?

Edward (*unenthusiastically*)   It's very nice.

Mrs Lyons   Oh, look, Edward . . . look at those trees and those cows. Oh Edward, you're going to like it so much out here, aren't you?

Edward   Yes. Are you feeling better now, Mummy?

Mrs Lyons   Much better now, darling. Oh Edward, look, look at those birds . . . Look at that lovely black and white one . . .

Edward (*immediately covering his eyes*)   Don't Mummy, don't look. It's a magpie, never look at one magpie. It's one for sorrow . . .

Mr Lyons   Edward . . . that's just stupid superstition.

Edward   It's not, Mickey told me.

Mrs Lyons   Edward, I think we can forget the silly things that Mickey said.

Edward   I'm going inside. I want to read.

Edward *exits*.

Mr Lyons (*comforting his wife*)   Children take time to adapt to new surroundings. He'll be as right as rain in a few days. He won't even remember he once lived somewhere else.

Mrs Lyons *forces a smile and allows herself to be led inside by her husband*.

Mickey *rings the doorbell of* **Edward**'*s old house*.

A **Woman** *answers the door*.

Woman   Yes?

Mickey   Is er . . . is Eddie in?

Woman   Eddie? I'm afraid Eddie doesn't live here now.

Mickey   Oh, yeh. (*He stands looking at the woman*.)

Woman   Goodbye.

Mickey   Do y' . . . erm, do y' know where he lives now?

Woman   Pardon?

Mickey   See, I've got some money, I was gonna go, on the bus, an' see him. Where does he live now?

Woman   I'm afraid I've no idea.

Mickey   It's somewhere in the country, isn't it?

Woman   Look, I honestly don't know and I'm rather busy. Goodbye.

The **Woman** *closes the door on* **Mickey**.

Mickey *wanders away, aimless and bored, deserted and alone. Music*.

Mickey (*singing*)   No kids out on the street today,
    You could be living on the moon.
    Maybe everybody's packed their bags and moved away,

Gonna be a long, long, long,
Sunday Afternoon
Just killing time and kicking cans around,
Try to remember jokes I knew,
I tell them to myself, but they're not funny since I found
It's gonna be a long, long, long,
Sunday Afternoon.

Edward, *in his garden, equally bored and alone. The scene appears in such a way that we don't know if it is real or in* **Mickey**'s *mind.*

My best friend
Always had sweets to share, (He)
Knew every word in the dictionary.
He was clean, neat and tidy,
From Monday to Friday,
I wish that I could be like,
Wear clean clothes, talk properly like,
Do sums and history like,

Edward (*together*)   My friend

Mickey   My friend

Edward   My best friend
He could swear like a soldier
You would laugh till you died
At the stories he told y'
He was untidy
From Monday to Friday
I wish that I could be like
Kick a ball and climb a tree like
Run around with dirty knees like

Edward (*together*)   My friend

Mickey   My friend

The Lights fade on **Edward** *as the music shifts back to 'Long Sunday Afternoon'.*

Mickey   Feels like everybody stayed in bed

Or maybe I woke up too soon.
Am I the last survivor
Is everybody dead?
On this long long long
Sunday Afternoon.

Mrs Johnstone *appears, clutching a letter.*

Mrs Johnstone (*singing*)   Oh, bright new day, We're movin'
away.

Mickey (*speaking*)   Mam? What's up?

Mrs Johnstone (*singing*)   We're startin' all over again.

Donna Marie *enters together with various neighbours.*

Donna Marie (*speaking*)   Is it a summons, Mother?

Mrs Johnstone (*singing*)   Oh, bright new day, We're goin'
away.

Mickey (*calling*)   Sammy!

Mrs Johnstone *addresses the various onlookers.*

Mrs Johnstone (*singing*)   Where nobody's heard of our name.

Sammy *enters.*

Sammy (*speaking*)   I never robbed nothin', honest, mam.

Mrs Johnstone (*singing*)   Where we can begin again,
     Feel we can win and then
     Live just like livin' should be
     Got a new situation,
     A new destination,
     And no reputation following me.

Mickey (*speaking*)   What is it, what is it?

Mrs Johnstone (*singing*)   We're gettin' out,
     We're movin' house,
     We're starting all over again.
     We're leavin' this mess

For our new address (*pointing it out*)
'Sixty five Skelmersdale Lane'.

Mickey (*speaking; worried*)   Where's that, mam?

Sammy (*speaking*)   Is that in the country?

Donna Marie (*speaking*)   What's it like there?

Mrs Johnstone (*singing*)   The air is so pure,
        You get drunk just by breathing,
        And the washing stays clean on the line.
        Where there's space for the kids,
        'Cos the garden's so big,
        It would take you a week just to reach the far side.
        (*Speaking*): Come on, Sammy, Mickey, now you've all gorra
        help. (*To the* **Neighbours**, *in a 'posh voice'*.) Erm would
        youse excuse us, we've gorra pack. We're movin' away.

Mrs Johnstone *and the children go in to pack.*

Neighbour   What did she say?

Milkman   They're movin' away.

All   Praise the Lord, he has delivered us at last.

Neighbour   They're gettin' out,
        They're movin' house,
        Life won't be the same as in the past.

Policeman   I can safely predict
        A sharp drop in the crime rate.

Neighbour   It'll be calm an' peaceful around here.

Milkman   AND now I might even
        Get paid what is mine, mate.

Neighbour   An' you'll see, graffiti will soon disappear.

Mrs Johnstone *marches out of the house carrying battered
suitcases, followed by the children who are struggling to get out
some of the items mentioned in the verse.*

Mrs Johnstone   Just pack up the bags,
We're leavin' the rags,
The wobbly wardrobe, chest of drawers that never close.
The two legged chair, the carpet so bare,
You wouldn't see it if it wasn't for the holes.
Now that we're movin'
Now that we're improvin',
Let's just wash our hands of this lot.
For it's no longer fitting, for me to be sitting
On a sofa, I know for a fact, was knocked off.

Her last line is delivered to **Sammy** *who indicates the* **Policeman**,
trying to get her to shut up.

We might get a car,
Be all 'lardie dah',
An' go drivin' out to the sands.
At the weekend,
A gentleman friend,
Might take me dancing
To the local bands.
We'll have a front room,
And then if it should happen,
That His Holiness flies in from Rome,
He can sit there with me, eating toast, drinking tea
In the sort of surroundings that remind him of home.

Mickey (*speaking*)   It's like the country, isn't it, mam?

Mrs Johnstone (*speaking*)   Ey, we'll be all right out here son,
away from the muck an' the dirt an' the bloody trouble. Eh, I could
dance. Come here.

Mickey   Get off . . .

Mrs Johnstone *picks up a picture of the Pope which is lying next
to one of the suitcases and begins to dance.*

Mrs Johnstone (*singing*)   Oh, bright new day,
We're movin' away,
We're startin' all over again.
Oh, bright new day,

We're goin' away,
Where nobody's heard of our name.
(*Speaking*): An' what are you laughin' at?

Mickey   I'm not laughin', I'm smilin'. I haven't seen you happy like this for ages.

Mrs Johnstone   Well, I am happy now. Eh, Jesus where's the others?

Mickey   They went into that field, mam.

Mrs Johnstone   Sammy. Sammy! Get off that bleedin' cow before I kill you. Oh Jesus, what's our Donna Marie stepped into? Sammy, that cow's a bull. Come here the pair of you.
Now we can begin again,
Feel we can win an' then,
Live just like livin' should be.
Got a new situation,
A new destination,
An' no reputation following me.

All   We're gettin' out. We're movin' house
We're goin' away. Gettin' out today.
We're movin' movin' movin' house.

Mrs Johnstone   We're goin' away,
Oh, bright new day.

Curtain.

Act Two

Mrs Johnstone *moves forward to sing.*

Mrs Johnstone   The house we got was lovely,
     The neighbours are a treat,
     They sometimes fight on Saturday night,
     But never in the week.

Mrs Johnstone *turns and looks 'next door'. Raised voices, and a dog barking, are heard, off.*

Neighbours (*off, speaking*)   What time do you call this then?

Time I got shot of you, rat bag!

Dog *barks.*

Mrs Johnstone (*singing*)   Since I pay me bills on time, the milkman

     Insists I call him Joe.
     He brings me bread and eggs.

Joe, *the milkman, enters.*

     Says I've got legs
     Like Marilyn Monroe.

Mrs Johnstone *and* **Joe** *dance.*

     Sometimes he takes me dancing
     Even takes me dancing.

Joe *exits, dancing.*

     I know our Sammy burnt the school down
     But it's very easily done.
     If the teacher lets the silly gets
     Play with magnesium.
     Thank God he only got probation,

A **Judge** *is seen, ticking* **Sammy** *off.*

The Judge was old and slow.

Mrs Johnstone *sings to the* **Judge,** *laying on a smile for him.*

Though it was kind of him,
Said I reminded him of Marilyn Monroe.

Judge (*lecherous*)   And could I take you dancing?
Take you dancing.

Mrs Johnstone *takes the* **Judge**'*s gavel and bangs him on the head.*

The **Judge** *exits, stunned.*

Mrs Johnstone   Our Mickey's just turned fourteen Y' know he's
at *that* age

Mickey *is seen in his room.*

When you mention girls, or courting,
He flies into a rage.

Mickey (*speaking*)   Shut up talking about me, Mother.

Mrs Johnstone   He's got a thing for taking blackheads out,
And he thinks that I don't know,
That he dreams all night of girls who look like
Marilyn Monroe. He's even started dancing, secret dancing.

(*Slower*):   And as for the rest, they've flown the nest
Got married or moved away
Our Donna Marie's already got three, she's
A bit like me that way . . .

(*Slower*):   And that other child of mine,
I haven't seen for years, although
Each day I pray he'll be OK,
Not like Marilyn Monroe . . .

On the other side of the stage **Mrs Lyons** *enters, waltzing with a
very awkward fourteen-year-old* **Edward**.

Mrs Lyons (*speaking*)   One, two, three. One, two, three.

(*Singing*):   Yes, that's right, you're dancing.
       That's right, you're dancing.

(*Speaking*):   You see, Edward, it is easy.

Edward   It is if you have someone to practice with. Girls. But in term time we hardly ever see a girl, let alone dance with one.

Mrs Lyons   I'll give you some more lessons when you're home for half term. Now come on, come on, you're going to be late. Daddy's at the door with the car. Now, are you sure you've got all your bags?

Edward   Yes, they're in the boot.

Mrs Lyons (*looking at him*)   I'll see you at half term then, darling. (*She kisses him, a light kiss, but holds on to him.*) Look after yourself my love.

Edward   Oh Mummy . . . stop fussing . . . I'm going to be late.

Mrs Lyons   We have had a very good time this holiday though, haven't we?

Edward   We always do.

Mrs Lyons   Yes. We're safe here, aren't we?

Edward   Mummy what are you on about? Sometimes . . . *A car horn is heard.*

Mrs Lyons (*hustling him out, good naturedly*)   Go on, go on . . . There's Daddy getting impatient. Bye, bye, Edward.

Edward   Bye, Ma.

Edward *exits.*

We see **Mrs Johnstone** *hustling* **Mickey** *to school.*

Mrs Johnstone   You're gonna be late y' know. Y' late already.

Mickey   I'm not.

Mrs Johnstone   You're gonna miss the bus.

Mickey   I won't.

Mrs Johnstone   Well, you'll miss Linda, she'll be waitin' for y'.

Mickey   Well, I don't wanna see her. What do I wanna see her for?

Mrs Johnstone (*laughing at his transparency*)   You've only been talkin' about her in your sleep for the past week . . .

Mickey (*outraged*)   You liar . . .

Mrs Johnstone   'Oh, my sweet darling . . .'

Mickey   I never. That was – a line out the school play!

Mrs Johnstone (*her laughter turning to a smile*)   All right. I believe y'. Now go before you miss the bus. Are y' goin'. *We see* **Linda** *at the bus stop.*

Linda   Hi-ya, Mickey.

Mrs Johnstone   Ogh, did I forget? Is that what you're waitin' for? Y' waitin' for y' mum to give y' a big sloppy kiss, come here . . .

Mickey   I'm goin', I'm goin' . . .

Sammy *runs through the house, pulling on a jacket as he does so.*

Sammy   Wait for me, YOU.

Mrs Johnstone   Where you goin' Sammy?

Sammy (*on his way out*)   The dole.

Mickey *and* **Sammy** *exit.*

Mrs Johnstone *stands watching them as they approach the bus stop. She smiles at* **Mickey**'s *failure to cope with* **Linda**'s *smile of welcome.*

The 'bus' appears, with the **Narrator** *as the conductor.*

Conductor   Come on, if y' gettin' on. We've not got all day.

Sammy, Mickey *and* **Linda** *get on the 'bus'.*

Mrs Johnstone (*calling to her kids*)   Tarrah, lads. Be good, both of y' now. I'll cook a nice surprise for y' tea.

Conductor (*noticing her as he goes to ring the bell*)   Gettin' on, Missis?

Mrs Johnstone *shakes her head, still smiling.*

(*Speaking*):   Happy are y'. Content at last?
        Wiped out what happened, forgotten the past?

She looks at him, puzzled.

        But you've got to have an endin', if a start's been made.
        No one gets off without the price bein' paid.

The 'bus' pulls away as the conductor begins to collect fares. No
one can embark without the price bein' paid.

(*To* **Mickey**):   Yeh?

Mickey (*handing over his money*)   A fourpenny scholar.

Conductor   How old are y'?

Linda   He's fourteen. Both of us are. A fourpenny scholar for me
as well.

The **Conductor** *gives out the ticket as* **Sammy** *offers his money.*

Sammy   Same for me.

Conductor   No son.

Sammy   What?

Conductor   You're older than fourteen.

Mickey (*worried*)   Sammy . . .

Sammy   Shut it. (*To the* **Conductor**.) I'm fourteen, I wanna
fourpenny scholar.

Conductor   Do you know the penalty for tryin' to defraud . . .

Sammy   I'm not defraudin' no one.

Conductor (*shouting to the* **Driver**)   'Ey, Billy, take the next left
will y'. We've got one for the cop shop here.

Sammy   What? (*He stands.*)

Mickey   He didn't mean it, Mister. Don't be soft. He, he was
jokin'. Sammy tell him, tell him you're really sixteen. I'll lend you
the rest of the fare . . .

Sammy (*considers; then*)   Fuck off. (*He produces a knife. To the* **Conductor**.) Now move, you. Move! Give me the bag.

Music.

Mickey   Sammy . . . Sammy . . .

Sammy (*to the* **Conductor**)   I said give. Stop the bus.

The **Conductor** *rings the bell to stop the 'bus'.* Come on, Mickey.

Linda   You stay where y' are, Mickey. You've done nothin'.

Mickey   Sammy, Sammy put that away . . . it's still not too late. (*To the* **Conductor**.) Is it Mister?

Sammy   Mickey.

Linda   He's stayin' here.

Sammy   No-mark!

Sammy *leaps from the 'bus' and is pursued by two policemen.*

The 'bus' pulls away leaving **Mickey** *and* **Linda** *alone on the pavement.*

Linda   He'll get put away for this, y' know, Mickey.

Mickey   I know.

Linda   He's always been a soft get, your Sammy.

Mickey   I know.

Linda   You better hadn't do anything soft, like him.

Mickey   I wouldn't.

Linda   Y' better hadn't or I won't be in love with y' anymore!

Mickey   Shut up! Y' always sayin' that.

Linda   I'm not.

Mickey   Yis y' are. Y' bloody well said it in assembly yesterday.

Linda   Well. I was only tellin' y'.

Mickey   Yeh, an' five hundred others as well.

Linda   I don't care who knows. I just love you. I love you!

Mickey   Come on . . . we're half an hour late as it is.

Mickey *hurries off, followed by* **Linda**.

Edward*'s school where* **Edward** *is confronted by a teacher (the* **Narrator***) looking down his nose at* **Edward**.

Teacher   You're doing very well here, aren't you, Lyons?

Edward   Yes, sir. I believe so.

Teacher   Talk of Oxbridge.

Edward   Yes, sir.

Teacher   Getting rather big for your boots, aren't you?

Edward   No, sir.

Teacher   No, sir? Yes, sir. I think you're a tyke, Lyons. The boys in your dorm say you wear a locket around your neck. Is that so?

Pause.

Edward   Yes, sir.

Teacher   A locket? A locket. This is a boys' school, Lyons.

Edward   I am a boy, sir.

Teacher   Then you must behave like one. Now give this locket to me.

Edward   No, sir.

Teacher   No sir? Am I to punish you Lyons? Am I to have you flogged?

Edward   You can do exactly as you choose Sir. You can take a flying fuck at a rolling doughnut! But you shall not take my locket!

Teacher (*thunderstruck*)   I'm going to . . . I'm going to have you suspended, Lyons.

Edward   Yes, sir.

Edward *exits.*

As **Edward** *exits a class in a Secondary Modern school is formed –
all boredom and futility. The school bell rings. The teacher becomes
the teacher of this class in which we see* **Linda** *and* **Mickey**.

Teacher   And so, we know then, don't we, that the Bora Indian of
the Amazon Basin lives on a diet of . . .

Perkins   Sir, sir . . .

Teacher   A diet of . . .

Perkins   Sir, sir . . .

Teacher   A diet of what, Johnstone? The Bora Indian of the
Amazon Basin lives on a diet of what?

Mickey   What?

Teacher   Exactly lad, exactly. What?

Mickey   I don't know.

Teacher (*his patience gone*)   Y' don't know. (*Mimicking.*) You
don't know. I told y' two minutes ago, lad.

Linda   Leave him alone will y'.

Teacher   You just stay out of this, Miss. It's got nothing to do
with you. It's Johnstone, not you . . .

Perkins   Sir!

Teacher   Oh, shut up Perkins. But you don't listen do you,
Johnstone?

Mickey (*shrugging*)   Yeh.

Teacher   Oh, y' do? Right, come out here in front of the class. Now
then, what is the staple diet of the Bora Indian of the Amazon Basin?

Mickey *looks about for help. There is none.*

Mickey (*defiantly*)   Fish Fingers!

Teacher   Just how the hell do you hope to get a job when you
never listen to anythin'?

Mickey   It's borin'.

Teacher   Yes, yes, you might think it's boring but you won't be sayin' that when you can't get a job.

Mickey   Yeh. Yeh an' it'll really help me to get a job if I know what some soddin' pygmies in Africa have for their dinner!

The class erupts into laughter.

Teacher (*to class*)   Shut up. Shut up.

Mickey   Or maybe y' were thinkin' I was lookin' for a job in an African restaurant.

Teacher   Out!

Linda   Take no notice Mickey. I love you.

Teacher   Johnstone, get out!

Linda   Oh, leave him alone you. Y' big worm!

Teacher   Right you as well . . . out . . . out . . .

Linda   I'm goin' . . . I'm goin' . . .

Teacher   You're both suspended.

Linda *and* **Mickey** *leave the class.*

The classroom sequence breaks up as we see **Mrs Lyons** *staring at a piece of paper.* **Edward** *is standing before her.*

Mrs Lyons (*incredulously*)   Suspended? Suspended? (*She looks at the paper.*) Because of a locket?

Edward   Because I wouldn't let them have my locket.

Mrs Lyons   But what's so . . . Can I see this locket?

There is a pause.

Edward   I suppose so . . . if you want to.

Edward *takes off the locket from around his neck and hands it to his mother. She looks at it without opening it.*

Mrs Lyons   Where did you get this?

Edward   I can't tell you that. It's a secret.

Mrs Lyons (*finally smiling in relief*)   I know it's from a girlfriend, isn't it? (*She laughs.*) Is there a picture in here?

Edward   Yes, Mummy. Can I have it back now?

Mrs Lyons   You won't let Mummy see your girlfriend. Oh, Edward, don't be so . . . (*She playfully moves away.*) Is she beautiful?

Edward   Mummy can . . .

Mrs Lyons   Oh, let me look, let me look. (*She beams a smile at him and then opens the locket.*)

Music.

Edward   Mummy . . . Mummy what's wrong . . . (*He goes to her and holds her steady.*) Mummy!

Mrs Lyons *takes his arms away from her.*

What is it?

Mrs Lyons   When . . . when were you photographed with this woman?

Edward   Pardon!

Mrs Lyons   When! Tell me, Edward.

Edward *begins to laugh.*

Edward!

Edward   Mummy . . . you silly old thing. That's not me. That's Mickey.

Mrs Lyons   What?

Edward   Mickey . . . you remember my friend when I was little. (*He takes the locket and shows it to her.*) Look. That's Mickey . . . and his mother. Why did you think it was me? (*He looks at it.*) I never looked a bit like Mickey.

Edward *replaces the locket around his neck.* **Mrs Lyons** *watches him.*

Mrs Lyons   No it's just . . . (*She stares, deep in thought.*)

Edward (*looking at her*)   Are you feeling all right Mummy? You're not ill again, like you used to be . . . are you?

Mrs Lyons   Where did you get that . . . locket from, Edward? Why do you wear it?

Edward   I can't tell you that, Ma. I've explained, it's a secret, I can't tell you.

Mrs Lyons   But . . . but I'm your mother.

Edward   I know but I still can't tell you. It's not important, I'm going up to my room. It's just a secret, everybody has secrets, don't you have secrets?

Edward *exits to his room.*

The **Narrator** *enters.*

Music continues.

Narrator (*singing*)   Did you really feel that you'd become secure
That time had brushed away the past
That there's no one by the window, no one knocking on your door
Did you believe that you were free at last
Free from the broken looking glass.
Oh y' know the devil's got your number
He's never far behind you
He always knows where to find you
And someone said they'd seen him walking past your door.

Narrator *exits.*

We see **Mickey** *and* **Linda** *making their way up the hill.*

Linda *having some difficulty in high heeled shoes.*

Linda   Tch . . . you didn't tell me it was gonna be over a load of fields.

Mickey   I didn't tell y' nothin'. I didn't ask y' to come, y' followed me. (*He walks away from her.*)

Linda (*watching him walk away*)   Mickey, Mickey . . . I'm stuck
. . . (*Holding out her helpless arms.*) Me foot's stuck. Honest.

Mickey *goes back, timidly takes a wrist and ineffectually pulls.*

Mickey, I think y' might be more successful if you were to sort of
put your arms around here. (*She puts her hands on her waist.*) Oh
Mickey, be gentle, be gentle . . .

Mickey (*managing to pull her free*)   Will you stop takin' the piss
out of me!

Linda   I'm not, I'm not.

Mickey *points down in the direction they have come from.*

Mickey   Look . . . y' can see the estate from up here.

Linda   Have we come all this way just to look at the bleedin'
estate? Mickey we're fourteen.

She beams at him. He can't take it and looks the other way.

Mickey   Look.

Linda   What?

Mickey   There's that lad lookin' out the window. I see him
sometimes when I'm up here.

Linda   Oh him . . . he's gorgeous, isn't he?

Mickey   What?

Linda   He's lovely lookin', isn't he?

Mickey   All right, all right! You've told me once.

Linda   Well, he is. An' what do you care if I think another feller's
gorgeous eh?

Mickey   I don't.

Linda   You . . . I give up with you, Mickey Johnstone. I'm off.
You get on my bleedin' nerves.

Linda *exits.*

Mickey   What . . . Linda . . . Linda . . . Don't . . . Linda, I wanna kiss y', an' put me arms around y' an' kiss y' and kiss y' an even fornicate with y' but I don't know how to tell y', because I've got pimples an' me feet are too big an' me bum sticks out an' . . .

He becomes conscious of **Edward** *approaching, and affects nonchalance.*

(*Speaking*):   If I was like him
      I'd know (*singing*) all the right words

Edward   If I was like . . . him
      I'd know some real birds
      Apart from those in my dreams
      And in magazines.

Mickey   Just look at his hair

Edward   His hair's dark and wavy
      Mine's mousey to fair

Mickey   Mine's the colour of gravy

Edward (*together*)   Each part of his face

Mickey   Is in just the right place
      Is he laughing at me
      At my nose, did he notice

Mickey   I should wear a brace

Edward   That I've got halitosis

Mickey (*together*)   When nature picked on me

Edward   She chose to stick on me

Edward   Eyes that don't match

Mickey   And ears that stand out

Edward (*together*)   She picked the wrong batch

Mickey   When she handed mine out
      And then she attacked me
      With permanent acne

Edward   I wish I was a bit like
Wish that I could score a hit like
And be just a little bit like
That guy
That guy

Mickey   I wish that I could be like
Just a little less like me
Like the sort of guy I see, like
That guy
That guy.

Edward   Hi.

Mickey   Hi. Gis a ciggie?

Edward   Oh, I don't smoke actually. But I can go and get you some.

Mickey   Are you soft? (*He suddenly realizes.*) A blood brother.

Edward   Mickey? Well, shag the vicar.

Mickey *laughs.*

What's wrong?

Mickey   You, it sounds dead funny swearin' in that posh voice.

Edward   What posh voice?

Mickey   That one.

Edward   Well, where do you live?

Mickey   The estate, look. (*He points.*)

Edward   My God, I only live . . .

Mickey   I know.

Edward   That girl I saw you with, was that . . .

Mickey   Linda. Do you remember Linda?

Edward   Wow, was that Linda? And is she your girlfriend?

Mickey   Yeh. She's one of them.

Edward   One of them.

Mickey   Have you got a girlfriend?

Edward   Me? Me? No!

Mickey   Haven't y'?

Edward   Look, you seem to have rather a lot of them, erm . . . perhaps you'd share one with me.

Mickey   Share one. Eddie I haven't even got one girlfriend.

Edward   But Linda . . . you said . . .

Mickey   I know, but she's not. I mean, I mean she would be me girlfriend, she even says she loves me all over the place, but it's just like dead difficult.

Edward   What?

Mickey   Like knowing what to say.

Edward   But you must, you must . . .

Mickey   I know that. But every time I see her I promise meself I'll ask her but, but the words just disappear.

Edward   But you mustn't let them.

Mickey   What do I say, though?

Edward   Mickey, it's easy, I've read about it. Look the next time you see Linda, you stare straight into her eyes and you say, 'Linda, I love you, I want you, the very core of my being is longing for you, my loins are burning for you. Let me lay my weary head between your warm breasts'! And then, Mickey, her eyes will be half closed and her voice may appear somewhat husky as she pleads with you, 'be gentle with me, be gentle'. It would work, you know. Listen, we can see how it's done; look the Essoldo for one week only, *Nymphomaniac Nights* and *Swedish Au Pairs*. Whoa . . .

Mickey   I'll have to go home and get some money . . .

As the boys are going, we see **Mrs Lyons** *appear. She has seen* **Edward** *and* **Mickey** *and she stares after them. Making up her* *mind she quickly goes and fetches a coat, then follows the two boys.*

The **Narrator** *enters.*

Music.

Edward   I've got plenty, I'll lend . . .

Mickey   No, it's all right, me Mam'll give it me . . .

Edward   Come on then, before my Ma sees me. She's off her beam, my Ma . . .

The boys exit, followed by **Mrs Lyons**.

Narrator (*singing*):   Did you really feel you were on solid ground,
     And that the past was tightly locked away,
     Did you really feel that you would never be found,
     Did you forget you've got some debts to pay,
     Did you forget about the reckoning day.
     Yes, the devil he's still got your number,
     He's moved in down the street from you,
     Someone said he wants to speak to you,
     Someone said they'd seen him leanin' on your door.

The **Narrator** *exits.*

We see **Mrs Johnstone** *in her kitchen as* **Mickey** *bursts in followed by* **Edward**.

Mickey   Mother, mam, look, look it's Eddie . . . Eddie . . . **Mrs Johnstone** *stands looking at* **Edward** *and smiling.*

Edward   Hi-ya, Mrs Johnstone. Isn't it fantastic. We're neighbours again.

Mickey   Mum, mum, mum, Eddie lives in that house, y' know that big house on the hill. Mam, can y' lend us a quid to go to the pictures . . .

Mrs Johnstone   Yes, it's, erm . . . it's in the sideboard . . .

Mickey   Oh thanks, mam. I love y'.

Mickey *exits to the next room.*

Edward   You're looking very well, Mrs Johnstone.

Mrs Johnstone   Am I? Do you . . . Do you still keep that locket I gave y'?

Edward   Of course . . . Look . . .

Mickey *enters.*

Mickey   Mam, Mam, can I bring Eddie back afterwards, for coffee?

Mrs Johnstone   Yeh. Go on . . . go an' enjoy yourselves but don't be too late will y'?

Mickey   See y', Mam . . .

Edward   Bye Mrs Johnstone.

The boys prepare to leave.

Mrs Johnstone   'Ey. What's the film you're gonna see?

Edward   Erm what?

Mrs Johnstone   What film . . .

Edward   *Dr Zhivago*   } (*together*)
Mickey   *Magnificent Seven*

Mrs Johnstone   Dr Zhivago's Magnificent Seven?

Edward   It's a double bill.

Mrs Johnstone   I see. An' where's it on?

Mickey (*together*)   WHAT?

Edward   The Essoldo.

Mrs Johnstone   Oh . . . the Essoldo eh? When I passed the Essoldo this mornin' they were showin' *Nymphomaniac Nights* and *Swedish Au Pairs*.

Edward   Ah yes, Mrs Johnstone, yes, yes they're just the trailers: a documentary and and . . .

Mickey   An' a travelogue. About Sweden!

Mrs Johnstone   Do the pair of you really think I was born yesterday?

Edward *can't hold it any longer and breaks into embarrassed laughter.*

Mickey (*trying to hold on*)   It is, it is . . . it's just a travelogue . . .

Mrs Johnstone   Showing the spectacular bends and curves of Sweden . . . Go on y' randy little sods . . .

Mickey (*scandalized*)   Mother!

Mrs Johnstone   Go on before I throw a bucket of water over the pair of y' . . .

Mickey *drags* **Edward** *out.*

I don't know about coffee . . . you'd be better off with bromide. (*She gets on with her work.*)

Edward (*outside the house but looking back*)   She's fabulous your ma, isn't she?

Mickey   She's a fuckin' head case. Come on . . .

As they run off we see **Mrs Lyons** *appear from where she has been concealed in the alley.*

Mrs Johnstone *is lilting the 'We Go Dancing' line as* **Mrs Lyons** *appears in the kitchen.* **Mrs Johnstone** *gets a shock as she looks up and sees* **Mrs Lyons** *there. The two women stare at each other.*

Mrs Johnstone (*eventually nodding*)   Hello.

Mrs Lyons   How long have you lived here?

Pause.

Mrs Johnstone   A few years.

Pause.

Mrs Lyons   Are you always going to follow me?

Mrs Johnstone   We were rehoused here . . . I didn't follow . . .

Mrs Lyons   Don't lie! I know what you're doing to me! You gave him that locket didn't you? Mm?

Mrs Johnstone *nods.*

He never takes it off you know. You're very clever aren't you?

Mrs Johnstone   I . . . I thought I'd never see him again. I wanted him to have . . . a picture of me . . . even though he'd never know.

Mrs Lyons   Afraid he might eventually have forgotten you? Oh no. There's no chance of that. He'll always remember you. After we'd moved he talked less and less of you and your family. I started . . . just for a while I came to believe that he was actually mine.

Mrs Johnstone   He is yours.

Mrs Lyons   No. I took him. But I never made him mine. Does he know? Have you told . . .

Mrs Johnstone   Of course not!

Mrs Lyons   Even when – when he was a tiny baby I'd see him looking straight at me and I'd think, he knows . . . he knows. (*Pause.*) You have ruined me. (*Pause.*) But you won't ruin Edward! Is it money you want?

Mrs Johnstone   What?

Mrs Lyons   I'll get it for you. If you move away from here. How much?

Mrs Johnstone   Look . . .

Mrs Lyons   How much?

Mrs Johnstone   Nothin'! Nothing. (*Pause.*) You bought me off once before . . .

Mrs Lyons   Thousands . . . I'm talking about thousands if you want it. And think what you could do with money like that.

Mrs Johnstone   I'd spend it. I'd buy more junk and trash; that's all. I don't want your money. I've made a life out here. It's not much of one maybe, but I made it. I'm stayin' here. You move if you want to.

Mrs Lyons   I would. But there's no point. You'd just follow me again wouldn't you?

Mrs Johnstone   Look I'm not followin' anybody.

Mrs Lyons   Wherever I go you'll be just behind me. I know that now . . . always and forever and ever like, like a shadow . . . unless I can . . . make . . . you go . . . But you won't so . . .

We see that throughout the above **Mrs Lyons** *has opened the knife drawer and has a lethal-looking kitchen knife in her hand.* **Mrs Johnstone**, *unaware, has her back to her. On impulse, and punctuated by a note*, **Mrs Johnstone** *wheels. On a punctuated note* **Mrs Lyons** *lunges.* **Mrs Johnstone** *moves and avoids it.* **Mrs Lyons** *lunges again but* **Mrs Johnstone** *manages to get hold of her wrist, rendering the knife hand helpless.* **Mrs Johnstone** *takes the knife from* **Mrs Lyons**' *grasp and moves away.*

Mrs Johnstone (*staring at her; knowing*)   YOU'RE MAD. MAD.

Mrs Lyons (*quietly*)   I curse the day I met you. You ruined me.

Mrs Johnstone   Go. Just go!

Mrs Lyons   Witch. (*Suddenly pointing.*) I curse you. Witch!

Mrs Johnstone (*screaming*)   Go!

Mrs Lyons *exits to the street.*

Kids' *voices are heard, chanting, off.*

Kids (*off*)   High upon the hill the mad woman lives,
Never ever eat the sweets she gives,
Just throw them away and tell your Dad,
High upon a hill there's a woman gone mad.
Mad woman, mad woman living on the hill,
If she catches your eye then you never will
Grow any further, your teeth will go bad
High upon a hill there's a woman gone mad.

Eddie *and* **Mickey** *emerge from the cinema, blinking as they try to adjust to the glare of the light in the street. They are both quite overcome with their celluloid/erotic encounter. As they pause and light up cigarettes by a corner lamp post they groan in their ecstatic agony. Each is in an aroused trance.*

Mickey   Ooh . . .!

Edward   Naked knockers, ooh . . .!

Mickey   Naked knockers with nipples . . .

Edward   Playing tennis. Ooh. Tennis with tits. Will Wimbledon ever be the same?

Mickey   Tits!

Edward   Tits, tits, tits . . . (*He begins a frustrated chant of the word, oblivious to everything.*)

Linda *and a mate enter.*

Finally **Mickey** *realizes* **Linda**'s *presence and knocks* **Edward**, *who becomes aware of the girls' presence. He goes into a song without missing a beat.*

> Tits, tits, tits a lovely way,
> To spend an evening . . .

Edward *grabs* **Linda**'s *mate and begins to waltz her around the street.*

> Can't think of anything
> I'd rather do . . .

Mate (*simultaneously with the above*)   Gerroff. Put me down, get y' friggin' paws off me you. Linda. Y' bloody lunatic, gettoff.

Edward *finally releases her and bows.*

Linda, come on. I'm goin' . . .

The **Mate** *begins to walk away.* **Linda** *makes no attempt to follow.*

Linda   What y' doin' in town, Mick?

Mickey   We've erm, we've . . .

Edward   We have been undergoing a remarkable celluloid experience!

Mate   We'll miss the bus, Linda.

Mickey   We've been the pictures.

Linda   So have we. What did y' go see?

Edward   *Nympho . . .*

Mickey   *Bridge Over the River Kwai.*

Linda   Ah, we've seen that. We went to see *Nymphomaniac Nights* instead. An' *Swedish Au Pairs*.

Mickey   You what!

Edward *begins to laugh.*

Mate   Oh, sod y' then. I'm goin'.

The **Mate** *exits.*

Mickey (*to* **Edward**)   What are you laughin' at? Take no notice. Remember Eddie? He's still a head case. Shurrup.

Edward (*shouting*)   Tits. Tits, tits, tits, tits, tits.

Edward *leaps around and hopefully ends up sitting at the top of the lamp post.* **Linda** *and* **Mickey** *laugh at him, while* **Edward** *chants.*

A **Policeman** *enters.*

The three do not see the arrival of the **Policeman**.

Policeman: An' what the bloody hell do you think you're doin'?

Edward   Adolph Hitler?

Policeman   Get down.

Edward *gets down from the lamp post.*

Policeman (*getting out his black book*)   Right. I want your names. What's your name?

Linda
Mickey } (*together*)   Waitin' for the ninety-two bus!

Edward
Linda } (*pointing upwards*)   Oh my God, look . . .

Policeman   Now listen . . .

The **Policeman** *falls for it and looks up.*

The three make their exit.

The **Policeman** *realizes and gives chase.*

Mickey, Linda *and* **Edward** *enter, laughing and exhausted.*

The **Narrator** *enters.*

Narrator   There's a few bob in your pocket and you've got good friends,
      And it seems that Summer's never coming to an end,
      Young, free and innocent, you haven't got a care,
      Apart from decidin' on the clothes you're gonna wear.
      The street's turned into Paradise, the radio's singing dreams
      You're innocent, immortal, you're just fifteen.

The **Narrator** *becomes the rifle range man at the fairground.*

Linda, Mickey *and* **Edward** *rush on.*

Linda, Mickey *and* **Edward** *pool their money and hand it to the rifle range man. He gives the gun to* **Mickey**, *who smiles, shakes his head and points to* **Linda**. *The man offers the gun to* **Edward** *but* **Linda** *takes it. The boys indicate to the rifle range man that he has had it now* **Linda** *has the gun. They eagerly watch the target but their smiles fade as* **Linda** *misses all three shots.* **Mickey** *and* **Edward** *turn on* **Linda** *in mock anger. They are stopped by the rifle range man throwing them a coconut which is used as a ball for a game of piggy-in-the-middle. When* **Linda** *is caught in the middle the game freezes.*

      And who'd dare tell the lambs in Spring,
      What fate the later seasons bring.
      Who'd tell the girl in the middle of the pair
      The price she'll pay for just being there.

Throughout the following we see **Linda, Mickey** *and* **Edward** *suiting their action to the words – coming out of the chip shop, talking, lighting a cigarette by the lamp post.*

> But leave them alone, let them go and play
> They care not for what's at the end of the day.
> For what is to come, for what might have been,
> Life has no ending when you're sweet sixteen
> And your friends are with you to talk away the night,
> Or until Mrs Wong switches off the chippy light.
> Then there's always the corner and the street lamp's glare
> An' another hour to spend, with your friends, with her,
> To share your last cigarette and your secret dream
> At the midnight hour, at seventeen.

Throughout the following we see **Linda, Mickey** *and* **Edward**, *as if at the beach,* **Linda** *taking a picture of* **Mickey** *and* **Edward**, *arms around each other camping it for the camera but eventually giving good and open smiles.* **Mickey** *taking a picture of* **Edward** *and* **Linda. Edward** *down on one knee and kissing her hand.* **Edward** *taking a picture of* **Mickey** *and* **Linda. Mickey** *pulling a distorted face,* **Linda** *wagging a finger at him.* **Mickey** *chastened.* **Linda** *raising her eyebrows and putting one of his arms round her.* **Linda** *moving forward and taking the camera.* **Linda** *waving the* **Narrator** *to snap them. He goes.* **Linda** *showing the* **Narrator** *how to operate the camera.* **Linda, Mickey** *and* **Edward**, *grouped together, arms around each other as the* **Narrator** *takes the picture. They get the camera and wave their thanks to the* **Narrator**.

> It's just another ferry boat, a trip to the beach
> But everything is possible, the world's within your reach
> An' you don't even notice broken bottles in the sand
> The oil in the water and you can't understand
> How living could be anything other than a dream
> When you're young, free and innocent and just eighteen.

Linda, Mickey *and* **Edward** *exit.*

> And only if the three of them could stay like that forever,
> And only if we could predict no changes in the weather,

And only if we didn't live in life, as well as dreams
And only if we could stop and be forever, just eighteen.

We see **Edward**, *waiting by a street lamp.*

Linda *approaches, sees him, and goes into a street walk.*

Linda   Well, hallo, sweetie pie; looking for a good time? Ten to seven. (*She laughs.*) Good time . . . ten to seven . . . it was a joke . . . I mean I know it was a lousy joke but y' could at least go into hysterics!

Edward *smiles.*

That's hysterics?

Edward   Where's Mickey?

Linda   He must be workin' overtime.

Edward   Oh.

Linda   What's wrong with you, misery?

Edward (*after a pause*)   I go away to university tomorrow.

Linda   Tomorrow! You didn't say.

Edward   I know. I think I've been pretending that if I didn't mention it the day would never come. I love it when we're together, the three of us, don't you?

Linda *nods.*

Can I write to you?

Linda   Yeh . . . yeh, if you want.

Edward   Would Mickey mind?

Linda   Why should he?

Edward   Come on . . . because you're his girlfriend.

Linda   No, I'm not.

Edward   You are, Linda.

Linda   I'm not, he hasn't asked me.

Edward (*laughing*)   You mean he still hasn't?

Linda (*laughing*)   No.

Edward   But it's ridiculous.

Linda   I know. I hope for his sake he never has to ask me to marry him. He'll be a pensioner before he gets around to it.

Edward (*after a pause*)   He's mad. If I was Mickey I would have asked you years ago.

Linda   I know *you* would. Cos y' soft you are.

Edward (*singing*)   If I could stand inside his shoes I'd say, How can I compare thee to a summer's day . . .

Linda (*speaking*)   Oh go away . . .

Edward   I'd take a page in all the papers, I'd announce it on the news

> If I was the guy, if I
> Was in his shoes.
> If I was him I'd bring you flowers
> And ask you to dance
> We'd while away the hours making future plans
> For rainy days in country lanes
> And trips to the sea
> I'd just tell you that I love you
> If it was me.
> But I'm not saying a word,
> I'm not saying I care,
> Though I would like you to know,
> That I'm not saying a word,
> I'm not saying I care,
> Though I would like you to know.
> If I was him I'd have to tell you,
> What I've kept in my heart,
> That even if we had to live
> Some worlds apart
> There would not be a day
> In which I'd not think of you
> If I was him, if I was him

That's what I'd do.
But I'm not saying a word
I'm not saying I care
Though I would like you to know
That I'm not saying a word
I'm not saying I care
Though I would like you to know.

But I'm not.

Linda   What?

Edward   Mickey.

Mickey *enters.*

Mickey!

Mickey   Hi-ya, Ed. Lind.

Linda   Where've y' been?

Mickey   I had to do overtime. I hate that soddin' place.

Edward   Mickey. I'm going away tomorrow . . . to University.

Mickey   What? Y' didn't say.

Edward   I know . . . but the thing is I won't be back until Christmas. Three months. Now you wouldn't want me to continue in suspense for all that time would you?

Linda   What are you on about?

Edward   Will you talk to Linda.

Linda   Oh Eddie . . .

Edward   Go on . . . go on.

Mickey *turns and goes to her.* **Linda** *tries to keep a straight face.*

Mickey   Erm . . . well, the er thing is . . . Linda, I've erm . . . (*Quickly.*) Linda for Christ's sake will you go out with me?

Linda (*just as quickly*)   Yeh.

Mickey   Oh . . . erm . . . Good. Well, I suppose I better . . . well er . . . come here . . . (*He quickly embraces and kisses* **Linda**.)

Linda (*fighting for air*)   My God. Y' take y' time gettin' goin' but then there's no stoppin' y'.

Mickey   I know . . . come here . . .

They kiss again. **Edward** *turns and begins to leave.*

Eddie . . . Eddie where y' goin'? I though we were all goin' the club. There's a dance.

Edward   No . . . I've got to, erm, I've got to pack for tomorrow.

Mickey   Are y' sure?

Edward *nods.*

See y' at Christmas then, Eddie? Listen, I'm gonna do loads of overtime between now and then, so the Christmas party's gonna be on me . . . right?

Edward   Right. It's a deal, Mick. See you.

Linda *rushes across and kisses* **Edward** *lightly.*

Linda   Thanks Eddie.

Mickey   Yeh, Eddie . . . thanks.

Linda *and* **Mickey**, *arms around each other, watch him go. They turn and look at each other.*

Mickey *and* **Linda** *exit.*

The Lights crossfade to the **Johnstone** *house.*

Mickey *enters and prepares to go to work.*

Mrs Johnstone *enters with* **Mickey***'s lunch bag.*

The **Narrator** *enters.*

> It was one day in October when the sun began to fade,
> And Winter broke the promise that Summer had just made,
> It was one day in October when the rain came falling down,
> And someone said the bogey man was seen around the town.

The **Narrator** *exits.*

Mrs Johnstone   Y' gonna be late Mick. I don't want you gettin'
the sack an' spendin' your days idlin' round like our Sammy.
Come on.

Mickey *instead of making an effort to go, stands looking at her.*

Mickey   Mam!

Mrs Johnstone   What?

Mickey   What!

Mrs Johnstone   Come on.

Mickey   Mam. Linda's pregnant! *A moment.*

Mrs Johnstone   Do you love her?

Mickey   Yeh!

Mrs Johnstone   When's the weddin'?

Mickey   We thought, about a month . . . before Christmas
anyway. Mam, could we live here for a bit?

She looks at him and nods.

Are you mad?

Mrs Johnstone   At you? Some hypocrite I'd be. No . . . I'm not
mad son. I'm just thinkin' . . . you've not had much of a life with
me, have y'?

Mickey   Don't be stupid, course I have. You're great, you are,
Mam. (*He gives her a quick kiss.*) Tar-ra I'd better get a move
on. They've started layin' people off in the other factory y' know.
Tarrah, Mam. Thanks.

Mickey *exits.*

Music.

Mrs Johnstone *watches him go. As 'Miss Jones' begins she whips
off her overall and a wedding suit is underneath. She acquires a hat.
A wedding party assembles.* **Mickey** *remains in his working clothes.*

Linda *is in white. Other guests are suitably attired. A* **Managing Director** *enters and sings as his secretary,* **Miss Jones**, *takes notes.*

Mr Lyons (*singing*)   Take a letter, Miss Jones (quote)
   I regret to inform you,
   That owing to circumstances
   Quite beyond our control.
   It's a premature retirement
   For those surplus to requirement,
   I'm afraid it's a sign of the times,
   Miss Jones,
   An unfortunate sign of the times.

Throughout the next verse we see the wedding party wave goodbye to **Mickey** *who goes to work, only to have his cards given to him when he gets there.*

   Take a letter, Miss Jones,
   Due to the world situation
   The shrinking pound, the global slump,
   And the price of oil
   I'm afraid we must fire you,
   We no longer require you,
   It's just another
   Sign of the times,
   Miss Jones,
   A most miserable sign of the times.

The **Guests** *at the wedding become a line of men looking for work.* **Mickey** *joins them as* **Linda** *watches. They are constantly met with shaking heads and by the end of the following verse have assembled in the dole office.*

   Take a letter Miss Jones, of course we'll
   Let the workforce know when
   Inflation's been defeated
   And recession is no more.
   And for the moment we suggest
   You don't become too depressed
   As it's only a sign

Of the times,
Miss Jones,
A peculiar sign of the times.
Take a letter Miss Jones:
My dear Miss Jones, we'd like to thank you
Many years of splendid service,
Et cetera blah blah blah
You've been a perfect poppet
Yes that's right Miss Jones, you've got it
It's just another sign
Of the times,
Miss Jones, it's
Just another sign of the times.

He shows her the door. Crying she approaches the dole queue but then hesitates. The men in the queue take up the song.

Doleites   Dry your eyes, Miss Jones
It's not as bad as it seems (you)
Get used to being idle
In a year or two.
Unemployment's such a pleasure
These days, we call it leisure
It's just another sign
Of the times,
Miss Jones, it's
Just another sign of the times.

Mickey *leaves the group and stands apart.* **Miss Jones** *takes his place. Behind* **Mickey** *we can see* **Linda** *and his* **Mother**.

There's a young man on the street, Miss Jones,
He's walkin' round in circles,
He's old before his time,
But still too young to know.
Don't look at him, don't cry though
This living on the Giro
Is only a sign of the times,
Miss Jones, it's
Just another sign of the times.

As they exit.

> Miss Jones,
> It's just another sign of the times . . .

Crowd *exits.*

Mickey *is left alone, sitting dejected. We hear Christmas Bells.*
Edward *enters in a duffle coat and college scarf, unseen by*
Mickey. **Edward** *creeps up behind* **Mickey** *and puts his hands*
over his eyes.

Edward   Guess who?

Mickey   Father Christmas.

Edward (*leaping out in front of them*)   **Mickey** . . . (*Laughing.*)
Merry Christmas.

Mickey, *unamused, looks at* **Edward** *and then looks away.* Come
on then . . . I'm back, where's the action, the booze, the Christmas
parties, the music and the birds. *No reaction.*

What's wrong, Mickey?

Mickey   Nothin'. How's University?

Edward   Mickey, it's fantastic. I haven't been to so many parties
in my life. And there's just so many tremendous people, but you'll
meet them Mick, some of them, Baz, Ronnie and Clare and oh, lots
of them. They're coming over to stay for the New Year, for the
party. Ooh it's just . . . it's great, Mickey.

Mickey   Good.

Edward   Come on, what's wrong? It's nearly Christmas, we were
going to do everything. How's Linda?

Mickey   She's OK.

Edward (*trying again to rally him*)   Well, come on then, let's go
then . . . come on.

Mickey   Come on where?

Edward   Mickey, what's wrong?

Mickey   You. You're a dick head!

Edward *is slightly unsure but laughs anyway.*

There are no parties arranged. There is no booze or music. Christmas? I'm sick to the teeth of Christmas an' it isn't even here yet. See, there's very little to celebrate, Eddie. Since you left I've been walking around all day, every day, lookin' for a job.

Edward   What about the job you had?

Mickey   It disappeared. (*Pause.*) Y' know somethin', I bleedin' hated that job, standin' there all day never doin' nothin' but put cardboard boxes together. I used to get . . . used to get terrified that I'd have to do it for the rest of me life. But, but after three months of nothin', the same answer everywhere, nothin', nothin' down for y', I'd crawl back to that job for half the pay and double the hours. Just . . . just makin' up boxes it was. But after bein' fucked off from everywhere, it seems like it was paradise.

Pause.

Edward   Why . . . why is a job so important? If I couldn't get a job I'd just say, sod it and draw the dole, live like a bohemian, tilt my hat to the world and say 'screw you'. So you're not working. Why is it so important?

Mickey (*looking at him*)   You don't understand anythin' do y'? I don't wear a hat that I could tilt at the world.

Edward   Look . . . come on . . . I've got money, plenty of it. I'm back, let's forget about bloody jobs, let's go and get Linda and celebrate. Look, look, money, lots of it, have some . . . (*He tries to thrust some notes into* **Mickey**'s *hands.*)

Mickey   No. I don't want your money, stuff it.

He throws the notes to the ground. **Edward** *picks them up and stands looking at* **Mickey**.

Eddie, just do me a favour an' piss off, will y'?

Pause.

Edward   I thought, I thought we always stuck together. I thought we were . . . were blood brothers.

Mickey   That was kids' stuff, Eddie. Didn't anyone tell y'? (*He looks at* **Edward**.) But I suppose you still are a kid, aren't y'?

Edward   I'm exactly the same age as you, Mickey.

Mickey   Yeh. But you're still a kid. An' I wish I could be as well Eddie, I wish I could still believe in all that blood brother stuff. But I can't, because while no one was looking I grew up. An' you didn't, because you didn't need to; an' I don't blame y' for it Eddie. In your shoes I'd be the same, I'd still be able to be a kid. But I'm not in your shoes, I'm in these, lookin' at you. An' you make me sick, right? That was all just kids' stuff, Eddie, an' I don't want to be reminded of it. Right? So just, just take yourself away. Go an' see your friends an' celebrate with them.

Pause.

Go on . . . beat it before I hit y'.

Edward *looks at* **Mickey** *and then slowly backs away.*
Sammy *approaches* **Mickey** *as, on the other side, we see* **Linda** *hurrying on passing* **Edward** *who stops and calls.*

Edward   Linda!

Sammy   Mickey.

Edward   Linda.

Reluctantly she stops, goes back a few paces.

Hello, Linda.

Linda   Hello, Eddie.

Edward   Why haven't you called to see me?

Linda   I heard you had friends, I didn't like butting in.

Edward   You'd never be butting in and you know it. It wouldn't matter if I never saw those friends again, if I could be with you.

Linda   Eddie . . .

Sammy   Look, I'm offerin' . . . all we need is someone to keep the eye for us. Look at y' Mickey. What have y' got? Nothin', like me Mam. Where y' takin' y' tart for New Year? Nowhere.

Edward   You might as well know, if I'm not going to see you again. I've always loved you, you must have known that.

Sammy   We don't *use* the shooters. They're just frighteners. Y' don' need to use them. Everyone behaves when they see a shooter. You won't even be where the action is. Just keep the eye out for us.

Edward   I'm sorry.

Sammy   Fifty quid Mickey. Fifty quid for an hour's work. Just think where y' could take Linda if you had cash like that.

Edward   I'm sorry, Linda.

Linda   It's all right. I suppose, I suppose I always . . . loved you, in a way.

Edward   Then marry me.

Linda   Didn't Mickey tell y'? We got married two weeks before you came home and I'm expecting a baby.

Mickey   Fifty notes?

Sammy *nods.*

All right.

Sammy   Great.

Mickey *nods.*

Cheer up, will y'? It's New Year.

Sammy *exits.*

Edward's Friends (*variously; off*)   Where's Lyo? Come on Lyons, you pillock, you're supposed to be helping us with the booze. Come on Lyonese. Edward, come on.

Linda   I'll see y' Eddie. Happy New Year. (*She moves away.*)

Edward *exits*.

Mickey   Linda . . . Linda . . .

Linda   Are you comin' in?

Mickey   Look . . . I'll be back about eight o'clock. An' listen, get dressed up. I'm takin' y' out.

Linda   What?

Mickey   We're goin' dancin'. Right? Then we're goin' for a slap-up meal an' tomorrow you can go into town an' get some new clothes.

Linda   Oh yeh? Where's the money comin' from?

Mickey   I'm . . . Doin' some work . . .

Linda   What?

Mickey   Look, stop arguin', will y'? I'm doin' some work and then I'm takin' you out.

Sammy (*off*)   Mickey!

Linda   Is that your Sammy?

Mickey   Now shut up, Linda. Right, right? Just make sure you're ready at eight . . . (*He starts to leave*.)

Linda (*as he goes*)   Mickey . . . Mickey . . . No!

Linda *exits*.

Mickey *moves away*.

The **Narrator** *enters*.

Sammy *enters*.

Narrator   There's a full moon shining and a joker in the pack, The dealers dealt the cards, and he won't take them back, There's a black cat stalking and a woman who's afraid, That there's no getting off without the price being paid.

We see **Mickey**, *nervously keeping look-out as behind him, as if inside a filling station office, we see* **Sammy**, *his back to us, talking to an off-stage character*.

Sammy Don't piss about with me, pal . . . I said give! (*Pause.*) Listen, it's not a toy y' know . . . We're not playin' games. Y' don't get up again if one of these hits y' . . . What are you doin'? I said listen to me, I said . . . don't you fuckin' touch that . . . Listen.

An alarm bell is heard, followed by an explosion from the gun. **Sammy** *reels backwards. He and* **Mickey** *run and enter their house.*

Narrator There's a man lies bleeding on a garage floor,

Sammy Quick, get in the house an' bolt the fuckin' door.

Mickey *stands unable to move, tears streaming down his face.*

Narrator And maybe, if you counted ten and kept your fingers crossed
It would all be just a game and then no one would have lost.

Mickey You shot him, you shot him.

Sammy I know I bloody did.

Mickey You shot him, you shot him.

Sammy Move, I've got to get this hid.

Linda (*off*) Mickey . . . Mickey, is that you?

Sammy Ooh, fuck . . . (*He quickly pulls back a mat, pulls up a floorboard and puts the gun beneath it.*)

Linda *enters.*

Two **Policemen** *arrive at the house.*

Sammy *splits out the back.* **Mickey** *remains silently crying.* **Linda** *goes to him and puts her arms around him. As* **Sammy** *is being apprehended at the back, the other* **Policeman** *enters and gently removes* **Linda** *from* **Mickey** *and leads him out and into the police station.*

Linda But I've ironed him a shirt.

Music.

Mickey, *placed in a prison cell, stands quietly crying.*

Mrs Johnston *enters.*

Mrs Johnstone (*singing*)   The jury found him guilty
    Sent him down for seven years,
    Though he acted like they gave him life,
    He couldn't stop the tears.
    And when we went to visit him,
    He didn't want to know,
    It seems like jail's sent him off the rails,
    Just like Marilyn Monroe
    His mind's gone dancing
    Can't stop dancing

A **Doctor** *enters the cell and examines* **Mickey**.

    They showed him to a doctor,
    And after routine tests,
    A prescription note the doctor wrote,
    For the chronically depressed.
    And now the tears have stopped
    He sits and counts the days to go
    And treats his ills with daily pills
    Just like Marilyn Monroe.

The **Doctor** *exits.*
    They stop his mind from dancing
    Stop it dancing.

A prison warder leads **Linda** *into the cell. He indicates a seat opposite* **Mickey**.

Linda   What are y' doin'?

Mickey   What? I'm takin' me tablet.

Linda   Listen, Mickey. I've told y'. They're just junk. You'll be home soon, Mickey, and you should come off them.

Mickey   Why? I need . . . I need to take them.

Linda   Listen, Mickey, you've . . .

Mickey   No! See, he says, the doctor, he said . . .

Linda   What did he say?

Mickey   He said, about me nerves. An' how I get depressed an' I need to take these cos they make me better . . .

Linda   I get depressed but I don't take those. You don't need those, Mickey.

Mickey   Leave me alone, will y'? I can't cope with this. I'm not well. The doctor said, didn't he, I'm not well . . . I can't do things . . . leave me alone . . .

The **Warder** *escorts* **Linda** *from the cell.*

Throughout the following verse **Mickey** *leaves the prison and goes home.*

Mrs Johnstone (*singing*)   With grace for good behaviour
        He got out before his time
        The family and the neighbours told him
        He was lookin' fine.
        But he's feelin' fifteen years older
        And his speech is rather slow
        And the neighbours said
        You'd think he was dead
        Like Marilyn Monroe
        No cause for dancing
        No more dancing . . .

Linda *approaches* **Mrs Johnstone. Linda** *is weighed down with shopping bags and is weary.*

Mrs Johnstone   Linda, where've y' been? We've gorra do somethin' about him. He's been out for months and he's still takin' those pills. Linda, he needs a job, you two need a place of your own an' . . .

Linda   Mam . . . Mam that's why I'm late, I've been to see . . . We're movin' at the end of the month. We've got our own place an' I think I've got Mickey a job . . .

Mrs Johnstone   Oh, Jesus, thank God. But how . . .

Linda   It's all right . . . I . . . someone I know . . .

Mrs Johnstone   But who . . .

Linda   It's all right Mam. Did y' get our Sarah from school?

Mrs Johnstone   Yeh, she's in bed, but listen how did y' manage to . . .

Linda   Never mind, Mam. Mam, isn't it great; if he's workin' an' we've got our own place he'll be able to get himself together an' stop takin' those friggin' things . . .

They start to leave.

Mrs Johnstone   But, listen Linda, who . . .

Linda   Oh just some . . . some feller I know. He's . . . he's on the housin' committee. You don't know him, Mam . . .

Mrs Johnstone *exits.*

Mickey *and* **Linda** *are in their new house. In the lounge* **Linda** *is preparing* **Mickey***'s working things.*

(*Shouting*): Mickey, Mickey, come on, you'll be late . . .

Mickey *enters his house.*

Mickey   Where's me . . .

Linda   Here . . . here's y' bag. Y' sandwiches are in there . . .

He ignores the bag and begins looking through a cupboard drawer.

Mickey, what y' lookin' for?

Mickey   Y' know what I'm lookin' for.

Linda   Mickey, Mickey listen to me . . .

Mickey   Where's me tablets gone, Linda?

Linda   Mickey you don't need your tablets!

Mickey   Linda!

Linda   Mickey. You're workin' now, we're livin' on our own –
you've got to start makin' an effort.

Mickey   Give them to me, Linda.

Linda   You promised.

Mickey   I know I promised but I can't do without them. I tried.
Last week I tried to do without them. By dinner time I was shakin'
an' sweating so much I couldn't even work. I need them. That's all
there is to it. Now give.

Pause.

Linda   Is that it then? Are y' gonna stay on them forever?

Mickey   Linda.

Linda   Look. We've . . . we've managed to sort ourselves out this
far but what's the use if . . .

Mickey   *We* have sorted ourselves out? Do you think I'm really
stupid?

Linda   What?

Mickey   I didn't sort anythin' out Linda. Not a job, not a house,
nothin'. It used to be just sweets an' ciggies he gave me, because I
had none of me own. Now it's a job and a house. I'm not stupid,
Linda. You sorted it out. You an' Councillor Eddie Lyons.

Linda *doesn't deny it.*

Now give me the tablets . . . I need them.

Linda   An' what about what I need? I need you. I love you. But,
Mickey, not when you've got them inside you. When you take
those things, Mickey, I can't even see you.

Mickey   That's why I take them. So I can be invisible. (*Pause.*)
Now give me them.

Music. We see **Linda** *mutely hand* **Mickey** *her bag.*

Mickey *quickly grabs the tablets.*

Mickey *exits.*

The **Narrator** *enters.*

The **Narrator** *watches* **Linda**. *She moves to telephone, but hesitates.*

Narrator   There's a girl inside the woman
    Who's waiting to get free
    She's washed a million dishes
    She's always making tea.

Linda (*speaking on the 'phone*)   Could I talk to Councillor Lyons, please?

Narrator   There's a girl inside the woman
    And the mother she became
    And a half remembered song
    Comes to her lips again.

Linda (*on the 'phone*)   Eddie, could I talk to you? Yeh, I remember.

Narrator   The girl would sing the melody
    But the woman stands in doubt
    And wonders what the price would be
    For letting the young girl out.

Mrs Johnstone *enters.*

Mrs Johnstone (*singing*)   It's just a light romance,
    It's nothing cruel,
    They laid no plans,
    How it came,
    Who can explain?

Linda *approaches* **Edward** *who is waiting at the park fence.*
    They just said 'hello',
    And foolishly they gazed,
    They should have gone
    Their separate ways.

The music continues.

Edward   Hey. (*He mimes firing a gun.*)

Linda   Missed.

Edward *laughs, grabbing* **Linda** *jokingly. Their smiles fade as they look at each other. Suddenly they kiss. They walk together, hand in hand. All this through the following verse.*

Mrs Johnstone (*singing*)   It's just the same old song,
Nothing cruel,
Nothing wrong.
It's just two fools,
Who know the rules,
But break them all,
And grasp at half a chance
To play their part
In a light romance.

Throughout the following chorus we see **Mickey** *at work.*

We see him go to take his pills. We see him make the effort of not taking them. We see the strain of this upon him but see that he is determined.

Living on the never never,
Constant as the changing weather,
Never sure
Who's at the door,
Or the price
You're gonna have to pay.

We see **Linda** *and* **Edward** *kicking up the leaves before parting.*

It's just a secret glance,
Across a room.
A touch of hands
That part too soon.
That same old tune
That always plays,
And lets them dance as friends,
Then stand apart,
As the music ends.

During the next chorus **Edward** *and* **Linda** *wave goodbye, as* **Edward** *and* **Mickey** *once did.*

Mrs Lyons *enters and goes to* **Mickey**.

She turns **Mickey** *round and points out* **Edward** *and* **Linda** *to him. By the end of the chorus* **Mickey** *is hammering on his own door.*

> Living on the never never,
> Constant as the changing weather,
> Never sure
> Who's at the door
> Or the price you're gonna have to pay.

As the music abruptly segues **Mickey** *is heard hammering on his door and calling for* **Linda**, *as he once did for his mother.*

The music pulsates and builds as he runs to his mother's house. He enters and flings back the floorboard to reveal the gun hidden by **Sammy**.

Mrs Johnstone *enters just as* **Mickey** *disappears with the gun.*

Mrs Johnstone (*screaming*)   Mickey . . . Mickey . . .

We see **Mickey** *comb the town, breaking through groups of people, looking, searching, desperate, not even knowing what he's looking for or what he is going to do. His mother is frantically trying to catch him but not succeeding.*

Narrator   There's a man gone mad in the town tonight,
> He's gonna shoot somebody down,
> There's a man gone mad, lost his mind tonight
> There's a mad man
> There's a mad man
> There's a mad man running round and round.
> Now you know the devil's got your number,
> He's runnin' right beside you,
> He's screamin' deep inside you,
> And someone said he's callin' your number up today.

As **Mrs Johnstone** *makes her way to* **Linda**'s *house.*

> There's a mad man/There's a mad man/There's a mad man.

Mrs Johnstone *hammers on* **Linda**'s *door, shouting her name.* **Linda**, *just returning home, comes up behind her.*

Linda   Mam . . . Mam . . . what's . . .

Mrs Johnstone (*out of breath*)   He's . . . Mickey . . . Mickey's got a gun . . .

Linda   Mickey? . . . Eddie? . . . The Town Hall . . .

Mrs Johnstone   What?

Linda (*beginning to run*)   Eddie Lyons!

Narrator   There's a mad man running round and round
You know the devil's got your number
You know he's right beside you
He's screamin' deep inside you
And someone said he's callin' your number up today
Today
Today
TODAY!

On the last three words of the chorus **Mrs Johnstone** *runs off.*

On the last 'Today' the music stops abruptly.

We see **Edward**, *standing behind a table, on a platform.*

He is in the middle of addressing his audience. Two Councillors stand either side.

Edward   And if, for once, I agree with Councillor Smith, you mustn't hold that against me. But in this particular instance, yes, I do agree with him. You're right, Bob, there is a light at the end of the tunnel. Quite right. None of us would argue with you on that score. But what we would question is this, how many of us . . .

From his audience a commotion is beginning. He thinks he is being heckled and so tries to carry on. In fact his audience is reacting to the sight of **Mickey** *appearing from the stalls, a gun held two-handed, to steady his shaking hands, and pointed directly at* **Edward. Edward** *turns and sees* **Mickey** *as someone on the platform next to him realizes the reality of the situation and screams.*

Mickey   Stay where you are!

Mickey *stops a couple of yards from* **Edward**. *He is unsteady and breathing awkwardly.*

Edward (*eventually*)   Hello, Mickey.

Mickey   I stopped takin' the pills.

Edward (*pause*)   Oh.

Mickey (*eventually*)   I began thinkin' again. Y' see. (*To the* **Councillor**.) Just get her out of here, mister, now!

The **Councillors** *hurry off.*

Edward *and* **Mickey** *are now alone on the platform.*

I had to start thinkin' again. Because there was one thing left in my life. (*Pause*.) Just one thing I had left, Eddie – Linda – an' I wanted to keep her. So, so I stopped takin' the pills. But it was too late. D' y' know who told me about . . . you . . . an' Linda . . . Your mother . . . she came to the factory and told me.

Edward   Mickey, I don't know what she told you but Linda and I are just friends . . .

Mickey (*shouting for the first time*)   Friends! I could kill you. We were friends weren't we? Blood brothers, wasn't it? Remember?

Edward   Yes, Mickey, I remember.

Mickey   Well, how come you got everything . . . an' I got nothin'? (*Pause*.) Friends. I've been thinkin' again Eddie. You an' Linda were friends when she first got pregnant, weren't y'?

Edward   Mickey!

Mickey   Does my child belong to you as well as everythin' else? Does she, Eddie, does she?

Edward (*shouting*)   No, for God's sake!

Pause.

From the back of the auditorium we hear a **Policeman** *through a loudhailer.*

Policeman 1   Now listen, son, listen to me; I've got armed marksmen with me. But if you do exactly as I say we won't need to use them, will we? Now look, Michael, put down the gun, just put the gun down, son.

Mickey (*dismissing their presence*)   What am I doin' here Eddie? I thought I was gonna shoot y'. But I can't even do that. I don't even know if the thing's loaded.

Mrs Johnstone *slowly walks down the centre aisle towards the platform.*

Policeman 2   What's that woman doin'?

Policeman 1   Get that woman away . . .

Policeman 2   Oh Christ.

Mrs Johnstone   Mickey. Mickey. Don't shoot him Mickey . . .

Mickey *continues to hold the gun in position.*

Mickey   Go away Mam . . . Mam you go away from here.

Mrs Johnstone   No, son. (*She walks on to the platform.*)

Mickey (*shouting*)   Mam!

Mrs Johnstone   Mickey. Don't shoot Eddie. He's your brother. You had a twin brother. I couldn't afford to keep both of you. His mother couldn't have kids. I agreed to give one of you away!

Mickey (*something that begins deep down inside him*)   You! (*Screaming.*) You! Why didn't you give me away! (*He stands glaring at her, almost uncontrollable with rage.*) I could have been . . . I could have been him!

On the word 'him' **Mickey** *waves at* **Edward** *with his gun hand. The gun explodes and blows* **Edward** *apart.* **Mickey** *turns to the* **Police** *screaming the word 'No'. They open fire and four guns explode, blowing* **Mickey** *away.*

Linda *runs down the aisle.*

The **Police** *are heard through the loudhailer.*

Nobody move, please. It's all right, it's all over, just stay where you are.

Music.

As the Light on the scene begins to dim we see the
Narrator, *watching.*

Narrator   And do we blame superstition for what came to pass?
Or could it be what we, the English, have come to know as class?
Did you ever hear the story of the Johnstone twins,
As like each other as two new pins,
How one was kept and one given away,
How they were born, and they died, on the self same day?

Mrs Johnstone (*singing*)   Tell me it's not true,
Say it's just a story.
Something on the news
Tell me it's not true.
Though it's here before me,
Say it's just a dream,
Say it's just a scene
From an old movie of years ago,
From an old movie of Marilyn Monroe.
Say it's just some clowns,
Two players in the limelight,
And bring the curtain down.
Say it's just two clowns,
Who couldn't get their lines right,
Say it's just a show
On the radio,
That we can turn over and start again,
That we can turn over; it's only a game.

Company   Tell me it's not true,
Say I only dreamed it,
And morning will come soon,
Tell me it's not true,
Say you didn't mean it,

Say it's just pretend,
Say it's just the end,
Of an old movie from years ago
Of an old movie with Marilyn Monroe.

Curtain.

Our Day Out – The Musical

Our Day Out was originally written for television and transmitted as a BBC 'Play for Today' in 1977. It was later adapted for the stage and first performed at the Everyman Theatre, Liverpool, on 8 April 1983.

Our Day Out – The Musical was first performed at the Royal Court Theatre, Liverpool, in September 2009, and subsequently returned to the Royal Court on 27 August 2010 with the following cast:

Les/Ronny/Zoo Keeper	Kieran Cunningham
Mrs Kay	Pauline Daniels
Mark	Stephen Fletcher
Mr Briggs	Mark Moraghan
Katie	Georgina White
Jackie	Sophie Fraser
Reilly	Chris Mason
Carlene	Abby Mavers
Digga	Jack Rigby
Amy	Mia Molloy
Young Actors	

Mickey Collins, Zoe Cozens, Rebecca Cummins, Kelly Forshaw, Jasmine Joel, Rio Samuels, Sinead Thompson, Miguel Trimon, Glenn Wild, Steven Williamson

The Red and Blue Teams performed on alternate nights
Red Team: Caitlin Evans, Taylor Fowlis, Aron Julius, Brittany McKay-Ellison, Abigail Middleton, Oliver O'Brien, Joe Slater
Blue Team: Kathryn Anderson, Jamie Davies, Olivia Galvin, Sofia Filipe, James Tudor-Jones, Georgia Jones, Aidan Walters-Williams

Directed by Bob Eaton
Musical direction by Howard Gray
Choreography by Beverley Norris-Edmunds
Designed by Mark Walters
Lighting by Ian Scott

Characters

Amy Chandler
Hoodies: Moler, Gonzo and Stack
Eunice Pilkington
Kelly
Chloe
Zoe
Reilly (Ryan)
Carly Croxley
Dennis
Digga (Dickson)
Jackie Morgan
Les
Sean
Steph
Brit (Brittany)
Milton
Caitlin
Georgia
Abi
Kath
Taylor
Oliver
Maurice
Katie
Mrs Kay (teacher)
Mark McDevit (teacher)
Kevin
Sophie
Briggs (teacher)
Ronson
Aaron Andrews
Ronny (the bus driver)
Little Ronny
Sir/Idealized Male Dancer (the Sir of Carly's imagination)
Zoo Keeper
Zoo Keeper's Helper
Stallholder

(/) means that the next line of speech should begin at this point.

Act One

Lights gradually coming up to reveal an inner-city area – morning. A road, streets, a patch of waste ground, the wail of an industrial building. We hear the sounds of the street – engines, a far-off siren, distant calls of kids, birdsong, the intermittent burst of a pneumatic drill, the bass thud thud of a muffled beat box.

Amy *appears. Into this mix comes a drum pattern and we hear voices (off) chanting on top of the tune as five* **Hoodies** *including* **Moler**, **Gonzo** *and* **Stack** *appear with spray cans.*

Kids   *If y' know where y' goin'*
      Then y' just keep goin'
      So there's no go-slowin'
      When y' . . . know y' goin'
      Our day out

Chant and drum pattern continue underscoring as **Hoodies** *spray walls in spray can dance routine.*

      If y' know where y' goin'
      Then y' just keep goin'
      So there's no go-slowin'
      When y' . . . know y' goin'
      Our day out

Amy *sings the following to herself as if it's a mantra – something that she's really had to concentrate on in order to get right and has to keep repeating to herself.*

Amy   *Miss said we've all gotta*
      Concentrate
      And not be late
      Because the bus won't wait

Hoodies *push past* **Amy** *as they run towards exit continuing chant.*

Kids   *If y' know where y' goin'*
          Then y' just keep goin'
          So there's no go-slowin'
          When y'. . . know y' goin'

Amy   *Miss said we've all gotta*
          Be on time
          Cos if we're not
          We'll be left behind

A group of **Kids** *begin to appear on the street, making their way to school as* **Amy** *is exiting.*

Kids   *If y' know where y' goin'*
          Then y' just keep goin'
          So there's no go-slowin'
          When y' know y' goin'
          Our day out

Eunice   Kelly!

Kelly   What?

Eunice   Get a move on! We're gonna be late. Miss'll be waitin'.

Kelly   She won't go without us.

Eunice   She might do. Come on! I wanna make sure we get a good seat on the coach.

They pick up the groove and sing –

Kids   *If y' know where y' goin'*
          Then y' just keep goin'
          So there's no go-slowin'
          When y' know y' goin'
          Our day out

A few nearby **Younger Kids** *rap <u>over</u> the tune as they all head off towards school, followed by different groups and combinations.*

Kids   *Who are the kids going . . . out today*
          Yes the Progress kids are on their way
          An' if you know where you're goin'

Then you just keep goin'
No there's no go-slowin'
When you . . . know you're goin'

All year round all the Progie kids
Are just mongs an' freaks an' stupid divs
But not when it's our day
. . . We're goin' our way
. . . We're havin' our say
. . . Cos this day is our day

Chloe/Zoe   *Got sweets*
Got drinks
Got money to spend
I'm gonna get a good seat near my best friend

Eunice   *I'm gonna take some pills so I won't be sick*

Kelly   *I'm gonna see if I can click*

(*Laughter*)

All   *Cos if y' know where y' goin'*
Then y' just keep goin'
No there's no go-slowin'
When y' know y' goin'
Our day out

Continue to underscore as this group exits. We see **Carly**, **Jackie**
and across the street, **Reilly** *and* **Digga**.

Reilly   Carly – come here.

Carly   No. I wanna get to school.

Reilly   Since when?

Carly   Since like, today's our trip isn't it? With Mrs Kay.

Digga   Where y' goin'?

Carly   What's it to you?

Reilly   Agh, it'll just be somewhere crap won't it – like Chester
or somewhere shite like that.

Jackie   Yeh, well we're not goin' for the scenery are we?

Carly   As long as Mr McDevit's goin' then we don't care *where*.

Reilly/Digga   Mister McDevit!

Reilly   D' you fancy him then Carly?

Carly   What if I do? (*Beat.*) What's it to you?

Reilly   Nott'n.

Digga   Agh Carly, behave yourself girl – He's a *teacher*.

Reilly   He's gettin' married to that posh one isn't he – Miss Whats-her-name?

Digga   Hey she's alright her, isn't she?

Reilly   So it seems like y' missed the boat there, Carly. (*Laughs.*)

Carly   Oh sod off!

Jackie   An' we're gonna miss the bleedin' bus as well if we don't get a move on. (*Pulling* **Carly**.) Carly, come on!

The girls walk away.

Jackie   *If y' know where you're goin'*
        Then y' just keep goin'

Carly *joins in – probably giving it a bit more in the knowledge that they're being clocked by* **Reilly**.

Carly/Jackie   *No there's no go-slowin'*
        When you know you're goin'

As **Carly** *and* **Jackie** *exit, another group of* **Progress Kids** *are making their way to school, various of them singing following lines.* **Les**, *a lollipop man, enters.*

Progress Kids   *Gotta get to school*
        Can't afford to be late
        When all our mates'll be
        Waitin' at the gate

Don't wanna miss the coach
Gotta be on time
Won't be one of those
Who gets left behind

So who are the kids going out today
Yes the Progress kids – we're on our way
An' if you know where you're goin'
Then you just keep goin'
No there's no go-slowin'
When you . . . know you're goin'

As **Kids** *move off we see* **Digga** *chasing* **Reilly***, the two of them barging past* **Les** *the lollipop man across the road and off.*

Underscore continues with minor key – Our Day Out motif.

Les (*berating them and following to other side of road*)   Hey! Hey! – there's little kiddies crossin' here.

Amy *arrives at the roadside and calls across to* **Les***.*

Amy   Les! Are y' alright?

Les   Who's that now? Who is it?

Amy   Les, it's me – Amy.

Les   Oh, alright there love – how are y' my little sweetheart? Listen, do us a favour will y' girl? See us back across the road will y'?

Amy *quickly crosses to retrieve him and leads him back to other side of road.*

My eyes aren't too good this mornin'. You're early today aren't y' love?

Amy   It's our day out, Les – we're goin' on our trip.

Les   Are they all goin'?

Amy   No, it's only for the kids who go the Progress Class, Les.

Les   The what class?

Amy   *Progress* class Les. It's Mrs Kay's class. Y' have to go there in the week if you're not very good at readin' an' writin' an' spellin' an' things like that.

Les   You mean if you're backward, love?

Amy   Les, y' shouldn't say, 'backward'. Mrs Kay says that nobody's 'backward'.

Les   Ah it's only my way, love – it's only ould Les. I never mean any harm do I? The kids all know me y' see sweetheart. An' I love them – the kiddies, I love the bones of them.

During the above, **Sean** *– a little 'kiddie' – has stepped off the kerb and is crossing the road.*

Hey! – y' little gobshite – what d' y think you're playin' at?

Sean   I'm crossin' the road. There's nott'n comin'.

Les   Hey! I'll be the one who decides if there's nott'n comin' or not.

Sean   You can't even see – you've got cataracts!

Les   I'll cataract you, y' hard-faced little get! From now on you can eff off to the pelican crossing an' when you end up under the wheels of a ten-ton Tesco delivery truck, see how you like your turkey fuckin' twizzlers then!

To **Amy***:*

Excuse my little bit of French there sweetheart.

Amy   It's alright Les – We don't do French. See y' Les.

Les   Au revoir sweetheart, au revoir!

(**Amy** *heads for school, singing – with* **Kids**)

Amy/Kids   *Oh yes we're going*
  Going going going
  Yes we're going
  Oh we're going
  We're going going

Oh we're going
Yes we're going
We're going

She is confronted by a group of non-Progress kids – **Moler***,* **Gonzo**
and **Stack***.*

Moler (*calling*)   Hey – Amy Chandler!

– y' little window-licker!

Gonzo   Agh – look, there's the rest of the mongs.

As a group of younger **Progress Kids** *enter.*

Stack (*whistling/jeering*)   Hey – retards.

All Three   *Y'll never see nott'n*
        That's half as thick as
        The mongs an' the spazzies
        An' the window-lickers

They begin to move mockingly around the **Progress Kids.**

        Mongs retards
        Mongs retards
        Mongs retards
        Special needs

Stack   *The meffs an' the divs*
        An' the window-lickers

All Three   *They dribble their food*
        An' they wet their knickers

        Mongs retards
        Mongs retards
        Mongs retards
        Special needs

As **Moler** *and co. torment the younger* **Kids** *they are unaware of*
the rest of the **Progress Kids** *entering, dancing/moving as the*
exaggerated grotesque stereotypes that **Moler** *and co. accuse them*
of being.

Mongs retards
Mongs retards
Mongs retards
Special needs

Progress Kids *suddenly move as one – dancing with power and strength, they front up their tormentors and 'dance' them back into a retreat.*

Eunice   *They call us loonies howling at the moonies*
They say that we're weird or we're gay

Steph   *They call us scaries away-with-the-fairies*
Just cos we go to Mrs Kay

Progress Kids   *But do we care*
Do we care
Do we care
No way

Cos we're goin' out
Goin' out
Goin' out
Today
Yes we're goin' out
Goin' out
With Mrs Kay

All Three   *Freaks dildos la-la-brains*
Spazzies dribblers ga-ga-brains

Jackie   *They call us dickheads loonies thickheads*
Just cos we go to Mrs Kay

Brit/Sophie   *They call us divs, meffs and biffs*
But do we care

Progress Kids   *No way*
Do we care
Do we care
Do we care
No way

Cos we're goin' out
Goin' out
Goin' out
Today
Yes we're goin' out

Goin' out
With Mrs Kay

All Three   *Psychos schizos*
OCD
Progress Kids
Agh – don't touch me

Milton   *They call us schizos look out it's those*
Kids who have to go to Mrs Kay

Caitlin/Georgia   *They call us psychos say we're like those*
Ones that get put away

Eunice   *They call us spastic chewing-on-the-plastic*
Just cos we go to Mrs Kay

Kelly   *We're all dyslexic fat or anorexic*
But are we arsed – no way

Progress Kids   *Are we arsed*
Are we arsed
Are we arsed
No way
Cos we're goin' out
Goin' out
Goin' out
Today
Yes we're goin' out
Goin' out
With Mrs Kay

Moler   Goin' back the funny farm?

Underscore following spoken lyric:

Carly   *Where we go is up to Miss*

Jackie   *But she doesn't tell us where it is*

Abi/Kath   *Till just before we get on the bus*

Amy   *An' then Miss comes and surprises us*

Sean   *An' it might be to Blackpool*

Milton   *Or Martin Mere*

Taylor/Oliver   *Or Chester Zoo*

Maurice   *Or Windermere*

Carly   *But wherever Miss takes us we don't care*
Cos we just love going out with her

Steph   *An' before you start calling anyone a fool*

Progress Kids   *We're going out an' you're stuck in school*

Non-Progress Kids   *Agh that's not fair*

Progress Kids   *Do we care*
Do we care
No way
Cos we're goin' out
Goin' out
Goin' out
Today
We're goin' out
Goin' out
With Mrs
Kay

During the above **Mrs Kay** *and* **Katie** *enter, signing the children off the register, all of them singing:*

All   *We're goin' goin' yes we're goin'*
Oh we're goin', oh yes we're goin'. . .

We're goin' goin' yes we're goin'
Oh we're goin', oh yes we're goin'. . .

Underscore continues as **Moler** *and co. continue to complain, not realizing that* **Mrs Kay** *is within earshot.*

Stack   If they're goin' out then we should be goin' out somewhere.

Gonzo   Yeah not just the retards.

Stack   And the spazzies.

Moler   Yeah – not just the mongs.

For a moment the music stops dead.

Mrs Kay   *Mongs!?*

Moler *and co. wheeling in shock and surprise.* **Mrs Kay** *approaches.*

Mrs Kay   What did you just say?

Moler   Nott'n! I never said nott'n.

Mrs Kay   What was the word you just used?

Gonzo   What word? No word, I . . . I never said, I never said nott'n.

Stack   Don't look at me, I never opened my mouth.

Music begins again. **Mrs Kay** *suddenly smiles at them and sings:*

Mrs Kay   *Oh – I'm delighted to hear you say*
    That you would never speak that way
    Because to use a word like 'mong'
    As well as being factually wrong
    Marks out the user as lacking wits
    But mostly it just gets on my tits

Moler (*unable to believe his ears*)   What!

Gonzo   Ah! What did she say?

Stack   She said . . . she *swore*!

Mrs Kay   Swore!? What do you mean, swore? (*Turns to* **Katie** *and* **Kids**.) Katie, did you hear me swear?

Katie   *Swear* Mrs Kay, you?

Mrs Kay   Children?

Kids   No Miss.

Mrs Kay (*to* **Moler** *and co.*)   You see – just the same as you – people think they hear you using words . . . when you haven't even opened your mouth!

> *So let me thank you once again*
> *For shunning words like 'spazzie-brain'*
> *'Window licker' and 'From the zoo'.*
> *Come here let me stick a big kiss on you*

(*She quickly cups the face of* **Stack** *and kisses him.*)

Stack (*appalled*)   Get off!

Moler (*agog*)   That's abuse that!

Stack   Come here, quick, we're late, come on.

Mrs Kay *stands watching them depart.*

Gonzo   She's more mental than the bleedin' mongs!

Progress Kids   *Miss, where we goin' Miss where we goin' Miss?*

> *Are we goin' on a coach Miss are we? Goin' on a . . .*

This repeated with variations but all the time rising in insistence and volume.

Mrs Kay *raises her arms before swiftly sweeping them apart in a silencing gesture.*

Mrs Kay   Stop!

There is immediate silence.

Sean (*trying it on*)   Miss where . . .

Mrs Kay (*warning finger*)   Sean!

Sean (*contrite*)   Sorry Miss.

Mrs Kay *surveys them for a second. Then she sings, rhythm reappearing under her singing:*

Mrs Kay   *Our destination, you want to know*
Where the Progress are about to go?
The envelope, Miss Appleby

Katie *dutifully places the sealed envelope into* **Mrs Kay**'s
outstretched hand.

Shall I take a look inside and see?

Kids   Yeah go on Miss, open it.

She slowly opens the envelope.

Mrs Kay   *Will it be Blackpool?* (**Kids** *cheer.*) *Or Wigan Pier?*
(**Kids** *groan.*) *Sherwood Forest?* (*Mixture of cheers and groans.*)
Or Martin Mere?

Sean   Yes!

Kids   That's just birds!

Brit/Sophie   Ah come on Miss.

Taylor/Oliver   Tell us Miss.

Sean   Stop messin' Miss.

Now she really clicks into the rhythm, almost rapping herself.

Mrs Kay   *Alright! Here goes. We have to know.*
This year the mighty Progress Class is going to go . . .
(Waving the envelope above her head.) to Alton Towers.

(*The* **Kids** *jumping up and down in delight – every one of them*
pulling out a mobile phone and either dialling or texting.)

Kids   Yeah

Alton Towers
Alton Towers
Alton Towers
Ah hey! (*Punching the air*)
Alton Towers
We're goin' there today
We just love goin' out with Mrs Kay

And we're goin' out, goin' out, goin' out Today!

*We're goin' out, goin' out, goin' out, goin' out, goin' out, goin'
   out, goin' out*
*We're goin' out, goin' out, goin' out, goin' out, goin' out, goin'
   out, goin' out*
*We're goin' out, goin' out, goin' out, goin' out, goin' out, goin'
   out, goin' out*
To ALTON TOWERS
Today
Yeah!

*Number ends with a tableau of kids all on mobile phones, all of
them delightedly, excitedly reporting their destination.*

Mrs Kay (*from box*)   Right!! What's the one thing we never take
with us on a trip?

*She reveals the large bag. The following singing is a cappella and
simultaneous with the **Protest Kids**' dialogue and **Katie** collecting
in the phones.*

Jackie   Ah Miss. Not that!

Sean Don't be tight Miss.	**Mrs Kay** *Give up those mobiles*
	Give me those phones
Caitlin/Georgia Please Miss.	*Give up those minging*
	ringing tones
Kelly Ah no Miss, no!	
	If you're expecting
Katie Come on, come on,	
come, every single phone in	
the bag now!	*To spend ,he day*
Sean Miss it isn't fair.	*Phoning and texting*
	Then think again
Jackie Miss! It's set on silent.	
	Give me those Nokias
Eunice Ah don't be rotten Miss.	*Those Vodaphones*

Milton   That's cruelty Miss.

I'm sorry if I shock y's
All to the bone
Give me those . . .

Eunice   Don't be mean Miss.

Mrs Kay *seeing* **Eunice** *trying to hide her mobile.*

Mrs Kay   Come on Eunice Pilkington, you as well!

Eunice   Miss, I've already put my phone in the bag! I haven't got it, I swear – cross my heart on our baby's life . . .

Mrs Kay   Eunice!

Eunice (*producing it*)   Ah, Miss! It's not fair – I get panic attacks if I don't have my phone with me!

Katie   They can all be collected from room 11 when we get back.

Andrews   Miss, that's really rancid, though, because how are we supposed to take pictures today if we've not got our phones with us?

Mrs Kay   Ah! Pictures! You want to take photographs?

Jackie   Miss, course we do.

Mrs Kay (*producing a camera which she flourishes above her head with a fanfare*) Da da da da! You want pictures! (*Handing it to* **Andrews**.) Here.

Andrews   Ogh Miss! This is a Lumix G1 12.1 megapixel!

Mrs Kay   Is it, really?

Andrews   Can I *use* this, Miss?

Mrs Kay   Of course you can use it. And not only that – for the next . . . twenty minutes or so you, Aaron, will be the Progress Class Official Photographer.

Andrews   Ogh Miss! Brilliant.

Mrs Kay   And then we'll pass it on so throughout the day everybody who wants to will get the chance to become our photographer.

Various groups of **Kids** *getting into position and posing for shots. As they do, we see a fleeting montage of the pictures being taken. Meanwhile singing:*

Kids   *Quick get a picture, I'm in the picture. Here get a picture, we're in the picture.*

Quick get a picture, I'm in the picture. Here get a picture, we're in the picture.

Quick get a picture, I'm in the picture. Here get a picture, we're in the picture.

Quick get a picture, I'm in the picture. Here get a picture, we're in the picture.

Quick get a picture, I'm in the picture. Here get a picture, we're in the picture.

Quick get a picture, I'm in the picture. Here get a picture, we're in the picture.

Quick get a picture, I'm in the picture. Here get a picture, we're in the picture.

Quick get a picture, I'm in the picture. Here get a picture, we're in the picture.

Quick get a picture, I'm in the picture. Here get a picture, we're in the picture.

Mark *enters, rushed and breathless.*

Mark (*to* **Mrs Kay**)   Sorry I'm late. I overslept and then the car wouldn't start.

He and **Katie** *acknowledging each other.*

Carly, *followed by* **Jackie** *immediately zoning in on him.*

Carly   Ogh . . . Hia sir.

Jackie   Sir, hia.

Mark   Hello girls. Mrs Kay, would it be best if I . . .

Carly   Sir, I was startin' to think you might not be coming on the trip. I was heartbroken.

Jackie   Sir, I was startin' to have palpitations.

Mark   Girls – please! Look, I, I really must . . .

Carly   Sir, I've got somethin' to show y'?

Mark   What, Carly?

Carly (*opening her jacket*)   Sir, d' y' like my new top?

Jackie   Sir, and mine! Look.

Mark   Carly, Jackie, they're very nice . . . but the thing is that . . .

Mrs Kay   Carlene Croxley, Jacqueline Morgan! Will you please give Mr McDevit a moment's peace!

Carly   Miss what have I done? I haven't done nott'n.

Jackie   Neither have I Miss.

Mrs Kay   I know you haven't sweethearts – but you must never forget that Mr McDevit is like a . . . a . . . precious . . . butterfly . . .

Mark *and* **Katie** *coughing and turning away.*

Carly ⎱   Oh go 'way Miss!

Jackie ⎰   Behave will y' Miss!

Mrs Kay   Beautiful . . . but delicate . . . and so *easily* crushed . . .

Carly ⎱   Miss stop it Miss!

Jackie ⎰   Miss!

Mrs Kay   *And* – he's probably not even had any breakfast yet.

Mrs Kay *produces a thermos flask from her bag.*

Have you?

Mark (*gratefully seizing the offered flask*)   Oh thanks.

Mrs Kay   And there's some fruit in the . . . Come on, I'll show you – I've got to put these (*phones*) away. Katie – before the coach arrives – we need to check who's not yet . . . (*Discreet gesture meaning 'paid'.*)

Katie (*picking it up immediately*)   Got it – yeh. Okay.

To **Kids** *as* **Mrs Kay** *and* **Mark** *exit:*

Okay, listen – everybody. (*Beat.*) I said, *everybody*, Kelly – thank you. (*Beat while she waits for full attention.*) Aaron? Okay. Now, all of you who've *signed* to come on this trip . . .

Moving a purposeful three strides away from the group.

. . . but haven't yet *paid* . . . I want you to come over here.

There is a moment's beat before every **Kid** *moves as one, engulfing her in a clamour of explanation – the following lines overlapping and crossing.*

Sean   Miss I'll bring me money next week.

Eunice   My Mam forgot Miss but she'll pay y' she will.

Caitlin/Georgia   Doesn't the school pay for it Miss?

Jackie   My Dad said he'd pay Miss but he never brought the money!

Kevin   Miss, I filled in the form but the dog ate it!

Brit/Sophie   Does that mean we can't go Miss?

Taylor/Oliver   My Mam said she'd pay y' after the holidays Miss.

Milton   Miss it's the credit crunch, my Gran said.

Briggs *enters on his way into school.*

Briggs   What's all this – what's goin' on? Move! All of you – move! – now! I said *move*! Come on, get yourselves sorted out! I've never seen such a rabble – what d'y' think you're playing at?

Katie   We're waiting for the coach, actually.

Briggs (*now turning his attention from the* **Kids** *and surveying her*)   Oh are we? *Actually.*

Katie   Yes!

Briggs (*beat*)   Student are you? Teaching practice?

Katie   No! NQT. I've been here for months, actually.

Briggs   Is that right? . . . Well you haven't learned so much about organization have you? Mind you, you work with her, don't you, Mrs Kay.

Katie   Yes, I do – I'm happy to say.

Briggs (*wry laugh*)   You'll learn. (*To* **Kids**.) Right! If you're waiting for a coach, what's the first thing you do?

Sean (*puts up his hand*)   Sir, go to the toilet.

Kids *laughing*.

Briggs (*barking at them*) Shuttup! I said be quiet! (*They immediately fall silent.*) If you're waiting for a coach you form a queue – in twos, a straight line, now come on, do it!

The **Kids** *get themselves formed into a reasonable semblance of a straight line.* **Briggs** *– indicating to* **Katie** *as if saying, 'That's how it's done.'*

Right. And keep it like that until your coach arrives.

As he's about to exit.

And where is it taking you then, this coach?

Andrews   Alton Towers, Sir.

Briggs (*beat – mental double-take*)   Alton *what?*

Kids   Alton *Towers*, Sir.

Briggs *shoots a glance at* **Katie** *before turning and purposefully striding off into the school – the queue immediately breaks down.*

Sean   Miss where's the coach?

Katie   It's alright / it'll be here soon.

Carly   / Miss where's Sir?

Katie   Don't worry. / He'll be back in a minute.

Kelly   / Miss when are we goin' / where's the coach?

Amy   Miss, where's Mrs Kay gone, Miss?

Reilly and **Dickson** *come running urgently out of school.*

Reilly	Digga
/Miss, don't go Miss, hold on Miss . . . Miss, Miss can we come with y' – ah don't be tight Miss, go on Miss.	Miss, wait wait Miss . . . Take us Miss, go on Miss take us to Alton Towers.

Sean	Eunice
Ah no!	Not them, Miss.

Milton	Reilly
Don't let them Miss.	Shut it, you!

Katie   Ryan!

Reilly   Ah but hey Miss don't be tight.

Digga   Go on Miss.

Reilly   Let us come to Alton Towers.

Kelly   They're not even in the Progie Class Miss.

Digga   Yeah, but we used to be.

Reilly   So that's not fair because we used to be in the Progress Class.

Mrs Kay *emerges from the school.*

Mrs Kay   Yes, but you're not any more, are you Ryan? Because now you can both read and write can't you – and that's why you're back in regular class. This trip's just for those in the Progress Class.

Digga   Miss, I'm OCD y' know.

Jackie   Miss he's not OCD he's just a dick!

Digga   'Ey, you!

Reilly (*to* **Katie**)   Agh 'ey Miss, come on Miss, say we can come.

Katie   Ryan! Mrs Kay's already explained – you're not in Progress Class any longer so . . .

Reilly (*to* **Mrs Kay**)   But Miss that's dead unfair that – half of *these* shouldn't be in the Progress Class.

Ronson   We should!   **Milton**   Yes, we should.

Eunice   *Why* shouldn't we eh?   **Taylor/Sophie**   Why not?

Reilly   Miss they shouldn't because they've got nott'n wrong with them!

Eunice   I've got A S D haven't I Miss?

Abi/Kath   I've got S A D.

Steph   I've got A D H D.

Kevin   I'm on the spectrum.

Sean   Miss, I'm antiseptic aren't I?

Mrs Kay   You mean 'dyslexic' Sean.

Sean   Oh yeah.

Carly   Aren't I phobic, Miss?

Jackie   An' psychic. I'm hyperactive!

Chloe/Zoe   We've got social issues.

Caitlin/Georgia   I've got allergies – all kinds.

Andrews   I've got Tourettes – fuck off!

Steph   Miss, he hasn't! Tell him! He just does that so he can swear!

Ronson   I've got wind.

Reilly   Ah, they're all liars – take no notice, Miss – they only wanna be in the Progress cos it's soft an' y' get to go to places like Alton Towers.

Slouches off a few yards, followed by **Digga**.

Carly   Ah Miss, let them come.

Jackie   Carlene!?

Carly   Ryan's alright now y' know Miss.

Jackie   Oh yeh!

Carly   He has! He's calmed down loads y' know Miss – now that he's not livin' with his Dad. Miss, go on, give them a chance.

Mrs Kay (*beat – to* **Katie**)   Have we got room?

Reilly   Ah, yes Miss, yeah!   **Digga**   Yes Miss!

Katie *nods to* **Mrs Kay**.

Mrs Kay (*to* **Reilly**)   But it's not up to me – you'd have to get permission from your form teacher.

Reilly (*reality dawns*)   Briggs? He won't let us come!

Mrs Kay   Well that's not my fault Ryan.

Mark *enters, handing the coffee flask back to* **Mrs Kay** *and shaking his head as he does*. **Reilly** *and* **Digga** *go back into school*.

Mark   Phoagh . . . Mrs Kay, what is in this coffee?!

Mrs Kay (*laughing*)   Oh my God! I forgot. Half a bottle of Johnny Walker! I thought it might warm us up if the weather got cold.

Mark   Well it's certainly warmed me up.

Carly *and* **Jackie** *are suddenly each side of him*.

Carly   Ogh Sir it *is* dead warm isn't it.

Removing her jacket and revealing the appropriately inappropriate 'flattering' top.

I'm boiling!

Jackie (*quickly getting in on the act and beginning to pull off her own jacket*)   Sir so am I!

Mrs Kay   Carly, Jackie! Don't you dare! Come on here's the coach. Aaron, come on take a picture.

Music as everybody gets into large group pose, singing as they do.

Kids   *Quick get a picture, I'm in the picture. Here get a picture,*
we're in the picture.
Quick get a picture, I'm in the picture. Here get a picture,
we're in the picture.
Our day out

During which we see on AV the image being shot as the coach
arrives. Music continues:

If y' know where y' goin'
Then y' just keep goin'
No there's no go-slowin'
When y' know that y' goin'
Our day out

If y' know where y' goin'
Then y' just keep goin'
No there's no go-slowin'
When y' know that y' goin'
Our day out

The driver, **Ronny,** *stands on the steps of the coach, barring the*
kids from climbing on. **Ronny** *is – or thinks he is – an imposing,*
intimidating figure and stops the **Kids** *and the music dead in their*
tracks.

Ronny   Right! Stop right there!

There's a suitably dramatic gesture – organ chords under the
following dialogue.

Sean   Miss said we could get on.

Ronny   Oh did she now?

Kids   Yeah!

Ronny   Well let me tell youse lot something now: '*Miss*' is not
the driver of this bus – *I* am! An' if I say you don't get on then you
don't get on!

He begins to build in oratorical fervour – almost as a gospel
preacher working his congregation, underscored with fervent organ.

Y' teachers might tell y' what to do in the playground or the classroom but this bus is . . . *my* domain – You got that? This is my bus. Whose bus?

Music starts to build to song tempo.

Kids (*incredulous*)   Wha . . .?

Ronny   I said *whose* bus?

Kids (*begrudgingly*)   Yours.

Ronny   *WHOSE* bus?

Kids (*louder, pissed off now*)   *YOUR bus*!

Ronny   That's right!

> *And I decide*
> *Who gets to ride!*

(*Number kicks in at full tempo.*)

> *This is my bus, I'm the boss of this bus,*
> *I've been drivin' it for twenty-five years*
> *This is my bus, I'm the boss of this bus*
> *So youse pin back your ears*
>
> *This is my bus, I'm the boss of this bus,*
> *You are lookin' at the number one*
> *This is my bus, I'm the boss of this bus,*
> *And you're not gettin' on.*

Kids   Why not?

Ronny   *Cos you 'aven't been checked*
> *And I suspect*
> *You'll be carryin chewing gum*
> *An' I can't have sweets getting stuck to the seats*
> *And respectable passengers' bums*

(*Rising chords.*)

> *We don't allow it!*

Mrs Kay   Driver . . .

Ronny   *We don't allow it!*

Mrs Kay   Driver!

Ronny   *We don't allow it!*

Mrs Kay   But *what* don't you allow?

Ronny   *None of it!*
Hubba Bubba, Juicy Fruit, Snickers
Not allowed!

Mars Bars, Crunchy Bars, Bounties
Not allowed!

(*The* **Kids** *begin to join him in his refrain.*)

Irn-Bru, Cherry Coke, Lilt

Kids   Not allowed!

Ronny   *Rolos, Polos, Crisps*

Kids   *Not allowed!*

Ronny   *Not allowed, not allowed, and of that I'm proud.*

Having been shooed away from the steps the **Kids** *start to express their frustration with* **Ronny** *in dance moves that express what a div they consider him to be.*

This is my bus, I'm the boss of this bus,
Now have you kids got that straight
This is my bus, I'm the boss of this bus,

Kids   *Yeah alright. We heard you mate*

RAP SECTION

Don't wet your knickers
We've got no snickers
No crisps no drinks
No sherbet dippers
Got no Mars
No crunchy bars
Any sticky shite, mate's
Yours not ours

Ronny   *Well I want this lesson learned right now*
If you wanna put one over on me
As far as this bus is concerned you're gonna need
A little more than a GCSE

This is my bus, I'm the boss of this bus,
And I've seen it all before
This is my bus, I'm the boss of this bus,
And I don't want no spew on the floor

So do youse understand

Kids   *Yeah*

Ronny   *What is banned banned banned?*

Kids   *Yeah!*

Ronny   *Let me hear you one more time*
Milky Way, Milk Tray, Tunes

Kids   *Not allowed!*

Ronny   *Penguins, Picnics, Twix*

Kids   *Not allowed!*

Ronny   *Ferrero Rocher Boost*

Kids   *Not allowed!*

Kids (*incredulous*)   Ferrero Rocher?

Ronny   *Not* allowed!

Ronny *is now carried away and in such full preacher mode that the* **Kids**, *despite their antipathy to him, or perhaps at first in ironic comment on him, go the whole way with his number.*

Ronny   Because this . . . I said this . . . I said this . . .

Kids   Yeah.

Ronny   . . . is . . .

Kids   Yeah.

Ronny   . . . my . . . my . . . my . . . my . . . my . . .!

Kids   *Bus bus*
   He's the boss of the bus, bus
   He's the boss of the bus, bus
   He's the boss of the bus, bus
   He's the boss of the bus, bus

Ronny   *Don't approach my coach.*
   An' you'll be . . . all . . . right!

Big gospel finish with **Kids** *collapsing. And then they are up again and dancing.*

Kids   *Bus bus*
   He's the boss of the bus, bus
   He's the boss of the bus, bus
   He's the boss of the bus, bus
   He's the boss of the bus, bus

Until **Ronny** *brings it to a climactic halt again with another big gospel finish.*

Ronny   *Do you feel . . . all . . . right?*

Kids (*now really enjoying the whole thing*)   Yeah!

Ronny (*spoken*)   Well y's are still not gettin' on.

Kids   Aah!

Mrs Kay   Driver, can I have a word with you – in private?

Leading **Ronny** *away from the main group.*

Shall we try and start again? Now – I'm Helen. And you are?

Ronny   The driver!

Mrs Kay   So the driver doesn't have a name?

Ronny   I don't normally have to give my name.

Mrs Kay   Oh, come on – what's your name? (*Beat.*) Handsome!

Ronny   Staples. Ronny Staples.

Mrs Kay   Ronny. Well, Ronny, I'd like you to do something for me.

Ronny (*suspicious*)   What!?

Mrs Kay   Ronny, I'd like you to take a good look at this school.

Ronny   We normally only do the better schools.

Mrs Kay   Oh yes, I'm sure you do Ronny – and I'm sure you must detest streets like these – and the kids who are raised in them.

Ronny   Detest them? I don't detest anyone. Anyway, I was raised in streets just like this.

Mrs Kay (*suddenly seeing her chance*)   Oh! Were you? And so things must have been pretty hard for you then?

Ronny   Hard? Hey, don't get me started. We had nothin' – us.

Mrs Kay   And that's why I can understand it Ronny – why it's such an ordeal for you to have to come back to streets like these, with kids like these. Because when you do, Ronny, it means you're reminded of that poor little lad that you once were – that little waif in rags who wandered the cold, cruel, heartless streets.

Ronny   How did you know that?

Mrs Kay (*guiding him to look and setting the scene before him as* **Little Ronny** *enters*)   Look, Ron, look – there he is now, that thin strip of a lost and hungry little boy, stood outside the sweet shop and gazing at the mint balls, the cough candy, the sherbet lemons and the Toblerone bars – all those sweets that the kids from the better streets and the better schools regularly get to eat while poor little Ronny can only look and imagine the taste of sweets that he can never buy.

Little Ronny *exits leaving* **Ronny** *still staring back at the nostalgic, crushed-lens vision of his romantically impoverished idealized childhood.* **Mrs Kay** *turns back to the* **Kids**.

Mrs Kay   Now I'm really sorry to have to tell you this children but it seems that the coach driver has deemed us entirely unsuitable to travel on his particular coach and so it means we'll have to . . .

Ronny   Hey – hold on hold on, what are y' say . . . what are y' sayin'? Here, look, you son . . .

Milton (*nervously*)   Me?

Ronny (*reaching into his pocket and pulling out wad of money*)   Come on, son, it's alright, here. Take this (*twenty-pound note*). Now you go to that sweet shop son and you tell that man in there that you want the best sweets that money can buy.

Milton *runs off.*

Katie (*aside*)   How did you manage that?

Mrs Kay (*winks*)   A touch of Charles Dickens and a splash of old nostalgia!

Ronny   Hey, come on what are y' all doin' waitin' there? On the coach, come on, everybody, on the coach now.

Kids *cheering as they assemble and board the coach.*

Kids   *We're goin' goin'*
       On the Galleons
       And the Skyride
       And the Toadstool
       We'll ride the Ripsaw
       And the Spinball
       And the Mine Train
       And the Rita

       We'll do the Nemesis
       The Congo
       And the Corkscrew
       The Oblivion

Kids *all chattering excitedly.*

Mrs Kay (*interrupting*)   Alright, alright . . . Now listen everyone. We'll be setting off in a couple of minutes and we want everyone to enjoy themselves so (*Suddenly snapping her fingers.*) Kelly I asked you to listen!

Kelly   Sorry Miss.

Mrs Kay   Now, in Progress Class we have a kindness rule don't we, which is . . .

Kids (*in unison with* **Mrs Kay**)   We try to think of others as well as ourselves.

Mrs Kay   That's right. Now . . .

Reilly *and* **Digga** *come rushing on to the coach and head for the back seat.*

Reilly   Miss, Miss. We're comin' with y'.

Mrs Kay   With Mr Briggs's permission?

Reilly   Yeah Miss, Briggsy' comin' himself.

Digga   He said you've gotta wait for him Miss.

As **Reilly** *and* **Digga** *make their way to the back of the coach,* **Mrs Kay** *turns to* **Mark** *and* **Katie**.

Mrs Kay   Oh that's just what we need.

Mark   Briggs at Alton Towers?

Katie   He probably thinks we're in grave danger of enjoying ourselves.

Mark   It'll be like Bin Laden Does Disney.

Mrs Kay (*considers, shrugs*)   We'll just have to do the best we can. (*She takes her seat next to* **Amy** *as* **Reilly** *and* **Digga** *approach the back seat.*)

Reilly (*to* **Maurice**, *the smallest kid on the back seat*)   Right, you! Come on, move!

Maurice (*all indignant outrage*)   Why?

Reilly   Cos we reserved the back seat didn't we?

Maurice   No y' never. Because there are no reserved seats, not for no one, even the teachers. Miss said it was first come first served.

Digga   And if you don't shift your arse it'll be first come, first smacked! Now do one!

Throughout the above and unseen by **Reilly** *and* **Digga**, **Briggs** *has boarded the coach and is stood at the front, glaring at them before, suddenly, he barks:*

Briggs   Reilly, Dickson, sit down!

Reilly   Sir we was only . . .

Briggs   I said sit down lad, the pair of you, now – get yourselves sat down!

Reilly *and* **Digga** *sit on* **Maurice**, *who is forced off the seat. He stands, exposed in the aisle, terrified of* **Briggs** *and not knowing where to sit.*

Briggs   You lad! What's your name?

Maurice (*almost in tears*)   Sir . . . Sir . . . I haven't got a seat.

Briggs   That's a stupid name lad! Sit there.

Maurice *moves down the coach and sits in a spare seat at the front.*

Briggs (*to* **Mrs Kay**)   You've got some real bright sparks here Mrs Kay. A right bunch! There's a few of them I could sling off right now!

Mrs Kay   Well . . . perhaps we'll just about survive; now that you've come to look after us.

Briggs   The boss thought it might be a good idea if you had an extra member of staff. Carlene Croxley! (*Approaching her.*) And what sort of an outfit do y' call that for a school visit?

Carly (*chewing, contemptuous, staring out of the window*)   What?

Briggs   Don't you 'what' me young lady! (*She merely shrugs.*) You know very well that on school trips you wear school uniform.

Carly   Yeah well I've got me school tie on, haven't I?

Briggs   Have you?

She displays the school tie tied around her waist.

Carly   What's *that*!?

Briggs   Ties are to be worn around the neck!

Carly   Well Mrs Kay never said nothin' about it!

Briggs   You're not talking to Mrs Kay now!

Carly   Yeh I know.

Briggs   Now you listen here madam, I don't like your attitude. I don't like it one bit!

Carly (*flashing sudden indignation*)   What have I said? I haven't said nothin' have I?

Briggs   I'm talking about your *attitude* Miss. (*She dismisses him with a glance and turns away.*) And if it carries on, the only place you'll be going today is back to the classroom. (*Glares at her.*) Is that understood? (*Beat.*)

Carly (*having to submit but doing nothing to disguise her attitude*)   Yeah!

Briggs   Yes *Sir*. And it better had be.

Mrs Kay   Mr Briggs, I don't think . . .

Briggs (*ignoring her, he turns to address the* **Kids**)   Right! Now listen. There's been a change of plan.

Mrs Kay   A what!

Briggs (*still addressing the* **Kids**)   Unfortunately we're not able, in fact, to go to Alton Towers today.

There is immediate uproar, various **Kids** *getting to their feet and all of them expressing their shock with cries of 'What?', 'Ah Hey', 'Why', 'Who says?', 'Why not'.*

Briggs   I said LISTEN! (*His bark and his glare silencing them, forcing them back into their seats.*)

Mrs Kay   Mr Briggs, would you be good enough to explain . . .

Briggs   If you'll allow me Mrs Kay, that is precisely what I am trying to do! (*Addressing the* **Kids** *but pointedly directing some of* *it in* **Mrs Kay**'*s direction.*) Now what's happened is that the school has just had a telephone call from Alton Towers to say that they're very sorry but because of a severe overbooking problem they cannot fit us in today.

The **Kids** *again erupt in protest.*

Kevin	Ah Hey!	**Kelly**	Why us?

Briggs Quiet!

Eunice What about the other schools?   **Andrews** That's not fair.

Briggs I said be quiet.

Mrs Kay But that's absolutely ridiculous!

Briggs It might be ridiculous Mrs Kay but it does not alter the fact that Alton Towers is off the agenda.

Briggs *delivers the following aside to* **Mrs Kay** *beneath the muted underscore of the* **Kids**' *moaning among themselves.*

Briggs Or would you prefer it Mrs Kay, if I told them they have a teacher who is a bare-faced liar! You know as well as me that after your last trip to Alton Towers you, and any children in your charge, are not allowed back there. Which is presumably why they have no booking under the name of this school. Although they do have a booking under the name – The Kay Academy for Gifted Children!

Mrs Kay But we should never have been barred in the first place!

Briggs But you were Mrs Kay, you were!

Andrews Sir, Sir, it's supposed to be our day out today.

Digga I'm not goin' back in school, I'm not.

Murmurs of agreement.

Briggs Did I say anything about going back to school for the day? You were promised a day out, and you'll have a day out – a very good day out.

Eunice   I bet it's Blackpool.

Kids (*various*)   Blackpool! I bet we're going to Blackpool. Ogh, Blackpool, Blackpool. Blackpool . . . YES!

The excited murmur of 'Blackpool' underscores the following.

Briggs   It's meant a lot of frantic last-minute telephone calls and some hasty reorganizing but, nevertheless, I have managed to arrange it so that today we can, all of us, enjoy what should be a highly interesting and stimulating trip to Wales.

There is a momentary stunned silence.

Reilly (*standing*)   I'm goin' back to school.

All the **Kids** *start to get up from their seats and follow* **Reilly** *down the aisle.*

Briggs   Sit down now! All of you!

Reilly   It's crap, Wales!

Digga   It's just fields.

Jackie   An' it's dead old-fashioned.

Chloe/Zoe   There's no shops.

Sean   It's all sheep!

Andrews   An' there's nothin' to do.

Under **Briggs**'s *withering gaze, the stand-off crumbles.* **Kids**, *dejected, grumbling, resume their seats with attitude pouring out of them.*

Briggs   'Nothing to do' – in Wales? Nothing to do? Wales is brimming with things to do. One of the sites we'll be visiting today is the remarkable Conway Castle – one of the great fortresses of medieval Europe. And mark my words, when you see the splendour of the eight . . . yes, *eight* magnificent Norman towers, you'll understand why no less a body than UNESCO has designated Conway Castle as a World Heritage Site. And if you'd only open your eyes and . . .

Milton (*rushing excitedly on to the coach, unaware of*
Briggs)   I've got them, I've got loads. The feller in the shop gave
us loads.

Briggs   Loads of what lad?

Milton   Sir, sweets Sir – from the shop.

Briggs   Sweets! Chocolates and sweets – on a school trip?

Ronny (*jabbing* **Briggs** *on the shoulder*)   Excuse me. Can I have
a word with you? (*Indicating the coach doors.*) In private.

A somewhat perplexed **Briggs** *follows* **Ronny** *off the coach.*

Eunice   Miss I don't wanna go to Wales.

Kevin   I've been there before Miss – it always rains!

Other **Kids** *joining in with calls of 'I don't wanna go neither,'*
'Miss nor me,' 'I don't wanna go.' Throughout the above **Mrs Kay**
stands facing them, momentarily lost in her own thoughts as she
tries to decide how to proceed.

Mrs Kay (*raising her hands for calm*)   I know it's a
disappointment and I'm sorry about that . . . But the fact is that
disappointments can . . . be . . . overcome! (*Talking now as much to*
herself as to the **Kids**.) And we are going to overcome this
disappointment!

Andrews   How though Miss?

Mrs Kay   Now look . . . just give me a moment.

The action inside the coach freezes as, outside the coach, we see
Ronny *waving his finger for emphasis as he 'lectures'* **Briggs**.

Ronny   An' so what you've gotta start understandin' mate! – is
that kids, like these, they hardly ever see a sweet or a bar of
chocolate! You just remember – they're nothin' but lost little waifs
and strays, left to wander the cold, cruel, heartless streets . . .

Ronny's *lecture continues, mute as we unfreeze the action inside*
the coach, then **Ronny** *and* **Briggs** *exit.*

Mrs Kay   Now Wales is not Alton Towers and there's no point pretending that it is. But, Wales is Wales. And we can, I know we can, have a very . . . good . . . time in Wales. It's not just castles. It's not just sheep. There are fantastic things to do in Wales.

Sean   Miss, like what?

Mrs Kay   Like . . . Sean . . . like . . . like . . . *beaches*! (*Beginning to run with it now.*) *Sand* . . . that stretches for miles and miles; an ocean, Sean, an ocean that stretches so far it reaches America.

Ronson   Will we be able to go to that beach Miss?

Mrs Kay   Yes! Yes, yes, yes. We'll go to the beach and play on the sand and walk in the water that touches America! And no matter what – we are going to have a great day out! Mark, Katie, the sweets? Who wants sweets?

Kids *cheer as* **Teachers** *begin handing out the sweets.*

Amy (*to* **Mrs Kay** *as she offers sweets*)   Miss, anyway, I like Wales.

Mrs Kay   Ah, do you Amy love? Why's that?

Amy   Because it's just empty Miss.

Mrs Kay   *Empty*, love?

Amy   Yea Miss. An' I like the kilts.

Mrs Kay   The kilts!

Mark (*at the back of the coach*)   You lads having sweets?

Reilly   How y' getting' on with Miss, then Sir?

Digga   We seen y' Sir – comin' outta that pub with her.

Mark (*trying to cover his embarrassment*)   Did you now?

Further down the coach, **Katie** *is watching and listening as she gives out sweets.*

Reilly   Sir, y' know in Wales, there's lots of woods aren't there?

Mark   Well, yes, forests, mountains and lakes.

Reilly   An' are you gonna show Miss the woods are y' Sir?

Mark (*making his escape*)   Alright, you've all got sweets have you?

Reilly   I'll show her the woods for y' if y' like Sir.

Katie (*snapping her fingers and fixing him with a pointed finger*)   Ryan!

Reilly (*all innocence*)   What? What Miss.

Katie   You know very well what.

Reilly   Miss, I was only askin' if he was gonna show y' all the trees an' the plants.

Digga   Miss, you an' Sir are getting' married aren't y'?

Katie   That's my business, thank you very much.

Reilly   Miss, you'd be better off with me Miss – I'm much fitter!

Katie (*gives up playing it straight, calling him to her*)   Ryan! (*Whispers to* **Reilly**.) Little boys shouldn't try to act like men. The day might come when their words are put to the test. (*She turns and* **Reilly** *makes his way back along the aisle.*)

Reilly   Any day Miss, any day!

Digga   What did she say?

Reilly   She said she fancied me.

Other **Kids** *laugh and jeer.*

Digga (*suddenly*)   Briggs – watch out.

Briggs *climbs back on board followed by* **Ronny** *who takes his place at the wheel.*

Briggs (*aside to* **Mrs Kay**)   Well we've got a right head-case of a driver!

As **Briggs** *takes a seat across the aisle from* **Mrs Kay** *the engine comes to life and the* **Kids** *cheer.*

Ronny   Okay everybody! Here we go!

Kids *all begin to sing while simultaneously waving enthusiastic V
signs through the windows. At this point the coach should move
and build a momentum which is sustained throughout the entire
duration of what follows so that the song underscore and dialogue
are all part of a sequence that creates the impression of a moving
coach.*

Kids   *We're off we're off*
    We're off in a motor car
    Sixty coppers are after us
    An' we don't know where we are
    We turn around a corner, WHOOOH (all leaning, as they do
      corner)
    Eatin' a Christmas pie
    Along came a copper
    An' he hit me in the eye

Kids   *Our day (clap clap)*
    This is our day
    If you're goin' our way
    Better get on board
    We're movin'

    Movin' (clap clap)
    Going somewhere
    Doesn't matter where cos
    It's gonna be better
    Than where we've come from

Kids   *I went to tell me mother*
    Me mother wasn't in
    I went to tell me father
    An' he kicked me in the
    Been to Madagascar
    Been to Spain and France
    Been to Paddy's Market
    With a monkey in my pants
    The monkey got the measles

The monkey went and died (AAAH)
My sister had a baby
And she pushed it down the slide

Kids   *Our day (clap clap)*
This is our day
If you're goin' our way
Better get on board
We're movin'

Movin' (clap clap)
Goin' somewhere
Doesn't matter where cos
It's gonna be better
Than where we've come from

The police caught the priest
And they put him in the dock
They gave him seven years
For lookin' up the lady's frock
Oh there's pervs in the precinct
An' there's paedos in the park
My mother's in the bettin' shop
My father's in a nark

Kids   *Our day (clap clap)*
This is our day
If you're goin' our way
Better get on board
We're movin'

Movin' (clap clap)
Goin' somewhere
Doesn't matter where cos
It's gonna be better
Than where we've come from

Music continues to underscore.

Ronny   Alright kids – let's hear it for the tunnel – we're goin'
through the Mersey Tunnel.

Kids *cheering.*

Kids   *The Mersey Tunnel is three miles long and the ceiling's*
             made of glass
          So that you can drive along and watch the ships go past
          There's a plug-hole every five yards
          They open it every night
          It lets in all the water an' it washes away the . . .

Briggs *leaps to his feet in anticipation of the obscenity he thinks*
they're about to sing.

          Sha na na na na na na na na na

Sidestepped, **Briggs** *resumes his seat.*

Music modulating to higher key.

Kids   *Sha na na na na na na na na na*
          They dug the Mersey Tunnel out of sand and soil and clay
          And all the tons of seagull dung they had to clear away
          It took them years and years working day and night
          With twenty thousand labourers just to shovel away the . . .

Briggs *again leaps to his feet in anticipation of the obscenity he*
thinks they're bound to sing this time.
          Sha na na na na na na na na na

Sidestepped again, **Briggs** *once more resumes his seat.*

Music again, modulating to higher key.

Kids   *Sha na na na na na na na na na*
          They made the Mersey Tunnel back in twenty-one BC
          It was built by the Romans who were good at history
          Caesar led his legions looking for a fight
          But the boys of Liverpool . . .

Not to be tricked a third time, **Briggs** *remains in his seat.*
          kicked them all to . . .

All the **Kids** *stand to shout:*

          shite!

Leaping to his feet **Briggs** *sees nothing but perfectly behaved* **Kids**
sat staring through the coach windows and singing quietly:

Kids   *Our day (clap clap)*
This is our day
If you're goin' our way
Better get on board
We're movin'

Movin' (clap clap)
Goin' somewhere
Doesn't matter where cos
It's gonna be better
Than where we've come from

Underscore continues quietly under:

Chloe/Zoe   *It's borin'*
It's bleedin' borin'
If it carries on like this
We'll soon be snoring

Coach trips are shockin'
They're all the bleedin' same
Just sittin' doin' nott'n
I don't know why we came

It's borin'
It's bleedin' borin'
We shoulda stayed in school
An' done some drawin'

Coach trips are mingin'
Y' can't even have a laugh
An' they start that stupid singin'
Songs that are bleedin' crap

It's borin'
It's bleedin' borin'

Kids   *Our day (clap clap)*
This is our day

If you're goin' our way
Better get on board
We're movin'

Movin' (clap clap)
Goin' somewhere
Doesn't matter where cos
It's gonna be better
Than where we've come from

Ronny   Get ready everyone – humpety backed bridge comin' up.

As they approach and go over the bridge:

Kids   Whooooooooh.

We're off we're off
We're off in a motor car
All the way to Wales
Where they all say 'yach y da'

Ronny   Okay everyone – there's the sign, comin' up . . . England, England.

Kids (*joining him*)   England . . . Waaaaaales!

Where the sun never shines
An' the rain never stops
An' they hate the bleedin' English
So they rob them in the shops
Our day . . .

Briggs (*up out of his seat*)   What are you talking about? 'They hate the bleedin' English? So they rob them in the shops?' Don't be so ridiculous! I've never heard such prejudice. The Welsh have a very strong sense of their own culture and identity, certainly, but that's no reason to say that they 'hate the English'. Where do you people get these ideas from?

Sean (*hand raised*)   Sir.

Briggs   What!

Sean   Sir I need the toilet.

During following, **Mrs Kay** *has a word with* **Ronny**.

Kevin   Sir so do I.

Briggs   Yes, well you should have thought of that before you got on the coach – shouldn't you?

Kevin   Sir, I didn't need the toilet before I got on the coach.

Eunice   Sir, I'm feeling dead sick.

Milton   Sir, I need the toilet too.

Briggs   Yes, and is it any wonder, the amount of sweets and drinks / you've been pouring down yourselves.

Milton   No Sir, it's because I've got a very weak bladder.

Jackie   Sir he has! He's almost incontinent.

Sean (*now desperate*)   / Ah Sir, I *really* need the toilet.

Jackie   Sir, I'm havin' palpitations.

Which cues all the **Kids** *to take up, in one form or another, groans, moans and cries of, 'I wanna go the toilet.'*

Mrs Kay (*to* **Kids**)   Alright everyone, we're pulling into a service area now. There are toilets there and shops and . . .

Briggs   Mrs Kay!

Mrs Kay   Mr Briggs! (*Spelling it out for him.*) I . . . want . . . to . . . go . . . to the toilet myself!

Briggs   Oh! Oh.

Mrs Kay (*as the coach pulls in and stops*)   Right, come on, all of you who need the toilets . . .

As they leave the coach, the **Kids** *chant through following* (**Eunice** *leads*) – **Briggs** *stands outside the door of the coach, his attention divided between* **Kids** *who have left the coach and those who are still getting off.* **Mrs Kay** *and* **Katie** *head for the ladies while* **Mark** *heads towards the gents.*

Eunice   *Everywhere we go*

Kids   *Everywhere we go . . .*

Briggs (*spoken*)   Come on, come on, less noise!

Eunice   *People wanna know*

Kids   *People wanna know*

Briggs (*spoken*)   This is strictly a stop for toilets.

Eunice   *Who we are*

Kids   *Who we are*

Briggs   Walk! Walk properly . . .

Eunice   *So we tell them*

Kids   *So we tell them . . .*

Briggs   Just five minutes, you understand.

Eunice   *We are the Progress*

Kids   *We are the Progress . . .*

Eunice   *The mighty mighty Progress . . .*

Kids   *The mighty mighty Progress*

Ronson   Sir which way's the boys' bogs?

Briggs   *Toilet* lad, not bogs! Over there!

Chloe *and* **Zoe** *– the bored girls – getting off the coach and heading in the opposite direction.*

Briggs   You two! Where do you think you're going?

Chloe/Zoe   To the shops Sir!

Briggs   This is a toilet stop, not a shop stop. Go on! (*Waving back in the 'right' direction.*) Go on!

Chloe/Zoe   God! – He's beyond borin'!

He stands, shaking his head and sighing his consternation at what he sees as the general lack of organization. His mood is not helped

*by the whoops and shrieks of laughter which come from the gents'
toilet.* **Mark** *returns.*

Briggs   What are they up to in there?

Mark   Well I wasn't taking notes but as it's a toilet and we are in
Wales, I'd say the chances are that they're taking a leak. (*Smiling
his pleasure at his little pun.* **Briggs** *ignores it.*)

Briggs   They're making enough noise about it!

Mark   Well they are kids aren't they?

Mark *moves away a few steps downstage of the coach, taking
advantage of the stop to look out at the view and get a few lungfuls
of country air.*

Briggs (*following* **Mark**)   You're not telling me you're the same
as her are you?

Mark   What do you mean?

Briggs   The same as her! Mrs . . . *Kay.*

We hear laughter from the gents.

Briggs (*automatically, over his shoulder*)   Be quiet! I said be
quiet! And get a move on! (*To* **Mark**.) I don't know.

Mark   Don't know what?

Briggs   I don't know what's going on! Didn't you see her, on the
coach – didn't you see how she undermined my authority?

Andrews *rushes out of the gents, sees* **Mark** *and* **Briggs** *and
rushes over to them addressing* **Mark**.

Andrews (*rushed, excited, holding out a pound coin*)   Sir, Sir
have you got two fifties for a pound?

Briggs (*to* **Mark**, *completely ignoring* **Andrew***'s presence.* **Mark**
reaching into his pocket and looking through his change)   We could
have driven on another half hour before stopping for the toilets.

Mark   Sorry Aaron, I haven't got any fifties.

Briggs   It's the staff who should be dictating when we stop, not the children.

Andrews (*urgent*)   Sir, Sir, have you Sir?

Briggs (*irritated*)   Have I what lad?

Andrews   Sir, two fifties for a pound.

Briggs (*absently, distractedly putting his hand into his pocket and pulling out loose change as he resumes pursuing his theme for* **Mark***'s benefit*)   And then, when we are stopped, what does she do? – just lets them stream off the coach any old how! I'll tell you what! I feel sorry for you having to work alongside her.

Andrews (*looking at the change in* **Briggs***'s hand*)   Sir there, thanks Sir.

Andrews *exits.*

Mark (*to* **Briggs**)   What do you mean 'having' to work with her? I choose to work with Mrs Kay.

Briggs   Choose? Well you're a fool – a young teacher like you, you're doing nothing for your career prospects working with a woman like that.

Mark   Look! I'm not interested in 'furthering my career'. I'm interested in becoming a good teacher.

Briggs   Well if you want to be a good teacher you should get yourself into a department where you can work with the kind of staff who set the right example.

Behind and beyond them, we see two inflated condoms protrude from out of the boys' toilet door and then fly off as they are released.

Andrews
              } (*as the 'balloons' ascend*)   Yes!
Sean

Briggs   You lads get back on the coach! (*To* **Mark**.) I mean all that child-centred let-the-kids-decide stuff. It doesn't do them a scrap of good. If you're going to do anything for kids like these you've got to risk being disliked.

Andrews *and* **Sean** *start in the direction of the coach but then quickly rush into the gents as* **Briggs***'s back is turned. At the back, and beyond* **Mark** *and* **Briggs***, we see* **Reilly** *and* **Digga** *emerge from the gents, arms akimbo, and legs taking faltering steps in their impression of grotesque creatures from another planet. To assist them in creating this effect, each of them is wearing a condom on his head. As they come out of the gents and then go back in, we and* **Briggs** *hear the laughter their 'act' is promoting from the other* **Kids** *inside the gents.*

Briggs   Freedom? Where does that lead? They've got enough freedom at home haven't they, with their twenty-quid pocket money, their eighty-quid training shoes, Sky Plus, iPad this, HD that, designer-this-that-and-the-other. I don't know about you but I think her philosophy's all over the place. Eh?

Behind and beyond them, **Maurice** *walks out of the toilet nonchalantly carrying a condom-dispensing machine under his arm. He disappears on to the coach with it.*

Mark   It's not a philosophy. Mrs Kay isn't some kind of theorist.

Briggs   Well what's the method she does work to then? You tell me. Mm?

Mark   Well . . . for one thing, she likes them.

Briggs   Who?

Mark   The kids. She likes the kids.

Briggs   What's that got to do with it? (*Spotting a group of noisy girls running out of the girls' toilet.*) You lot – where do you think you're going to – on the coach, get back on the coach now!

As he ushers them off towards the coach, **Carly** *and* **Jackie** *appear. Throughout the following, all the remaining* **Kids** *and staff make their way back on to the coach.*

Carly   Oh Sir!

Jackie   Sir where've you been?

Carly   Sir we've been looking everywhere for y' – we thought you might have been hi-jacked.

Mark (*looking at* **Briggs**)   So did I for a minute!

Carly   Oh God Sir, don't say that. I'd have been distraught!

Jackie (*as they both go to link arms with him*)   And me Sir.

Mark (*managing to free himself*)   Alright girls, come on. Come on, back on the coach now.

Carly   Sir are y' gonna come and sit by us?

Jackie   Ah go on Sir. Sir go on, say you will.

They grab him again. **Briggs** *returns.*

Mark   We'll see, we'll see.

Briggs   What are you doing!? Get on the coach, now!

Carly (*to* **Mark**, *ignoring* **Briggs** *as they move back to coach*) Don't forget, Sir – we're on a promise.

Mark, *under the disapproving gaze of* **Briggs**, *follows them on to the coach.*

Briggs (*shouting towards the gents*)   Right, come on! Come on, now, everybody back on board. Come on, we've waited long enough as it is. Everybody back on board, now!

Mrs Kay (*leaning out of the coach door*)   Mr Briggs, do you think you could get a move on? Everybody's waiting for you!

Briggs *turns and looks and sees everybody sat in their seats, awaiting him. He strides off. The kids reassemble the coach as they sing:*

Kids   *Our day*
       This is our day
       If you're goin' our way
       Better get on board
       We're movin'

       Movin' (clap clap)
       Goin' somewhere

> *Doesn't matter where cos*
> *It's gonna be better*
> *Than where we've come from*

*By now the **Kids** have reassembled on the bus and sing as **Briggs** hurries to get on board:*

> *Whoah whoah whoah whoah*
> *Sir's missed the bus*
> *Sir's missed the bus*
> *He's missed the bloody bus*
> *Whoah whoah whoah whoah Sir's missed the bus*
> *He can't get out of bed in the morning*

*The **Kids** cheer as the coach sets off again.*

> *Our day (clap clap)*
> *This is our day*
> *If you're goin' our way*
> *Better get on board*
> *We're movin'*

> *Movin' (clap clap)*
> *Goin' somewhere*
> *Doesn't matter where cos*
> *It's gonna be better*
> *Than where we've come from*

*On board the coach, **Jackie** now has the camera and is out of her seat, taking pictures. Seeing his opportunity, **Reilly** quickly slips into her seat, next to **Carly**.*

***Kids** sing, as underscore minor key 'Our Day Out' motif – possibly with escalating key change to point where it naturally segues into underscore prelude to 'I'm in Love with Sir'.*

Reilly   Alright Carlene.

Carly   Hia.

(*Pause.*)

Reilly   Are y' okay?

Carly   Yeah. Are you?

Reilly   Yeah. (*Pause.*) Good. Yeah. (*Pause.*) Have y' erm . . . have y' seen that? (*Pointing out of window.*) See the mountain.

Carly   Oh yeah. Yeah. It's good isn't it?

Segue from vocal underscore to instrumental – 'I'm in Love with Sir'.

Reilly   Yeah, they are good aren't they – mountains.

Carly   Yeah, they're good. I bet they'd look even better in winter. Y' know when they've got snow on them.

Reilly   Ogh yeah, they'd be brilliant then wouldn't they? Yeah.

Jackie (*returning to her seat*)   'Ey you, that's my seat.

Reilly   Well find another one.

Jackie   I've been sitting there all the time.

Reilly   Well live dangerous for once an' sit somewhere else. Go sit up at the back, with Digga.

Jackie   I'm not sitting with him, that Digga one, he's a biff! Carly, tell him to move!

Reilly   Go on, just sit up at the back for five minutes, that's all.

Jackie   Carly!

Carly   Oh go on, just for a minute!

Jackie   You! (*She goes and perches, prim and huffy, next to* **Digga**.)

Reilly   Listen, maybe me and you could come out here in the winter.

Carly   Could we?

Reilly   Yeah, y' know, just to look at the mountains when they've got some snow on them. (*Pause.*) Do y' think?

Carly   Yeah. Yeah, that'd be good that. (*A moment, a smile.*) Yeah.

Reilly (*chuffed*)   Alright.

Carly   Sir was tellin' me and Jackie before, about the mountains.

Reilly   Sir?

Carly   Mr McDevit. He said that, erm, all of these mountains were . . . glacial.

Reilly   Did he?

Carly   Y' know, the mountains were made like when the glaciers melted, y' know at the end of the ice age.

Reilly   Yeah!

Carly   He was really interesting.

Reilly   Oh yeah! Well he would be wouldn't he?

Carly   What?

Reilly   I mean he's a right little Stephen Fry isn't he?

Carly   Why d' y' have to say somethin' like that?

Reilly   Cos he's soft isn't he?

Carly   Oh is he? Well he might be soft – but he's really nice as well!

Reilly   Is he now? Well why don't you get him to take you lookin' at the snowy bleedin' mountains then.

Carly   Maybe I will!

Reilly *looks at her before hurriedly getting up and going to the back where he addresses* **Jackie** *who is now relaxed deep in conversation with* **Digga**.

Reilly   Hey you, get out of my seat!

Jackie   I'm talkin' with Dennis.

Reilly (*derisory*)   Who?

Jackie   Digga! I'm talking with Digga, alright!

Digga　Leave her where she is Reil!

Reilly *gives up and bunks in alongside a nervous* **Milton** *who sits there, staring apprehensively at his uninvited travelling companion.*

Reilly　What are you lookin' at, gobshite?

Milton *quickly looks the other way. Seeing* **Mark** *walking along the aisle,* **Reilly** *turns away and fixes his gaze on the window.*

Carly (*as* **Mark** *approaches*)　Sir, y' comin' to sit by me?

Mark　No I'm not, Carly.

Carly　Sir you promised.

Mark　I did no such thing.

Carly　Oh Sir go on, just for a minute, go on sit down. I wanna tell you something.

Mark　Well tell me now.

Carly　Sir, I don't want everyone else to hear!

As he tentatively sits, **Jackie** *sees him and immediately moves, fast, to the seat behind* **Carly** *and* **Mark***, poking her head through the space between the seats.*

Jackie　Hia Sir!

Mark (*long-suffering*)　Hello Jackie. Now come on, what is it you want to tell me?

Carly *and* **Jackie** *laughing.*

Mark　Come on! It's not a joke is it?

Carly　No Sir, it's serious. It's dead serious!

They laugh again.

Mark (*going to get up*)　Look, I've got to go, I've . . .

Carly (*hastily linking her arm through his and trying to hold him there. From behind him,* **Jackie***, pushing down on his* *shoulders*)   Sir I'll tell y', I'll tell y'. I'll tell y' now, I will I'll tell y'. She said I haven't got the nerve but I have! Sir, I just wanna tell y' that I think you . . . are . . . really gorgeous!

Mark (*quickly getting up and making his escape*)   Carlene!

Carly   I told him – I said I would. Ogh God, he's fitter than Friday him, isn't he?

Jackie   But you're just wastin' your time girl. You've got no chance. He's getting' married to Miss, isn't he?

Carly   Yeah, but he's not married her yet, has he? He might give her the elbow; might start going out with me instead. For all you know, it might just be me who he marries!

Jackie (*shrieking derision*)   Shut up – you mental mare! You'll never get a husband like Sir. If you marry anyone, it'll be someone like your old feller!

Carly   You're just jealous you girl!

Jackie   Oh get lost!

Carly *turns and dismisses her. As she does so, she sees* **Reilly**, *sitting, watching her.* **Carly** *turns away and stares through the window and begins to sing.*

Carly   *I'm in love with Sir*
        But Sir doesn't care
        Cos Sir's in love with her
        Over there
        With the hair
        The bleedin' mare

        If I was the wife of a man like Sir
        My life would not be full of trouble and care
        I'd look forward to the nights
        And we'd make a perfect pair
        Me and Sir

        I'm in love with Sir
        But Sir doesn't care

Cos Sir's in love with her
Over there
With the hair
I'm in despair

Kids *sing 'ah ah ah' backing vocals during following verse.*

If I could marry Sir I'd be alright
I wouldn't need to work
And he'd take me out each night
Dancing and romancing
And dining by candlelight

Kids   *Oh don't talk shite*

How could she even dare
To think that Sir and her
Could ever be a pair
Hark at her / Over there
The dozy mare

Jackie   *You'll be the wife of a man like your dad*
He'll disappear
When you grow fat
You'll be left with the kids
On your own in a council flat

Music segues as the scene is transformed into a romantic and idealized 'Strictly Come Dancing' world of crushed focus and swirling mirror ball light. An equally romanticized/idealized male **Dancer** *appears – it is the* **Sir** *of* **Carly**'s *imagination, singing to her as he approaches, effortlessly, elegantly dancing his way towards her.*

Sir   *I'm told you sometimes think of me*
I'm told that sometimes you sing
My name and whisper you love me
Love me
You lovely thing

Taking **Carly** *in his arms and singing to her as they dance:*

I know the fears that confound you
For what the future might bring

But no more tears now
That I've found you
Found you
You lovely thing

Instrumental break – tango.

As **Sir** *literally sweeps* **Carly** *off her feet, all the* **Kids** *form into dancing pairs and take to the floor for their own dance, with* **Sir** *and* **Carly** *performing, at the centre, their virtuoso routine.*

Kids (*as they dance*)

Wouldn't it be good
If it only could
Happen like it happens
In Hollywood
Where everything that happens to you
Happens just the way it should

Instrumental break – waltz.

Sir   *And from this heart now I bring you*
The gift of this golden ring

Which he now slips on to **Carly**'s *finger.*

Along with a love you can cling to
I bring you
You lovely thing

Carly *stares, entranced, at the ring on her finger as* **Sir** *exits.*

Kids   *Wake up y' dozy mare*
You're never goin' there
It's just stupid dreams
And castles in the air

Cos nothing ever happens
Like it happens
In Hollywood
And you'll end up
With the kind of man
Who'll promise you the world

In the back of a van
That he robbed with his mate
Off a ferry from the Isle of Man

Carly, *as if coming out of a trance, looks at her finger – and the ring has now gone.*

Carly *I'm in love with Sir*	**Kids** *She's in love with Sir*
But Sir doesn't care	*But Sir doesn't care*
Cos Sir's in love with her	*Cos Sir's in love with her*
Over there	*Over there*
With the hair	*With the hair*
The bleedin' mare	*The bleedin' mare*
I'm in love with . . .	*She's in love with . . .*

Carly *slowly makes her way back to her seat next to* **Jackie** *as the* **Kids** *form the coach back into being.*

All   *Sir*

As the song comes to a close **Jackie** *is shaking* **Carly** *who has fallen asleep.*

Jackie   Carly! Will y' wake up! Carly . . .

As **Carly** *wakes,* **Briggs** *rises from his seat and hands a thermostop cup back to* **Mrs Kay**.

Briggs   Well I've got to hand it to you Mrs Kay – you certainly make a marvellous cup of coffee.

Mrs Kay *beams a big and knowing smile, which* **Katie** *has to look away from.*

Kevin (*wildly excited*)   Miss . . . Miss there's a zoo over there!

Kelly   Miss, Miss ah Miss, go on Miss; say we can go the zoo Miss ah please Miss please.

Ronson
Eunice (*unison*) ⎫ Miss I love zoos, please Miss.
            ⎬ Miss we could see all the lovely animals
            ⎭   Miss we love animals, don't we?

Caitlin/Georgia (*unison*)   Miss, the tigers are lovely.

Kids   Ah Miss, Miss . . . please Miss.

Mrs Kay *standing before them, hands held aloft and exaggeratedly shaking her head.*

Mrs Kay   I'm very sorry. As has been made abundantly clear to me, this is an educational trip. I don't think Mr Briggs would appreciate us wasting our time visiting a zoo.

Briggs   Wasting time? Why would it be a waste of time? A zoo is an environment where you can learn a great deal.

Mrs Kay   Oh, I'd forgotten. Yes, that's right you're something of an expert on natural history aren't you Mr Briggs?

Briggs   Well I wouldn't exactly say expert but . . .

Mrs Kay   A bit of a David Attenborough in your spare time.

Briggs   Well I'm, y' know.

Milton   Ah Sir, go on Sir.

Taylor/Oliver   Go on, say yeah Sir.

Abi/Kath   Let's go the zoo, Sir, please!

Brit/Sophie (*unison*)   Go on Sir let us go the zoo Sir!

Briggs (*looking at the* **Kids**)   You're genuinely fond of animals are you?

Eunice   Sir we love them. Don't we?

Kelly   Yeah. We do Sir, we love furry animals.

Briggs   Well not *every* animal is a furry creature.

Ronson   There's scaley ones and feathered ones aren't there Sir?

Briggs   That's right Ronson. The various species all have their own particular coats.

Kevin   Sir please Sir. Please let us see the zoo.

Sean   Go on Sir.

Beat – as he considers.

Briggs   Driver pull into the zoo.

The **Kids** *around him cheering and song beginning as coach pulls into zoo.*

Kids   *Yeah yeah*
We're off to see the monkeys
And the kangaroo
Yeah yeah, the big black bear
The creepy spiders, tigers cockatoo
Too Too Too
At the zoo zoo zoo zoo

Leaving the coach.

Yeah yeah
We're off to see the penguins
And the pandas and the baby caribou
Yeah yeah
The mountain hare
The puma, the leopard, the lynx the big gnu
Nu Nu Nu
At the zoo zoo zoo zoo

Briggs *suddenly stood before them barring the way.*

Briggs   *But listen to me*
I want to see
You all behave responsibly
Have you got that?

Kids   Yes Sir/Sir we will/Honest Sir.

Briggs   *Any of you*
Who think a zoo
Is a place for games and hullabaloo
You can stop that

Kids   Sir no sir/We won't Sir/We'll be dead good Sir.

(*Rising key change beginning here.*)

Briggs   *Don't act like fools*
  You are the school's
  Ambassadors
  So hark the rules
  And heed them

Kids   Sir, *what*?

(*Rising key change.*)

Briggs   *Signs that read*
  'Please do not feed
  The penguins'
  Really do mean
  Do not feed them

Kids   Sir we wouldn't, we'd never.

(*Rising key change.*)

Briggs   *If you expect*
  To get respect
  Then please ensure
  That you respect
  The creatures

Kids   Sir we love the animals.

(*Back to original key here*)

Kids   *The cuddly ones*
  The lovely ones
  The slimy grimy
  Ugly ones

Kids   *Like teachers!*

Briggs   Now you listen here . . . I don't want . . .

Kids   *Yeah yeah*
  It's okay Sir
  We won't do what we're not supposed to do
  Yeah Yeah
  You can trust us Sir

You know we'd never make a show
Of you
You you you
At the zoo zoo zoo zoo

Music continues as underscore throughout following.

Briggs   Right – those of you who want to see the reptiles, follow me.

(*As* **Steph**, **Taylor/Oliver**, **Caitlin/Georgia** *and* **Abi/Kath** *go to link arms with him.*)

What do you think you're doing?

Steph   Ah hey Sir – all the other teachers let you link them.

As **Kids** *and* **Teachers** *disperse,* **Chloe** *and* **Zoe** *remain.*

Chloe/Zoe   *It's borin'*
It's bleedin' borin'
The tigers look half dead
They're not even roarin'
It's like they're all on Prozac
Or they've all been on the drink
Zoos are really borin'
An' as well as that – they stink

I don't wanna see no parrot
No penguins or giraffe
It isn't worth a carrot
Y' can't even have a laugh

(*Without a shred of enthusiasm.*)

Zoe   Come on – shall we go see the monkeys?

Chloe   What'll that be like?

Zoe   Borin'.

Chloe   Oh come on then.

As they exit the music segues and **Reilly, Digga, Carly** *and* **Jackie** *cautiously approach a cage which houses the lion. They are joined by* **Eunice, Kelly, Sean, Ronson** *and* **Kevin**.

Reilly *reaches out with the sweets.*

Carly   Ryan – be careful – it's a lion.

Reilly   Look at it, the poor bleedin' thing.

Jackie   It looks like one of the auld ones in the Day Centre –
when they just sit there, never movin' all day.

Carly   Agh it's dead sad isn't it?

All   *Poor bloody lion*
He must be in pain
He's lost all his teeth
An' most of his mane
When he should be
Running wild
Living free

Reilly   I know – an' it's supposed to be the lord of the jungle
isn't it?

Digga (*laughing*)   The lord of the *what*?

Carly   You heard.

All   *The boss of the beasts*
Shouldn't be behind bars
The king of the cats
Should be under the stars
Where he could be
Running wild
Living free

No no
The king of the jungle
Should never be
Made to do
The freak show
The peep show
Locked up in a box
For me and you you you you
At the zoo zoo zoo zoo

Unnoticed by **Reilly** *and the others,* **Briggs** *and his group enter.*

Reilly   *If I was in charge I'd let them all out*
Leave them to roam and go running about
And then they'd be
Running wild
Living free

Briggs   What are you on about, Reilly? You'd set what free?

As music shifts to underscore.

Reilly   The animals, all of them.

Briggs   And what would be the consequence of that? Eh? You let animals just go loose, don't you think there'd be death, or serious injury?

Reilly   But that's only because they're been caged up. An' if y' keep animals locked up like that well it's bound to make them mad so when they get loose they do wanna kill . . . (*Shrugs.*) an' that.

Briggs   So how the hell do you know that Reilly?

Reilly   Because I've seen my auld feller's dog – after it's been chained up an' left – for ages. Sometimes all the weekend.

Briggs   Don't be ridiculous Reilly, I hardly think you can compare your father's domestic dog situation with what goes on in a zoo. Without places like this how do you think they'd be able to conduct research, promote conservation. Well?

Reilly   I don't know.

Briggs   No you don't lad. I don't think you know very much at all.

Eunice   Ah come on Sir, let's go and see the elephants an' that.

Steph   No way! Sir let's go to the Pets' Corner.

Briggs   Be patient, just be patient. We'll get around them all eventually.

Seeing **Reilly** *walking off.*

Reilly! Where are you going? Reilly!

Reilly   The coach! I'm goin' back the coach!

Briggs *stalled from remonstrating further by the arrival of*
Mrs Kay *with a small group of* **Kids**.

Mrs Kay   How you getting on? Still plying you with questions?

Briggs   Yes. They've been very good actually. Excellent. Well,
most of them!

Mrs Kay   I'm just going to the café. Do you want to join me?

Briggs   Well I was just on my way to the Pets' Corner . . .

Andrews   It's alright Sir, we'll go on our own.

Mrs Kay   Come on. They'll be alright.

Briggs   But will they Mrs Kay? (*Turns to* **Kids**.) Will you?

Kids   *Yeah yeah*
    It's okay Sir
    We won't do what we're not
    Supposed to do

A beaming **Mrs Kay** *linking a not entirely comfortable* **Briggs** *and*
leading him off.

    Yeah yeah
    Cross my heart and swear
    We'd never ever make a show of you you you
    At the zoo zoo zoo zoo

Various of the younger **Kids**, *conspiratorial, whispering, looking*
to make sure that **Briggs** *has gone. Beginning to leave in the*
opposite direction.

Steph   The Pets' Corner, come on . . .

Eunice   What about the elephants?

Steph   Forget the elephants you. You can't pick up an elephant
can y'?

Eunice   What?

Steph   But y' can pick up the animals in the Pets' Corner can't y' . . .

Amy   Can yer?

Ronson   No you can't!

Kids *move to where a low fence or arc of boxes represents Pets' Corner.* **Steph, Caitlin/Georgia** *and* **Amy** *lean in, looking at the various creatures in the small compound.*

Eunice   We'll get in trouble.

Steph (*starting to feed crisps to one of the animals*)   No we won't, it'll be alright.

Ronson   No! No, I'm gonna tell!

Amy   We're not doin' any harm.

Eunice   *Y' dozy mare*
        Now can't y' read
        It says up there
        You shouldn't feed
        The rabbits

Steph   Well! What harm's it doin'?

Eunice   *Givin' it crisps*
        And sweets, you div!
        You'll make the poor thing
        Grow up with
        Bad habits

Steph   No I won't! Because the crisps I'm giving it are low-fat crisps aren't they?

Caitlin/Georgia   An' these sweets are diabetic – so they'll be alright.

As **Amy** *reaches down to pick up one of the cuddly creatures:*

Ronson   Agh! Hey, you, Amy Chandler!

Eunice   *What y' doin'*
        Y' stupid mare
        Y' shouldn't touch
        The creatures' fur
        Or stroke them

Amy   I'm only playin' with it

Eunice   *An animal isn't*
        A toy y' div
        It can't be fixed
        Or mended if
        It gets broken

Ronson   You better put that down, you – now.

Amy   I won't.

Ronson   Well I'm gonna tell the *man*! An' he'll tell your social worker! An' then you'll get taken back in care, Amy Chandler.

Amy   *All I'm doin'*
        Is strokin' it
        I'm hardly gonna
        Be chokin' it
        With a cuddle

Kids   *It isn't allowed*
        If Sir could see
        You holding it
        You know you'd be
        In trouble

Amy   But I'm only giving the little thing a love! That's all. And it's dead happy – look. It's smiling isn't it?

Eunice   Gerbils don't *smile*!

Amy   Look!

Amy *displays the animal, letting each of them stroke it.*

Kids   Agh!

Eunice   It is – it's smilin'.

Caitlin/Georgia   Ah isn't it dead cute eh?

Kelly   It's lovely.

Maurice   Ah it's just like a little baby isn't it?

Ronson   Feel its fur – it's dead warm.

Amy *moving beyond their reach.*

Eunice   Amy, let's stroke it again.

Amy   No – you're wearin' it out.

Eunice   Don't be tight – give us a go of it.

Amy   No. It's mine.

Kids, *as one, all look round to check that nobody is around.*

Eunice   I'm gettin' one.

Ronson   An' me!

Which is the cue for them all to pick up animals.

Kelly   *I'll get my own*

Taylor/Oliver   *Me as well*

Milton   *Feel its fur*

Abi/Kath   *Doesn't it smell*

All   *Lovely*

All   *Guinea pig, hamster*
Gerbil, mice
Chicks and ducks
They're all so nice
And cuddly

Yeah, yeah,
Lovely cuddly creatures
If you only knew
Yeah yeah

How much we care
And just how much
We all love all of you
You you you
In the zoo zoo zoo zoo

Repeated as they exit.

Zoo zoo zoo zoo
Zoo zoo zoo zoo

Mrs Kay *and* **Briggs** *in the café/picnic area.*

Mrs Kay   Will you take another drop?

Briggs   I won't say no – if you can spare it.

Mrs Kay   I've got another flask.

Briggs   Well, lovely, thanks.

Beat.

I'll tell you something – it's marvellous to be out in this country air isn't it?

Mrs Kay (*breathing it in*)   Intoxicating isn't it?

Briggs   They're really enthusiastic aren't they? Really interested.

Mrs Kay   In the animals? Oh yes. Can I say it's such a help having you here because you know so much about this sort of thing.

Briggs   Well I'm not exactly an expert but . . . you know what I was thinking, when we're back at school, perhaps I could arrange for some of your kids to come up to my department. I've got some marvellous stuff – I think some of them might find it really interesting.

Mrs Kay   Oh I'm sure they would. That's marvellous. Would you really do that?

Briggs   Of course.

We see **Mark** *and* **Katie** *approaching* **Mrs Kay** *and* **Briggs**.

Briggs (*to* **Mrs Kay**)   I'll sort out which free periods I've got and we'll get it organized.

Mrs Kay   That's tremendous. Thanks (*To* **Mark** *and* **Katie**.) Hi. Want some coffee?

Katie   We've had some, thanks.

Mark   I think they're all ready to go actually.

Mrs Kay   Are they all back?

During the following the **Kids** *are revealed, neatly lined up.*

Katie   It's amazing. We came around the corner and they were all getting themselves lined up, waiting for the coach.

Mrs Kay   Lined up? Wonders will never cease. (*To* **Briggs**.) You see, you *can* trust them.

Briggs (*affable*)   Well I'm glad to hear it. They're all ready? Good. Well it's on to Conway then.

The **Teachers** *leave the café and see an orderly line of patiently waiting* **Kids**. **Briggs** *is impressed.*

Briggs   Well! My word! Look at this Mrs Kay. Well done – well done indeed. Right. All checked and present. Come on, on board the . . .

The **Kids** *go to follow him just as a* **Zoo Keeper** *comes rushing up to them.*

Keeper   Hold it right there! Are you supposed to be in charge of this lot?

Mrs Kay   Why, what's wrong?

Keeper   Children? They're not bloody children, they're animals. Zoo? It's not the zoo back there. This is the bloody zoo!

Briggs   Excuse me! Would you mind controlling your language and telling me what's going on?

Keeper (*ignoring him, as he pushes past and confronts the*
Kids)   Right! Now where are they?

Innocent faces and replies of 'What?' 'Where's what?' 'What do y'
mean?'

Keeper   What! You know bloody well what!

Briggs (*intercepting him*)   Now look, this has gone far enough.
Would you mind just explaining what your problem . . .

Tailing off as he hears the loud clucking of a hen. The **Keeper**
strides up to one of the **Kids** *and pulls open his jacket, revealing a*
bantam hen.

Keeper (*taking possession of the hen and addressing the* **Kids**)
Right! And now I want the rest!

There is a moment's hesitation before the floodgates open and
animals begin to emerge from every conceivable hiding place. The
Teachers *look on as* **Keeper** *and* **Helper** *round up the animals and*
take them off. The **Kids** *are left withering under the explosive gaze*
of **Briggs** *as underscoring begins.*

Briggs   I trusted you! I trusted you. And this! This is how you
repay me!

Ronson   Sir we only borrowed them!

Briggs (*exploding*)   Shuttup! (*Glares and breathes.*) No wonder!
No wonder that people are prepared to do nothing for the likes
of you! Trust! You don't even understand the meaning of the
word.

Mrs Kay (*muted, to* **Kids**)   Come on now. All of you, on to the
coach.

Kids *exit, ushered off by* **Mark** *and* **Katy**. **Briggs** *continues*
berating them as they go.

Briggs   The moment you are treated like real people, what
happens? Well that man was right. You're animals! All of you,
animals! (*He turns on* **Mrs Kay**.) When we get to the castle we'll
split into four groups, with one member of staff responsible for

each group. If they behave like animals they'll be treated like animals. Is that understood?!

Mrs Kay *nods and turns to go.* **Briggs** *sings.* NB *– his lyrics are rhetorical – not directly addressed to the audience. During the first verse the* **Kids** *gradually appear behind him.*

Briggs *What happens to society when honour and respect*
 And rules of common decency fall into neglect
 When standards and authority are trampled in the mud
 And hooligan brutality is all that's understood
 What do you get?

Amy *What do you get?*

Briggs *Children who grow up to be*
 Devoid of all morality
 Like animals

Behind him we now see the **Kids** *silhouetted and shadowed looking like animals in cages.*

Briggs *Kids who lie and cheat and curse*
 And kids who turn out to be worse
 Than animals

Kids *Animals animals that's all he sees*
 A horde of screaming hyenas

Briggs *How can we call a child a child*
 When he's no better than the wild
 Animals

Kids *Animals monkeys a gaggle of geese*
 With barely a brain cell between us

Briggs *Brutes who kick and maul and maim*
 Beasts and creatures all the same
 As animals

Kids *Animals parrots rabbits and sheep*
 Dumb and dim-witted retarded

Briggs   *Who violate and vandalize*
          And rob and steal and terrorize
          Animals

Kids   *Animals let's just make sure that we keep*
          Them locked up and caged up and guarded

Briggs   *Stupidity dumb insolence*
          Apathy and indolence
          Animals

Kids   *Animals pigs with their snouts in the trough*
          Slimy and grimy and greedy

Briggs   *Mindless senseless vile obscene*
          Filthy vulgar foul unclean

Kids   *Animals with everything that they've got*
          They're lewd and they're crude and they're creepy

Briggs   *Brutal wretched malcontent*
          Beyond the pale beneath contempt
          Animals

Kids   *Animals are ugly animals are sly*
          Animals give you the rabies
          Animals are evil and so that is why
          They're coming to eat up your babies

Kids *chant 'zoo zoo zoo zoo zoo' under the following verse:*

All   *Animals   Animals*
          Animals   Animals
          Animals   Animals
          Animals   Animals
          Animals   Animals
          Animals   Animals
          Animals   Animals
          Animals   Animals
          Animals   Animals
          Animals   Animals
          Animals   Animals

As the refrain repeats and builds we see the **Kids** *in the cages become a grotesque tableau of writhing creatures, volume and intensity building and building relentlessly until the final scream/ roar of:*

Briggs/Kids   *ANIMALS!*

Blackout and end Act One.

Act Two

Lights come up to reveal courtyard, turrets and towers of the castle. Music as **Mr Briggs** *leads his group, regimented, two-by-two into the courtyard.*

Briggs   *Now here you see the gatehouse sits*
  Inside the drawbridge
  Notice its
  Portcullis
  The enfilading arrow slits
  The way the ancient
  Stonework fits
  The turrets

Music continues to underscore dialogue throughout sequence.

Briggs   Alright! Now pay attention. Now just take a close look at the thickness of those walls.

Chloe/Zoe   *It's borin', it's bleedin' borin'*
  The bloody castle wasn't worth restorin'
  It's just old stones
  And windows without glass
  The walls haven't even been painted!
  I think castles are last
  An' borin'
  Bleedin' borin'

Briggs   Of course it's not boring!

Zoe   Sir, it is!

Briggs   No! *You* might find it boring. But do you ever stop to ask yourselves *why* you're bored.

Chloe   No!

Briggs   You don't use your minds, your imaginations; you've no curiosity have you – and that's why you're bored.

Zoe   No it's not!

Briggs   Oh well you tell me then! – why you're bored.

Chloe   Cos we like proper castles.

Briggs   '*Proper*' castles.

Zoe   Yeh! Like the ones at Disney.

Sean   Ogh, they're brilliant Sir, the castles at Disneyland – they've got all lights an' like . . .

Briggs   *Disneyland!* Forget Disneyland. Alton Towers, Disneyland . . .! This is real! This is history, heritage, antiquity – you can feel it . . . you can touch it – but don't touch anything! Not unless I say you can.

>   *Now pay some real attention*
>   *To the outer wall dimensions*
>   *And the towers*
>   *There's such a wealth of detail there*
>   *A man could easily stand and stare*
>   *For hours*

Chloe/Zoe   Oh Sir, what are you like!?

Briggs   What am I like? What do you mean what am I like?! (*To offstage.*) Hey you lad get down from there!

As they exit, **Mark** *enters, slavishly followed by* **Carly** *and* **Jackie**.

Mark   And in winter, you see, without any real heating it would have been absolutely freezing.

>   *So when this place was occupied*
>   *How do you think that they survived*
>   *Cold weather?*

Carly/Jackie   *Sir, I'll bet they huddled up*

As they now try to do with **Mark**.

And snuggled up and cuddled up
Together

Mark   Girls! Girls! (*Wriggling free.*) Well yes but, more importantly – they would have worn much thicker clothing in those days so that . . . (*Looking around.*) Where the . . . where are the others, where's the rest of the group gone?

Jackie   Sir, they were bored! They kept droppin' out while you were talkin'.

Carly   But it's alright Sir. We're dead interested. You can keep showing us around. We're fascinated, aren't we?

Jackie   Oh God, yeah. Go on Sir, go on, you keep fascinating us.

Carly   Sir – we're learnin' so much with you – we could probably go on 'Mastermind' y' know.

Mark   Well that's very flattering of you but . . .

Carly   You influence us y' know Sir . . .

Mark   Well that's very kind of you to say . . .

Jackie   But it's true Sir – you're just – the *best*.

Carly/Jackie   *Yeh Sir*
We'd be really brainy Sir
If all the other teachers were like you
We'd be right there
Day and night Sir
If you were the one
Who was showing us what to
Do do do do Sir
you you you Sir
Ooh ooh ooh Sir

Mark (*extricating himself*)   Girls girls girls . . .

Perhaps I'd be fooled
By this passion to learn
If we saw you at school
More than twice in one term

How can you hope to thrive
When you never arrive at school

Carly/Jackie   *Sir I swear Sir*
On the life of our baby
That we'd never sag off school again oh no
Or be bad Sir
If we had Sir
Just you to teach us all we need
To know know know Sir
Oh oh oh Sir . . .
Oh oh oh Sir

Mark (*freeing himself from their clutches*)   Girls come on!
(*Beat.*) Oh look!

As **Mark, Carly** *and* **Jackie** *exit we see* **Briggs** *and his group.*

Briggs   Right wait for me! Stay back from the edge! Wait
for me!

Sean   Look how high it is!

Steph   I can't look I've got vertigo.

Briggs   Now the defenders of the castle, what could they do, to
try and repel their attackers? Now think.

Sean   Come up here on the battlements?

Briggs   Good, good! And from up here, above the enemy, what
would they be able to do to them?

Sean   Sir, drop fridges on their heads?

Briggs   Fridges?

Sean   Sir, yeah an' Tesco trolleys.

But before he gets a response, **Andrews** *and* **Eunice** *come rushing
up.*

Andrews   Sir, Sir, Maurice McNally Sir, he's got his head stuck
in the iron bars of the dungeon an' we can't get him out.

Eunice   An' Sir, Sir, Mohamed O'Shea's fallen in the moat an'
he's all covered in mud and slime Sir – an' now he keeps tryin' to
pull everyone else in.

Briggs   You what! Where's your teacher – who's in charge of
your group?

Andrews   I don't know.

Briggs   For God's sake, what's going on here . . . quick,
quick – follow me, all of you follow me.

As **Briggs** *moves off and they all follow.*

Eunice   An' Sir, look! (*Pointing.*) Sir, Digga Dickson's climbing
up the flagpole – he said he's gonna rescue the flag Sir.

Briggs (*yelling as he runs*)   Dickson! . . . Dickson! . . . Get down
from there now!! . . .

Andrews (*running after him*)   It's brilliant, the castle isn't it,
Sir – isn't it just *great*?

*As they exit, the grounds of the castle explode with life and music
as* **Kids** *pour into the courtyard, on to the battlements and down
the turrets and towers, all of them singing and dancing in a joyous
display of exuberant play.*

Defenders   *Quick pull up the drawbridge*
            And watch it round the back
            The scum and all the lowlife
            Are startin' to attack

Attackers   *Raiders an' marauders*
            Climbin' up the walls

Defenders   *An' we're all under orders*
            To bash them in the balls

Attackers   *Balls balls cannon balls*
            It's all a load of bluff
            We'll meet y' on the walls
            If you think you're hard enough

Defenders   *Our place*
This is our space
Get your own place
Cos there's no room here
For the hard-faced
Or the lard-faced
Or the scarred-faced
Only down in the dungeon

Attackers   *Dungeon*
Where the rats live
An' when you're sleepin'
They all come crawlin' out
To eat your fingers
Mingers!
We're gonna sling y's
In that dungeon

Defenders   *You haven't got a bleedin' chance*
Think you're hard
Think you're hard
Think you're hard
No way
We'll be the kings
Be the kings
Be the kings
Today

All   *We'll be the kings*
Be the kings
Of the castle today

Attackers   *If y' don't surrender*
We're comin' to slit y' throat
An' all of you defenders
We'll drown y' in the moat
We'll have y' drawn an' quartered
We'll put y' on the rack
An' when you've all been slaughtered
There's none of y' comin' back

Defenders   *Na na na na*
You're all just talk
If y' wanna rule the castle
Then you've gotta walk the walk
Your dummies really suit y'
Run home to your mam
An' tell her that in future
She should keep y' in y' pram

Defenders   *Our place*
This is our space
Get your own place
Cos there's no room here
For the hard-faced
Or the lard-faced
Or the scarred-faced
Only down in the dungeon

Attackers   *Dungeon*
Where the rats live
An' when you're sleepin'
They all come crawlin' out
To eat your fingers
Mingers!
We're gonna sling y's
In that dungeon

Defenders   *You haven't got a bleedin' chance*
Think you're hard
Think you're hard
Think you're hard   **Andrews**   Whoa whoa
                                                     hold on . . .

No way   Stop.
We'll be the kings   Listen!
Be the kings   Hold it.
Be the kings . . .   Stop.

*Singing trails to a halt. Music continues to underscore, segueing to
'No Go Slowin'.*

Andrews   Look, what are we doin' all fightin' each other? It's ridiculous. There's the Welsh comin' at us from over there, the Taliban from over there – an' Al-Qaeda comin' that way – all of them after the castle. But if we stayed together . . . we could *share* the castle – why don't we all own it together?

Kevin   Us? Wit' youse?

Andrews   Yeah! We're all from the Progie aren't we?

Sean   He's right! It's the Progies who should own the castle.
(*raps*)

Who are the kids who rule this castle
The Progress Kids – don't give us no hassle
Don't give us no dis no aggravation
Now we are the rulers of this nation

All   *Who are the kids who've come to rule us*
The Progress kids they're the best and the coolest
Don't give us no dis no aggravation
Now we are the rulers of this nation

We're the kings
We're the kings
We're the kings
Okay
We are the kings
Are the kings
Of the castle today
An' there's no one here
Who can take
Our castle away
We are the kings   *Our Day Out (x3)*
Are the kings
Are the kings
Are the kings
Are the kings
Are the kings
Are the kings

We are the kings
Are the kings
Are the kings
Are the kings
Are the kings
Are the kings
Are the kings
We are the kings
We are the kings
We are the kings
Today!

As we come to the close of the song we see **Mrs Kay** *and* **Amy** *on the battlements. From off we hear snatches of exuberant yells and cheers, all mixed in with music which lightly underscores following.*

Mrs Kay   Amy, love, don't you want to play with the others?

Amy   No Miss I'd rather sit here with you and look at the lake.

Mrs Kay   That's the sea, Amy.

Amy   That's what I meant, Miss. (*Beat.*) Miss? Miss y' know when I grow up – *I'm* gonna be a teacher.

Mrs Kay *barely able to suppress a double-take.*

An' I'll be nice to the kids, Miss. Like you.

Mrs Kay   A teacher?

Amy   *confidently nodding.*

Mrs Kay   Well! In that case I'm just going to have to work even harder at teaching you how to read – aren't I?

Amy *nods.* **Andrews** *enters and comes to join* **Mrs Kay** *and* **Amy**.

Andrews   Miss wouldn't it be smart, eh, if we had somethin' like this castle round our way. Then the kids wouldn't get into trouble, would they, if they had somewhere like this to play.

Amy   Miss, we could never have somethin' like this round our way.

Mrs Kay   Why not?

Amy   Cos if we had somethin' like this we'd just wreck it all wouldn't we?

Andrews   No we wouldn't.

Amy   We would. That's why we never have nothin' nice round our way – because we'd smash it all up an' make a mess of it.

Andrews   Miss, d'y' know what I think about it Miss?

Mrs Kay   No, go on Aaron, what?

Andrews   Miss, Miss if all this belonged to us – like if it wasn't the council's but really *ours* we'd look after it an' . . . an' defend it. D'y' know what I mean, Miss?

Mrs Kay   Yes, I think I do know what you mean Aaron. What you're saying . . .

Amy   But Miss, we don't deserve to have nice things do we?

Mrs Kay   Why not love?

Amy   Cos, Miss, by us the bus shelters always get smashed up don't they – an' when y' go the chippie or the Aldi there's always glass everywhere; an' y' go the paper shop it's always dark even in the summer because the shutters are always down. An' even if people try an' put nice things . . .

Music as **Briggs** *enters, remonstrating with a group of* **Kids** *running across stage.*

Briggs   Get down from there – get down now! I've told you – keep to the marked pathways! This is just . . .

Sees **Mrs Kay** *and hurriedly approaches. Sings:*

> *What's this?*
> *You tell me! What's this?*
> *And just exactly what do you*
> *Intend to do*
> *To stop this?*

Mrs Kay   Stop what?

Briggs (*seeing* **Amy** *and* **Andrews**)   You two – move!

Andrews   Sir where?

Briggs   Never mind where! Go on – the pair of you.

The two **Kids** *reluctantly wander off.* **Briggs** *waiting until they are out of hearing.*

Mrs Kay (*quietly angry*)   I was talking to those children.

Briggs (*equally angry*)   Yes and I'm talking to you!

A group of **Kids** *chase each other across stage, shouting as they do. Various groups of* **Kids** *shout and run throughout the following number providing examples for* **Briggs**'s *annoyance at such rowdy behaviour.*

Briggs   *All this!*
　　　What do you call this?

Mrs Kay   *I call it just a bunch of kids*
　　　Behaving
　　　Like children

Briggs   *Children!*
　　　You can't leave children
　　　To run and shout
　　　And chase about
　　　And act like children

Mrs Kay   *Children!*
　　　That's right they're children
　　　Letting off some steam
　　　And running round
　　　Like children

Briggs   *Order!*
　　　They're out of order
　　　Beyond control
　　　Ignoring every
　　　Boundary and border
　　　Disorder

I'm going to order
Everyone back home
If you don't bring
This trip to order

Mrs Kay   *Orders!*
Always orders!
They're kids Mr Briggs!
Not vandals
And marauders

Music continues to underscore throughout following dialogue.

Mrs Kay   Kids, Mr Briggs, children.

Briggs   Children who need to be checked! And stopped from haring and tearing round the place. God knows what the castle authorities must think. This is a *World Heritage Site*!

Mrs Kay   Yes, and I hardly think the antics of a few over-exuberant kids are going to bring it crashing to the ground.

Briggs (*beat*)   You really are on their side aren't you?

Mrs Kay   I didn't know it was a question of *sides*, Mr Briggs – but if that's how you choose to see it then absolutely, yes, I am on their side.

A couple of **Kids** *shouting to try and hear the echo of their names.*

Briggs   *Bedlam!*
It's worse than Bedlam
Left to shout
And run about
Wherever their fancy's led them

Mrs Kay   *Did no one tell you, Mr Briggs*
That kids do tend to act like kids
And in the process, God forbid!
They sometimes make a noise

Briggs   I've had enough of this – all I want to know now, right now, is what you intend to do about this . . . mayhem?

Mrs Kay   Look – can't you just relax? Alright, so classes
you teach probably are a lot more ordered. But this is *my* lot,
Mr Briggs, my *Progress* kids. And each day almost every one
of these kids comes to school carrying an invisible bag on his or
her shoulder. And do you know what that bag's full of, Mr Briggs?
Shit! From the life that you don't see – the life at home; the same
life that shaped their parents who now shape their own kids in
the same twisted way. Yes, Mr Briggs, I'd love to see them all
educated, all sitting neatly at their desks. But for these kids of
mine there are still rather a lot of obstacles in the way before
they can even begin to see the benefits of an education. And I
don't see much point in behaving as if a day out to Wales is
going to furnish them with one. We're not going to solve anything
today Mr Briggs. So can't we at least just try and give them a good
day out? Mm?

Briggs   Well that's a fine attitude isn't it, for a member of the
teaching profession?

Mrs Kay   And so what's your alternative? Pretending?
   Pretending that these kids of mine
   Will somehow all start doing fine
   If they can learn to stand in line
   Keep quiet and obey

   Pretending that a trip to see
   Some crumbling old antiquity
   Will mean that academically
   These kids are on their way

Briggs   *Enough Miss*
   I've had enough Miss
   I'm warning you
   Informing you
   If you don't do your stuff Miss

   It's over
   I'm taking over
   And ordering everybody

Back to school
It's over

Mrs Kay   *Well you must do what you must do*
Forgive us, though, not joining you
But when you've come all this way to
The sea it's such a shame

Not to go down to the beach
And hear the waves, the seagulls' screech
Pick driftwood that the sun has bleached
And write your massive name

Briggs   The beach! You're going to the beach!

Mrs Kay   Oh yes. You can't come all the way to the seaside and not go down to the beach. We're not going home yet. So if you are – you'd better start walking.

Music.

Come on everybody, round yourselves up now. We're going to the seaside!

Briggs *and* **Mrs Kay** *exit.*

Kids   *Seaside*
We're goin' the seaside
An' getting a bronzy
An' catchin' little fishies
In the rock pools

Seaside
We're goin' the seaside
An' havin' a sand fight
Running
With no shoes and socks on

Seaside
We're goin' the seaside
An' makin' sand-pies
Finding shells that
Look like diamonds

Seaside
We're goin' the seaside

Melody segues to verse of 'Our Day (We're Off)' and underscores
Chloe/Zoe.

Chloe/Zoe   *I'm bored*
I'm bored
I'm bored to bleedin' death
I'm so bleedin' bored that I
Could breathe my dyin' breath
It's just borin' sand
An' borin' bleedin' sea
I've never ever known a more
Borin' place to be

Music back to chorus of 'Our Day (We're Off)'.

Kids   *Seaside*
We're goin' the seaside
We're goin' the seaside
We're goin' the seaside

Music shifts, dropping rhythm track so that singing becomes
*rubato, reflecting a sense of awe as the **Kids** become aware of the*
immensity of the ocean, sand and sky before them, transfixing them
as they stand, squelching their toes in the wet sand. Music slow
and wave-like.

Amy   *The sea's gi'bleedin-gantic*
It must be really wide

Kids   *Cos we can't even see across*
To the other side

The sound of the ocean.

Mrs Kay   Right, who's for a game of footie?

*Lights fade on the **Kids**, while lights come up on **Ronny**, who is*
sat on a rock, feeding the seagulls and enjoying a cup of tea.
***Briggs** enters and goes to walk on past.*

Roı ny   Whoagh (*Putting cup away*). Y' caught me havin' a sly cuppa there. Suppose I'll get detention, eh?

Briggs *doesn't laugh.*

Ronny   Only a joke, boss.

Briggs   Oh . . .

Ronny   You're very, erm . . . Well I've noticed you're strict with them, aren't you, the kids?

Briggs (*defensively*)   And what if I am?

Ronny   No, no I was only saying . . . Here d'y' wanna sit down?

Briggs   No erm, no thanks.

Ronny   When *I* was at school, all the teachers were like that, discipline, authority, make sure the kids know who's in charge. I dunno. I suppose kids need that, don't they?

Briggs (*softening*)   Yes well, I believe they do, yes.

Ronny   Yeah.

Briggs   Look at yourself. Robbie isn't it?

Ronny   It's Ronny, Mr Briggs.

Briggs   When you were at school, you had discipline didn't you?

Ronny   Too right, when we got into a classroom, we sat down properly, we opened our books and we copied what was on the blackboard.

Briggs (*sitting alongside*)   You see? A disciplined environment produces a disciplined mind.

Ronny   We had none of this freedom and free expression and . . . finger paintin'. Teachers then talked properly, wore suits. When we did poems we did poems that *rhymed*; you know:

'*So here's to the eldest son of Dunne*
And likewise to the eldest Dunne

> *And here's to the eldest Dunne*
> *When the eldest Dunne is done*
> *For any man can be well done*
> *In this big wicked world*
> *What's done by Dunne*
> *Must be well done*
> *So well done good ole Dunne.'*

See . . . Still remember that poem to this day.

Briggs Very good, very good. See, you got a good solid grounding Robbie – and that's invaluable.

Ronny Like . . . gettin' the basics right, isn't it?

Briggs Yes! That's right – basic values and why not.

Ronny Yeah, I was thinking about all that, 'cos in my job you get a lot of time to just think. Like driving here today, I was thinking, Mr Briggs, he's the sort of teacher we all used to respect.

Briggs Thank you.

Ronny I thought about how we all lined up, sat straight in our desks, it brought back all that. Then I found myself thinking – with all that brilliant education I had; how come I've spent all my life drivin' a fuckin' coach!

Music underscore as **Ronny** *moves across to join the other* **Teachers** *and the* **Kids**. **Briggs** *goes off in the other direction.*

Ronny Over here! On me head.

Amy (*tugging at* **Mrs Kay**'s *sleeve as some of the* **Kids** *rush off with* **Ronny**) Miss, when we do we have to go home?

Mrs Kay What's the matter love? Aren't you enjoying yourself?

Amy Yeh. But I don't wanna go home.

Mrs Kay Why Amy? Why don't you want to go home?

Amy (*shrugs*) I just wanna stay here.

Mrs Kay   Amy love, we're here for at least another hour yet. Now why don't you start enjoying yourself instead of worrying about going home.

Amy   Cos I don't wanna go home.

Mrs Kay   Amy! We have to go home in the end, sweetheart. This is a special day. It can't be like this all the time.

Amy   Why not?

Mrs Kay (*looks at her and sighs, puts her arm around her.*)   I don't know, love. Come on, let's go and play football with the others.

Amy   Nah. (*She breaks away and wanders off.*)

Mrs Kay (**Mrs Kay** *watching* **Amy** *for a moment and then, her attention drawn by a sigh of boredom, turning to* **Chloe** *and* **Zoe**.)   Come on you two; let's go and play football.

Chloe   Miss what for?

Mrs Kay   What for?

Zoe   Miss we don't wanna play football.

Mrs Kay   Oh, football's *borin'* isn't it? (*Suddenly mimicking them.*) Football's bleedin' borin', dead bleedin' borin', it's borin' – scorin'. An' even more borin' when you're only bleedin' drawin'.

They stare at her as though she's lost a screw.

You don't like football!

Zoe   Miss, we do!

Mrs Kay   Well come on then. (*She begins to go.*) Come on.

Chloe   Miss where?

Mrs Kay (*almost screaming*)   To play football, you said you like football.

Zoe   On the *telly* Miss!

Chloe/Zoe   We don't like *playin'* it though, playin' football's dead . . .

Mrs Kay, *screaming/yelling, hands outstretched to throttle the pair, rushing at them, and the two* **Girls** *suddenly moving, being chased off by* **Mrs Kay**.

Mark, **Katie**, **Carly**, **Jackie** *are examining the rock pools.*

Reilly, **Digga** *and a small group of followers are having an illicit can of beer behind some large rocks.*

Andrews (*to* **Reilly**)   Gis a swig, go on Reil.

Digga   Get y' your own, you bum.

Andrews   Don't be a rat. Come on.

Reilly *holds out the can but as* **Andrews** *goes to take it* **Reilly** *throws it to* **Digga**. **Reilly** *moves out from behind the rocks and shouts over to* **Katie**.

Reilly   All right, Miss?

Mark (*quietly*)   Oh oh – Here we go.

Reilly (*shouting across*)   Y' comin' for a walk with me, Miss?

Mark (*standing and shouting back*)   Look I'm warning you Reilly . . .

Katie   Leave it . . .

Mark   I'm just about sick of him.

Katie   Well go over and have a word with him.

Mark   I've tried that but whatever I do I can't seem to get through to our friend Ryan.

Katie   I wonder if *I* could.

Reilly (*shouting over*)   What's wrong, Miss – what y' frightened of?

Katie (*to* **Mark**)   You go back with the others.

Mark   What are you going to . . .

Katie   Go on . . .

Mark *and the group of* **Girls** *begin to move away.*

Carly   Is Miss gonna sort him out, Sir?

Jackie   He needs sortin' out doesn't he Sir?

Carly   He's all right y' know. He's great when y' get him on his own, away from his mates – he's lovely.

Jackie   Oh! An' how do *you* know that?

Carly   I just do!

They go off and **Katie** *begins to walk towards* **Reilly**, *slow and determined, staring straight at him, focused, provocative and intimidating.* **Reilly**'s *smile begins to disappear as* **Katie** *advances towards him.*

Katie   Well Ryan . . . here I am.

Reilly   What, Miss?

Katie   I'm here! I'm all yours! Handsome, sexy Ryan!

As the music begins **Katie**, *in a single movement, whips off her dress to reveal a figure-clinging swimsuit.*

>   *Oh*
>   *Oh*
>   *OOOOGGH*
> *Beach boy*
> *Big bad be bad*
> *Beach boy*
> *Let me be your beach toy*
> *Come on an' play with me*

Reilly   Stop it Miss!

Katie   *I can feel those undertones*
> *I can smell those pheromones*
> *I can feel them running through my bones*
> *And deep down inside my erogenous zones*

>   *Ah, aahhh, ahhhhhh*

During the orgasmic groan prelude to the next verse we see **Andrews**, **Digga** *and other* **Kids** *as they raise their heads above*

the rocks where they've been hiding – each of them gawps
in open-mouthed awe. **Katie** *suddenly turns and all the*
Kids *– as one – drop down behind the rocks and out of sight*
again.

Reilly   Miss – don't Miss!

Katie   *Sexy*
        Young and hung and sprung
        And sexy
        I love the way he affects me
        Come on let's do it in the sand

Reilly   Miss – behave!

Katie (*draping arms around him*)   Oh – I am misbehaving!

        I'm ready and I'm waiting and I'm hot
        Anticipating what you've got
        So come on big boy
        Hit . . . the . . . spot
        What you got
        I want the whole damn lot

(*She gets into* **Reilly**'s *arms, moaning as if in the throes of orgasm.*
At which point **Briggs** *enters and stands transfixed and jaw-*
dropped by what he thinks he is witnessing. **Katie** *and* **Reilly**
remain unaware of him.)

Katie   *Ah, ahhhh, ahhhhhh*

(**Briggs**, *having seen more than enough, turns on his heels and*
hurriedly exits.)

        Big boy
        Big bad be bad
        Beach boy
        I wanna wanna wanna wanna
        Be your beach toy
        Come on and play with me
        Come on and play with me

Katie (*only now acknowledging his lack of response*)   Ryan?
Ryan what's wrong?

Reilly   Miss, stop it Miss – y' know I was only jokin' y'.

Katie   'Joking? Only joking'? (*Pulling on her dress as if devastated and embarrassed. Walks back to* **Reilly** *now dropping the act.*) Now you listen to me Ryan Reilly, the next time you want to . . . *joke* . . . at a teacher's expense – or anyone else's for that matter – just pause for a minute and remember what it was like when the joke was on you.

(*Beat.*)

Did you hear what I said.

Reilly (*nodding*)   Miss.

Katie (*beginning to leave but returning*)   Oh, and Ryan – you're a really good-looking lad you know.

Reilly   Miss, shut up!

Katie   So I don't know why you're wasting all those 'come on' lines on me – unless, of course, you're just practising lines that are really intended for someone else.

Reilly   What? – Like who?

Katie   Oh? Erm . . . like Carly?

Reilly   Carlene Croxley, Miss, go 'way. She's only got eyes for Sir. No one else can get a look in.

Katie   I wouldn't be too sure about that.

Reilly   What do y' mean?

Katie   Find out for yourself. See you Ryan.

Reilly   See y' Miss.

As **Katie** *exits,* **Reilly**'*s mates, laughing and jeering, emerge from behind the rocks where they've been hiding and watching.*

Digga   Agh – 'I was only jokin' Miss.'

Andrews   'Don't mess Miss, don't mess.'

Kevin   Reilly the 'hard case'.

Andrews   Big *fruit* – more like it.

Reilly   Shut it, you! (*To* **Digga**.) Come on let's go.

Digga   What?

Reilly   Let's go!

Digga   You can go where y' like Reilly – but I'm not comin' with y'.

Andrews (*shouting*)   Digga – look, there's Jackie Morgan an' that lot. They're goin' the arcades.

Digga   Quick, come on. (*Calling as he and the others leave.*) Jackie . . . hold on, hold on girl . . .

Reilly (*calling after them*)   Digga . . . Digga . . . Knobhead.

Reilly, *alone, turns and begins to walk off in opposite direction. As he does so* **Ronny**, **Mrs Kay** *and* **Kids**, *including* **Carly**, *rush on, playing football.* **Reilly** *stands apart, a spectator.*

Mrs Kay (*as someone scores and she gives up being goalie*) Whoooooh. I've had enough, I'm all in.

Eunice   Ah Miss, we've got no goalie now.

Mrs Kay   Ryan can go in goal.

Caitlin/Georgia   Oh not him!

Mrs Kay   Come on Ryan.

Reilly   Miss I don't play football.

Mrs Kay   Ogh, come on.

Carly   Yeh, go on Ryan. Be goalie for *us*.

Mrs Kay   I suppose we could ask Amy – she likes to go in goal doesn't she?

Reilly   No Miss. It's alright. I'll . . . I'll go in goal for y'.

Mrs Kay (*as the game resumes*)   Actually (*Looking around.*) where is Amy? Kelly, Eunice . . . have you seen Amy Chandler?

Kelly/Eunice (*playing football*)   No Miss.

Mark *and* **Katie**, *with their group of* **Kids**, *enter.*

Mrs Kay   Is she with you?

Mark   Who?

Mrs Kay   Amy Chandler?

Mark   No, haven't seen her.

Katie   We thought she was with you.

Mrs Kay   She was – earlier. But . . . Everybody, listen, just listen for a moment. Has anyone seen Amy Chandler in the last hour or so?

Kids *shaking their heads and mumbling, 'No Miss.'*

Mrs Kay (*looking around*)   Oh, God – she couldn't could she?

Katie   Wandered off?

Mrs Kay (*groans*)   Don't say it. I wonder if he's seen her. (*Calling – off.*) Mr Briggs . . . Mr Briggs . . . (**Briggs** *enters.*)

Briggs   Is that it then? Are we finally headed home?

Mrs Kay   Have you seen Amy Chandler?

Briggs   Who?

Mrs Kay   Amy Chandler, year eight, small, she's . . . I'm worried she might . . . have wandered off somewhere.

Briggs   You mean you've lost her?

Mrs Kay   No! I mean she might have wandered off somewhere!

Briggs   Well what's that if it's not losing her? All I can say is it's a wonder you haven't lost half a dozen of them today. (*He turns to go.*)

Mark   Listen Briggs, it's about time someone told you just what a prat you can . . .

Briggs (*wheels on him*)   And you listen sonny! Don't you try and tell me a thing, because you haven't even begun to earn the right.

Don't you worry, when we get back to school your number's up, as well as hers (*To* **Mrs Kay**). And you! (*To* **Katie**.) Yes. Don't worry, I saw what was going on between you and Reilly!

Katie   Oh, for God's sake!

Briggs   Call yourselves *teachers*! Well when we get back, I'm submitting a report on everything that's gone on today and I . . .

Mrs Kay   Would you mind just . . . postponing your threats until we have found Amy Chandler? At the moment I'd say the most important thing is to find the girl.

Briggs   Don't you mean *try* and find her?

Mrs Kay   Mark, Katie, you keep the rest of them playing football. We'll split up and look for her.

They go off in separate directions. We see **Amy** *appear on the cliff top where she stands, looking out, waving at seagulls. She sings.*

Amy   *Why can't it always be this way*
     Why can't it last for more than just a day
     The sun in the sky and the seagulls flying by
     I think I'd like to stay
     Then it could always be this way

     Shouting to the seagulls,
     Seagulls say 'hello'
     Wonder how they stay up there so high
     Looking at the seashore miles and miles below
     Makes me wish that I could fly

The action moves to **Carly**, *sat alone on some rocks by a cove.* **Reilly** *suddenly appears.*

Reilly   Oh! I was just . . . erm . . . lookin' for someone.

Carly   Amy Chandler? No one can find her.

Reilly   So erm . . . Do you wanna see what I did find?

Carly   Yeah.

Reilly (*taking a pebble from his pocket*)   It's nothin' much really, it's just a pebble. Can y' see the way the sea's sort of smoothed it? (*Showing this to* **Carly**.)

Carly   Oh yeah, yeah, it's lovely isn't it. I like the way those blue bits shine out. (*Pause.*) Well what are y' gonna do with it?

Reilly   Well I dunno. (*Pause.*) I got it for you. I was thinking of giving it to you.

Carly   Well go on then. (*She puts out her hand and he gives her the pebble. She kisses his cheek and sits down. He joins her.*)

Reilly   It's been a great day today, hasn't it?

Carly   Yeah it's been brilliant.

Reilly   But we could make it even better couldn't we?

Carly   Yeah.

Reilly *moves in to kiss* **Carly**, *the action returns to* **Amy** *on the cliff. The other* **Kids** *and* **Teachers** *start to enter in silhouette during the following solo and sit as if on the beach.*

Amy   *Why can't it always be this nice*
Why can't it be a bit like paradise
Where troubles disappear
And there's nothin' left to fear
Listen to the seagulls' cries
Why can't it always be this nice

All   *Sunlight on the water*
Sea salt in your clothes
Haven't felt like this since God knows when
Tangled up in seaweed sand between your toes
Like a little kid again

Carly   *Why can't it always be this good*
Once just for once
It feels just like it should

Reilly and Carly   *Suddenly it seems*
Even better than your dreams

Better than you ever thought it could
Why can't it always be this good

All   *If someone could hold the day*
So it would never end

Amy   *Shouting to the seagulls,*
Seagulls say 'hello'
Wonder how they stay up there so high
Looking at the seashore miles and miles below
Makes me wish that I could fly

Kids *and* **Teachers** *exit leaving* **Amy** *alone on stage.*

Amy   *Why can't we just stay where we are?*
Away from the noise and the buses and the cars
If I close my eyes and try and try and try
To wish upon a special star,
Then we could all just stay where we are.

As the song ends, **Briggs** *appears on the cliff and sees* **Amy**.

Briggs   Amy Chandler, just come here. Who gave you permission to come on these cliffs?

Amy (*moving to the edge*)   No one. (*She turns and dismisses him.*)

Briggs   I'm talking to you Miss Chandler.

She continues to ignore his presence. He moves a pace closer.

Now you listen to me young lady, you've got . . .

Amy (*suddenly turning*)   Don't you come near me!

Briggs (*taken aback by her vehemence, he stops*)   Pardon?

Amy   I don't want you to come near me. You go. (*Beat.*) I'm not comin'.

Briggs   You're not what?

Amy   I'm not comin' back! You tell Mrs Kay – she can go home without me. 'Cos I'm stoppin' here. By the sea.

Briggs   Now you listen here! I've had just about enough today, more than enough and I'm not about to start putting up with some silliness from a slip of a thing like you. Now move!

He starts towards her but she moves to the very edge of the cliff.

Amy   You try an' get me, take one more step an' I'll jump over.

Briggs *stops in his tracks, astounded and angered.*

Briggs (*shouting*)   Listen you stupid girl, get yourself over here this minute. (*She ignores him.*) I'll not tell you again!

They stare at each other. It's obvious that she will not do as he bids.

I'll give you five seconds! Just five seconds. One, two, three . . . I'm warning you! . . . Four . . .

Amy   I've told y', I'm not comin' with y'. I will jump y' know. I will.

Briggs   Just what are you tryin' to do to me?

Amy   Just leave me alone. (*Beat*) I wanna stay here. Where it's nice.

Briggs   *Stay here?* How could *you* stay here?

Amy (*she shrugs*)   I dunno. (*Beat.*) But it's nice. I like the little white houses.

Briggs   You couldn't stay *here*. You don't belong here.

Amy (*turning on him*)   I don't know why you're wastin' your breath – 'cos you don't care, do y'?

Briggs   About what? About you? Of course I care, if I didn't care why would I be up here now, trying to make you realize just how dangerous it is to be on these cliffs? Trying to make you see some sense and get yourself back down to the beach.

Amy   That's not carin' about me. If I fell off these cliffs – or jumped off them, well you'd be in big trouble when you get back to school. That's why you're up here Briggsy, so stop goin' on. You hate me.

Briggs   Hate you? Don't be ridiculous. Just because I'm a schoolteacher it doesn't mean to say that . . .

Amy   Don't lie, you! I know you hate me. I've seen you goin' home in your car, passin' us on the street. An' the way you look at us. You hate all the kids.

Briggs (*beat*)   I don't . . . *hate* you. I don't . . . hate anyone.

Amy   Why can't I just stay here an' live in one of them nice white houses, an' do the garden and that?

Briggs   Look . . . Amy . . . The way you talk – it's almost as if you've given up on life. Now why can't . . . I mean, what's to stop you from working hard at school from now on, getting a good job and then moving out here when you're old enough? Eh?

Amy (*she turns and looks at him with pure contempt*)   Are you thick? (*She turns and looks out to the sea.*) It's been a brilliant day today. I loved it. I don't wanna leave here an' go home. (*Pause.*) If I stayed it wouldn't be any good though, would it? You'd send the social workers wouldn't y', and the police, to come an' get me.

Briggs   We'd have to. You're just a child.

Amy   I know. (*Pause.*) I'm not goin' back though.

She kneels at the cliff edge, looks over.

Briggs   Amy . . . please . . .

Amy   Sir . . . you know, if you'd been my old feller . . . I would've been all right wouldn't I?

Briggs *slowly and cautiously creeping forward, holding out his hand.*

Briggs   Please – come away from there.

She looks down over the cliff.

Please.

Amy   Sir . . . sir you don't half look funny y' know.

Briggs (*smiling*)   Why?

Amy   Sir, you should smile more often. You look like a nice person when y' smile.

Briggs (*holding out his hand*)   Come on Amy.

Amy   Sir . . . what'll happen to me for doin' this?

Briggs   Nothing . . . I promise.

Amy   Sir, you're promisin' now, but what about back at school?

Briggs   I give you my word – it won't even be mentioned. There's nothing to fear.

Amy   Sir I'm frightened. I'm going to fall.

His hand outstretched and gently reassuring her, **Briggs** *edges along the cliff to* **Amy**. *He eventually reaches her and pulls her into his arms.* **Briggs** *stands and holds* **Amy** *in a safe embrace.*

The scene shifts back to the beach. **Ronny** *and* **Mrs Kay** *enter.*

Ronnie   No sign?

Mrs Kay   No. I'm just praying that one of the others has found her. If not . . . I'm going to have to phone the police.

Ronnie   She'll turn up! You know what they're like, kids, always wanderin' off.

Mrs Kay   But it's my job to make sure that kids *don't* go wandering off. Especially a kid like Amy Chandler.

Ronnie   Yeh but you can't be expected to have eyes in the back of your head can y'? Y' tell the kids where they should go, where they shouldn't – if they ignore y', well that's their choice isn't it? You can't be held responsible for that can' y'?

Mrs Kay   Oh yes I can.

Ronnie   By who?

Mrs Kay   By me Ronnie! Me. A kid like Amy Chandler relies on me. There' no one *else* to look after her.

Katie *and* **Mark** *come on with a group of kids playing football.*

Carly   Go on Ryan, go on, go on . . . (*As he scores.*) Yes.

Reilly *letting on to her.*

Katie (*as she approaches* **Mrs Kay**)   No luck?

Mrs Kay (*shaking her head*)   I think we better let the police know.

Katie   Shall we keep them playing . . .

Jackie (*seeing* **Briggs** *and* **Amy** *enter*)   Miss!

Katie   Oh look . . . he's found her.

Mark   I'll bet he makes a bloody meal out of this.

Mrs Kay   It doesn't matter. She's alright, she's safe, that's the main thing.

Mark   We'd better round them up. It'll be straight home now.

Mark *begins to do so.*

Mrs Kay (*approaching* **Briggs** *and* **Amy**)   Amy, where've you been?

Amy   On the cliff, Miss.

Mrs Kay   On the . . .

Briggs   It's all right Mrs Kay, we've been through all that. It's all been dealt with.

Mrs Kay *putting her arm around* **Amy**.

Mrs Kay   Amy! The worry you've caused. Oh . . . love . . .

Briggs   Come on . . . everyone on the coach.

Ronnie   Back to the school then boss?

Briggs   School? Back to school? It's still early isn't it? Anyway – you can't come all the way to the seaside and not pay a visit to a pleasure park.

Mrs Kay   Pleasure park?

Briggs   Yes, play your cards right Mrs Kay I might take you for a ride on the waltzer.

Steph (*to* **Milton**)   Pleasure park!

Eunice (*to* **Sean**)   Sir's takin' us to a pleasure park.

Sean (*to* **Kevin**)   Pleasure park – we're goin' the pleasure park.

Kevin (*to* **Digga**)   Hey, we're goin' the pleasure park.

Digga   Pleasure park!

Ronson   What's a pleasure park?

Andrews   It's like Alton Towers. Only shite!

Music begins. The **Kids** *create a fairground. 'Scream if you wanna go faster' choruses are dance sequences.* **Mrs Kay** *takes photos throughout,* **Mr Briggs** *happens to feature prominently in most of the photos.*

Kids   *This might not be what you would call*
      The greatest fairground of them all
      It isn't Alton Towers, but we don't care
      They might not have a Nemesis
      A Mine Train or a Ripsaw, Miss
      But Sir is gonna take us to the fair
      And we are . . .

      Goin' on the Waltzer gonna have some fun
      Gonna get well dizzy gonna get well spun
      Comin' down the Helter Skelter with a . . .
      Whaaah!

Briggs   *Roller coaster?*

Kids   *Yes Sir please*

Mrs Kay   *Hold on everybody now, say cheese*

All   *Cheeeeeeeeeese! (music starts to speed up)*
Scream if you wanna go faster, scream
If you wanna go faster, scream if you wanna go faster
Scream if you wanna go . . .
Aaaah!
Scream if you wanna go faster, scream
If you wanna go faster, scream if you wanna go faster
Scream if you wanna go . . .
Aaaah!

Back to tempo for a semi-rapped section as various groups of **Kids**
check out the arcades and stalls – imagined across the front of the
balls, guns, prizes etc. coming out of the pit.

Kevin   *Try your luck. Hook a duck*
There's a prize every time, but the prizes suck

Sean   *Ball in the bucket. No matter how you chuck it*
The ball just bounces out. Agh! . . . f . . .

Mrs Kay   Sean!

Sean   Sorry Miss.

Chloe/Zoe   *Well if y' haven't got a chance of scorin'*
That just makes it really

All   *Borin'*

Tempo starts to speed up again.

Kids   *Scream if you wanna go faster, scream*
If you wanna go faster, scream if you wanna go faster
Scream if you wanna go . . .
Aaaah!
Scream if you wanna go faster, scream
If you wanna go faster, scream if you wanna go faster
Scream if you wanna go . . .
Aaaah!

Music returns to tempo.

Kelly   *But ey, that's what you call a prize*

Eunice   *Never seen a toy that size*

Steph   *You'd hardly get it through the bedroom door*

Jackie   *Isn't it cuddly, isn't it cute?*

Digga   *Yeah, but never mind how well you shoot*
There's no way you could ever reach that score

Briggs   Erm . . . If you'll allow me . . .

Briggs *takes the air rifle and takes aim.*

Kids   *Yeah come on Sir, yeah have a go*

Digga   *He'll never do it he won't, y'know*

Briggs *takes one shot. Applause. Second shot. More applause. Pause. Third shot.*

Kids *cheer and dance around ecstatically. An enormous stuffed toy lion, at least twice the size of the smaller kids, is produced from the rifle range.* **Briggs** *offers it to* **Amy** *who backs away from it, shaking her head.* **Briggs** *hands it to nearest kid who happens to be* **Digga**. *He gives it to* **Jackie** *who is made up and gives him a big kiss on the cheek.* **Briggs**, *during the following verse, enquires in dumbshow what* **Amy** *would like and she indicates the 'hook a duck' stall. One of the little rubber ducks (not supposed to be a prize) is produced and* **Briggs** *gives it to* **Amy**, *despite the apparent protests of the* **Stallholder**. *Meanwhile music speeds up . . .*

Kids   *Scream if you wanna go faster, scream*
If you wanna go faster, scream if you wanna go faster
Scream if you wanna go . . .
Aaaah!
Scream if you wanna go faster, scream
If you wanna go faster, scream if you wanna go faster
Scream if you wanna go . . .
Aaaah!

Music returns to tempo.

Kids   *Look at old Briggsy, what's the score?*
Never seen him like this before

Who'd have thought he'd take us to the fair
He's paid for us to go on rides
Bought us sweets an' loads besides
Think there must be somethin' in the air
Scream if you wanna go faster, scream

If you wanna go faster, scream if you wanna go faster
Scream if you wanna go . . .
Aaaah!
Scream if you wanna go faster, scream
If you wanna go faster, scream if you wanna go faster
Scream if you wanna go . . .
Aaaah!
Scream if you wanna go faster!

*Number ends in big tableau, with one final photo of the entire
group,* **Briggs** *surrounded by delighted, grinning* **Kids** *relishing
the whole experience. As the number ends, the* **Kids** *immediately
re-form the coach.*

Briggs   Come on, everybody, on the coach – everybody on the
coach now – last one on is . . . a monkey's bum!

Kids   Sir!

The **Kids** *singing without accompaniment as they re-form the
coach.*

Kids   *Everywhere we go*
    Everywhere we go
    People wanna know
    People wanna know
    Who we are
    Who we are
    So we tell them
    So we tell them
    We are the Progress
    We are the Progress
    The mighty mighty Progress
    The mighty mighty Progress

Ronny   Okay everybody – where we headed now?

Kids   *We're off we're off*
We're off in a motor coach
The driver's wearin' lipstick
And he's signin' on the soash

Ronny   Hey! We'll have less of that.

Kids   *Over the humpety-backed bridge*
Eatin' a vindaloo (Urghh!)

Girls   *There's gorgeous girls in Toxteth*

Boys   *An' there's cats in Katmandu*

Kids/All   *Our day* (*clap clap*)
Back from our day
Everybody say 'Hey'
If y' comin' back round our way
Our day (*clap clap*)
Such a star day
Everybody say 'Hey'
If y' comin' back round our way

Kids   *Back across the water*
Goin' back to see my mam
I hope that when she sees me
She remembers who I am
There's a lodger in my bedroom
An' he's got a yellow beard
The baby's in the bagwash
An' my father's disappeared

Kids/All   *Our day* (*clap clap*)
Back from our day
Everybody say 'Hey'
If y' comin' back round our way
Our day (*clap clap*)
Such a star day
Everybody say 'Hey'
If y' comin' back round our way

Chloe/Zoe   We just think it's really borin'.

Everyone except **Chloe** *and* **Zoe** *stand as one and shout:*

All   SHUTUP!

Briggs, *wearing cowboy hat, at back seat with* **Kids**, *remains on his feet and enthusiastically leads another chorus*

Briggs/All   *Our day* (*clap clap*)
    Back from our day
    Everybody say 'Hey'
    If y' comin' back round our way
    Our day (*clap clap*)
    Such a star day
    Everybody say 'Hey'
    If y' comin' back round our way

    Our day out
    Our day out . . .

But weariness and tiredness overcome them, the song fading into a collective yawn until most of them are asleep or dozing. Music segues to piano underscore of 'No One Can Take This Time Away'.

Briggs *wearing the cowboy hat makes his way along the aisle, pausing to take in* **Digga** *and* **Jackie** *who appear to now be an item – similarly,* **Reilly** *and* **Carly** *draped together on seat. When he reaches* **Mrs Kay** *she turns the camera on him. It is as if at that moment the flashlight signals the beginning of a return to reality for* **Briggs**. *He becomes conscious of the hat he is wearing and, smiling at* **Mrs Kay**, *he removes it and places it on the head of* **Brittany**.

Mrs Kay   We've got some real gems of you here. Have to make sure we get one of these up in the staff room.

Briggs   Of *me*? What for?

Mrs Kay   Oh don't worry – I'm not going to let you forget the day you enjoyed yourself. Be good for the rest of the staff to see as well – when I can get them developed, or whatever it is you do with photographs these days.

Briggs (*watching her return the camera to her bag*)   You just, you know, print them out. Load them up on computer and . . .

Mrs Kay   Oh don't! Computers – and me?

Briggs   Do you want me to do them for you?

Mrs Kay   Oh! Would you?

Briggs   Come on, give it to me. I'll have those done in no time.

Mrs Kay (*handing over the camera*)   Thanks.

Briggs (*looking out of window*)   Well . . . here we are. Almost home again. (*Calling – but somewhat softer than usual.*) Come on everybody. Wake up now. Be home in a moment – Time to get your things together.

Cue intro music for 'We Had a Really Great Day Out'. During the following all the seats of the coach are removed.

Kids   *We had a really great day out*
       We went to the beach
       And went daft and ran about
       We went to the zoo

       And the fair and castle too
       And Briggsy let us sing and shout
       Coming back from our day out.

Ronny   *That's the end of that one then*
       Another job another day
       Maybe somewhere down the road
       We'll meet once again

Kids   *Thanks Ron, we had a lovely day*
       Thanks Sir and Miss, it was brilliant Mrs Kay
       The best we ever had
       Even Briggsy's not so bad
       Never seen him mess about
       He must have had a great day out

Briggs   OK, everybody off.

Kids   *Climbing off the bus now*
Back in Liverpool
Better get off home now for me tea
Looking at the streets, the playground and the school
Seems a long way from the sea.

Continue melody as underscoring.

Everybody is now off the coach. **Ronny** *and various* **Kids** *have moved off.* **Reilly** *and* **Carly**, *arms around each other, pass* **Briggs**. *Melody of 'We Had a Really Great Day Out' continues to underscore following dialogue.*

Reilly   'Night Sir.

Briggs   Yes. Goodnight . . . erm . . .

Carly   'Ryan'.

Briggs   Reilly, yes. Night.

Reilly   Enjoyed yourself today didn't y' Sir?

Briggs   Mm?

Reilly   I didn't know you could be like that sir – y' know, havin' a laugh an' that. Nice one, Sir.

Carly   See y' Sir.

Briggs (*clears his throat and nods goodbye to them*)   Oh . . . Carlene, by the way.

She stops and turns.

We'll say nothing further about the uniform on this occasion. But don't let me catch you dressing like that again on a school outing.

Reilly (*as they exit*)   I think y' look dead nice.

Reilly *and* **Carly** *exit.*

Chloe *and* **Zoe** *enter, each of them glued to her mobile.*

Zoe (*into phone*)   Well there were mountains . . .

Chloe (*into phone*)   . . . and a load of sheep.

Zoe (*into phone*)   . . . and a beach.

Chloe (*into phone*)   . . . something called a pleasure park.

Zoe/Chloe (*unison into their respective phones*)   . . . and it was all really . . . boring? No! It was brilliant!

They run off. **Georgia** *crosses the street nonchalantly with a 'live' penguin sticking out of her backpack.* **Mrs Kay** *enters.*

Mrs Kay   Well that seems to be it. (*She sees* **Amy** *hovering nearby.*) Are you going home Amy?

From off we hear a whistle and **Ronny** *enters.*

Ronny   Hold on, hold on . . . You wouldn't happen to have left something behind on the coach, would y'? Erm, a condom machine!

Mrs Kay   What!

Ronny *suddenly laughing.*

Ronny   Ah no, y' alright. Just checkin' that's all. Little joke, y' know. Someone did leave this though – didn't they?

From behind his back **Ronny** *produces the yellow plastic duck and hands it to* **Amy**.

They always forget somethin'.

Mrs Kay   Thanks Ronny.

Ronny   Thanks Helen. Goodnight. (*To the others as he exits.*) Bye now. See y'.

Mark⎫
    ⎬ Goodnight.
Katie⎭

Ronny   Goodnight Mr Briggs.

Briggs   Goodnight Robbie.

Ronny *pauses for a moment. Then, shaking his head, exits.*

Mrs Kay   Well that's that. I don't know about anyone else but I'm for a drink.

Katie   Oh I'll second that.

Mark   I could murder one.

Mrs Kay (*to* **Briggs**)   You going to join us?

Briggs   Erm . . . I'd er . . . I'd better not.

Katie   No? . . . Oh come on.

Mr Briggs   No, honestly. Thanks anyway but, erm, I've got a stack of marking to do when I get home. Thanks though.

Mrs Kay   No – thank *you*. For today, thank you. Come on. Car's over here. (*Seeing* **Amy** *still in the shadows.*) Amy? You going home love?

Amy *nods.*

You've got my number, haven't you? If you need it.

Amy   Yes Miss.

Mrs Kay   Alright. See you tomorrow sweetheart.

Mrs Kay, Katie *and* **Mark** *leave.*

Briggs *reaches into his pocket and produces his car keys. There's something else in the pocket though and reaching in again,* **Briggs** *absently brings out the camera, remembering it now. He goes to return it to his pocket but pauses and stands looking at it for a moment unaware of the* **Kids**, *each one appearing individually from behind and around him and standing in the shadows watching as* **Briggs** *activates the camera and stands, scanning through the day's images which now appear in* AV, *the entire set becoming a photo montage of images captured throughout the day.* **Briggs** *ponders for a moment, looks up, checking that no one is around (to him there's nobody) before pressing a select button so that on* AV *we see a series of picture of himself and* **Kids**, *taken during the day, each picture remaining on screen so that a collage of about eight pictures fills the frame. Across this the words* DELETE?

YES/NO *appear. Looking round again,* **Briggs** *selects* 'YES' *and the images disappear leaving a blank screen.* **Briggs** *exits.*

Eunice   *No one can take this time away*

Sean/Milton   *No matter what they cannot take the day*

Jackie   *No one can steal*
           Something you just feel

Taylor/Oliver and Jackie   *And although the pictures fade*
           No one can take this time away

Amy   *Someone said the camera*
           Got dropped into the sea
           Someone said that sand
           Had got inside
           Someone said the problem
           Was with the memory
           Or the battery had just died

All   *But who needs a picture*
           Pictures always fade
           Just get lost
           Or stuck behind a drawer
           And I can always find
           A picture in my mind
           Of some far and distant shore

Boys   *Someone said the memory*
           Was washed out with the tide

Girls   *But you can't wipe a memory*
           That I'll hold safe inside

Full Chorus   *No one can take this time away*
           No matter what they do
           No matter what they say
           We couldn't give a shit 'cos it was

Spoken.

    Brilliant

Magic

Fit!

And although the pictures fade

*But instead of it being the last line of this verse, the following
becomes the first line of a reprised first verse, sung by all.*

> *No one can take this time away*
> *No matter what, they cannot take the day*
> *No one can steal*
> *Something you just feel*
> *And although the pictures fade*
> *No one can take this time away*

Curtain.

Shirley Valentine

Shirley Valentine was first performed at the Everyman Theatre, Liverpool on 13 March 1986. The part of Shirley Valentine was played by Noreen Kershaw. The director was Glen Walford, designer Claire Lyth and the lighting was by Brian Harris.

Shirley Valentine was subsequently produced in London at the Vaudeville Theatre on 21 January 1988. The part of Shirley Valentine was played by Pauline Collins. The director was Simon Callow, designer Bruno Santini and the lighting was by Nick Chelton.

Shirley Valentine was made into a film in 1989, starring Pauline Collins.

Act One

Scene One

The kitchen of a semi-detached house. It is a well-established kitchen, bearing signs of additions and alterations which have been made over the years. It is not a highly personalized palace of pitch pine and hanging baskets but nevertheless has signs of personality having overcome the bleakness of the chipboard and formica . . . It is quite a comfortable and reassuring place.

Specifically the kitchen contains (apart from the obvious cooker, fridge, etc.) a door which leads out of the house, a wall with a window, a dining table and chairs.

As we open, **Shirley** *is beginning preparations for cooking the evening meal – this includes opening a bottle of white wine from which she pours a glass. Throughout the following scene she sets a table for two and she prepares, cooks and finally serves one of the truly great but unsung dishes of world cuisine – chips and egg.*

Shirley   Y'know I like a glass of wine when I'm doin' the cookin'. Don't I wall? Don't I like a glass of wine when I'm preparing the evenin' meal. Chips an' egg! (*Takes a sip of wine.*) I never used to drink wine. It was our Millandra who started me on this. She said to me, she said 'Mother! Mother, nobody drinks rum an' coke these days. Everybody drinks wine now. Oh Mother have a glass of Riesling instead.' Kids. They know everything don't they? Our Millandra was goin' through her slightly intellectual phase at the time. Y'know her, an' her mate – Sharron-Louise. Because it was all white wine an' Bruce Springsteen at the time. Y' know the pair of them stopped goin' down the clubs in town an' started hangin' out in that Bistro all the time. Y' know where the artists go. They seen, erm, what's his name one night, erm Henry Adrian, yeh. Apparently Sharron-Louise got his autograph. And breakfast as well I believe. Anyway, the pair of them are out of that

phase now. And am I glad? Because y' know the two of them'd sit
at the table for hours an' all's y'd hear from the pair of them was:
'It was great. It was great. Was a laugh wasn't it?' Then they'd
both go back into trance for half an hour an' you'd suddenly hear:
'It was brilliant last night. It was more than brilliant. It was mega
brill.' 'Yeh it was, it was double fab wasn't it?' And d' y' know, no
matter how long they sat there, you'd never get to know what it
was that was so double fab an' mega brill. (*Pause.*) Maybe it was
the breakfasts! Mind you I do miss them, the kids. Our Millandra
shares a flat with Sharron-Louise now. An' our Brian's livin' in a
squat. In Kirkby. I said to him, I said, 'Brian, if you're gonna live
in a squat, son, couldn't y' pick somewhere nice. Y' know
somewhere like Childwall?' 'Mother,' he said to me. 'Childwall is
no place for a poet.' 'Cos that's our Brian's latest scheme y' see.
He's always got a scheme. This one is – he's become Britain's first
ever busker poet. What's he like wall? The language. 'I hate the
fuckin' daffodils/I hate the blue remembered hills.' He's loop the
loop. Mind you, I'm glad he's given up archery. Oh God, look at
the time. What am I doin' sittin' here talkin' and he'll be in for his
tea won't he. An' what's he like? My Feller. What's he like wall?
Well he likes everything to be as it's always been. Like his tea
always has to be on the table as he comes through that door. If the
plate isn't landin' on the table just as his foot is landin' on the mat,
there's ructions. I've given up arguin'. I said to him, once, I said,
'Listen Joe, if your tea isn't on the table at the same time every
night it doesn't mean that the pound's collapsed y' know, or that
there's been a world disaster. All it means Joe, is that one of the
billions of human bein's on this planet has to eat his tea at a
different time.' Well did it do any good? I could've been talkin' to
that. Couldn't I wall, I could've been talkin' to you. (*Pause.*) I
always said I'd leave him when the kids grew up – but by the time
they'd grown up there was nowhere to go. Well you don't start
again at forty-two do y'? They say don't they, they say once you've
reached your forties life gets a bit jaded an' y' start to believe that
the only good things are things in the past. Well I must have been
an early developer; I felt like that at twenty-five. I'm not sayin'
he's bad, my feller. He's just no bleedin' good. Mind you, I think
most of them are the same aren't they? I mean they're lovely at

first. Y' know when they're courtin' y'. Y' know before you've had
the horizontal party with them, oh they're marvellous then. They'll
do anything for y'. Nothin' is too much trouble. But the minute, the
very minute after they've first had y' – their behaviour starts to
change. It's like that advert isn't it? I was watchin' it the other
night – y' know, Milk Tray Man. Oh he's marvellous isn't he? Y'
see him, he dives off a thousand-foot cliff an' swims across two
miles of water, just to drop off a box of chocolates. An' y' learn
from that that the lady loves Milk Tray. And that the lady's been
keepin' her legs firmly closed. Because if she hadn't, if he'd had
his way with her he wouldn't go there by divin' off a thousand-foot
cliff an' swimmin' through a ragin' torrent. He'd go by bus. An'
there'd be no chocolates. If she mentioned the chocolates that he
used to bring he'd say, 'Oh no. I've stopped bringin' y' chocolates
babe, cos y' puttin' a bit too much weight on.' D' y' know when y'
think about it, Cadbury's could go out of business if women didn't
hold back a bit. I don't hate men. I'm not a feminist. Not like Jane.
Jane's my mate. Now she's a feminist. Well she likes to think she
is, y' know she reads Cosmopolitan an' says that all men are
potential rapists. Even the Pope. Well Jane does hate men. She
divorced her husband y' know. I never knew him, it was before I
met Jane. Apparently she came back from work one mornin' and
found her husband in bed with the milkman. With the milkman,
honest to God. Well, apparently, from that day forward Jane was a
feminist. An' I've noticed, she never takes milk in her tea. I haven't
known Jane all that long, but she's great. She's goin' to Greece for
a fortnight. Next month she's goin'. God what will I do for two
weeks? She's the only one who keeps me sane. Jane's the only one
I ever talk to, apart from the wall – isn't she wall? She is. I said to
her this mornin', 'Jane I won't half miss y'.' You know what she
said to me? 'I want you to come with me.' (*Laughs.*) Silly bitch.
Hey, wall, wall, imagine the face on 'him'. Imagine the face if he
had to look after himself for two weeks. Jesus, if I go to the
bathroom for five minutes he thinks I've been hijacked.

She takes a sip of her wine.

Oh it's lovely that. It's not too dry. Some of it'd strip the palate off
y' wouldn't it. But this is lovely.

She takes another sip and savours it.

It's nice. Wine. It's like it's been kissed by the sun. 'He' doesn't
drink wine. 'He' says wine is nothin' but a posh way of gettin'
pissed. I suppose it is really. But it's nice. Know what I'd like to do,
I'd like to drink a glass of wine in a country where the grape is
grown. Sittin' by the sea. Lookin' at the sun. But 'he' won't go
abroad. Well y' see, he gets jet lag when we go to the Isle of Man.
An' I wouldn't mind – we go by boat. We've been goin' there for
fifteen years – he still won't drink the tap water. He's that type Joe.
Gets culture shock if we go to Chester. See what Jane says is, he's
entitled to his own mind an' that's fine. If he doesn't wanna go
abroad, well that's up to him. But that shouldn't stop me goin'.
If I want to. An' I know Jane's right. I know. It's logical. Dead
logical. But like I said to her, 'Jane, y' can't bring logic into this –
we're talkin' about marriage.' Marriage is like the Middle East
isn't it? There's no solution. You jiggle things around a bit,
give up a bit here, take a bit there, deal with the flare-ups when
they happen. But most of the time you just keep your head down,
observe the curfew and hope that the ceasefire holds. (*Pause.*)
Course, that was when Jane handed me the time bomb. She's only
gone an' paid for me to go, hasn't she? She handed me the tickets
this mornin'.

*She goes to her bag and produces an air ticket from which she
reads.*

'Bradshaw. S. Mrs. BD. 581. 23 June. 19.00. From Man. to Cor.'
Jane said she didn't want to go on her own. She'd just got the
money through from the sale of their house. Well how the hell
could I tell her it was impossible? I'll . . . I'll give her the tickets
back tomorrow. She'll easy find someone else to go with her. I
shouldn't have taken the bloody tickets off her in the first place.
Well I tried to like, tried to expl . . ., to tell her it was impossible.
But y' know what feminists are like. If something's impossible,
that's the perfect reason for doin' it. Hey, wall, it'd be fantastic
though, wouldn't it? I just lay his tea in front of him an' I turn
away all dead casj an' say, 'Oh by the way Babe – I'm just poppin'
off to Greece for a fortnight. Yeh. I just thought I'd mention it so's

y' can put it in y' diary. You won't mind doin' y' own washin' an'
cookin' for a couple of weeks will y'? There's nothin' to it Doll.
The white blob on the left of the kitchen is the washin' machine an'
the brown blob on the right is the cooker. An' don't get them mixed
up will y' or y' might end up with socks on toast.' Some chance eh
wall? Some chance.

She returns the ticket to her bag.

Y' know if I said to him . . . if I said I was off to Greece for a
fortnight, he'd think it was for the sex. Wouldn't he wall? Well . . .
two women, on their own, goin' to Greece. Well it's obvious isn't
it? I wouldn't mind – I'm not even particularly fond of it – sex, am
I wall? I'm not. I think sex is like Sainsbury's – y' know, over-
rated. It's just a lot of pushin' an' shovin' an' y' still come out with
very little in the end. Course it would've been different if I'd been
born into the next generation, our Millandra's generation. 'Cos it's
different for them isn't it? They discovered it, y' see, the clitoris.
'The Clitoris Kids' I call them. And good luck to them, I don't
begrudge them anythin'. But when I was a girl we'd never heard of
this clitoris. In those days everyone thought it was just a case of in
out, in out, shake it all about, stars'd light up the sky an' the earth
would tremble. The only thing that trembled for me was the
headboard on the bed. But y' see, the clitoris hadn't been
discovered then, had it? I mean, obviously, it was always there, like
penicillin, an' America. It was there but it's not really there until
it's been discovered, is it? Maybe I should have married
Christopher Columbus! I was about, about twenty-eight when I
first read all about it, the clitoris. It was dead interestin'.
Apparently it was all Freud's fault. Y' know, Sigmund. You see,
what happened was, Freud had said that there were two ways for a
woman to have, erm, an orgasm. An' erm the main one could only
be caused by havin' the muscles, inside, stimulated. An' the other,
erm, orgasm, it was supposed to be like an inferior, second rate
one, caused by the little clitoris. Now y' see, that's what Freud
had said. An' everyone had believed him. Well, you would
wouldn't y'. I mean, Sigmund Freud, who's gonna argue with
someone called Sigmund Freud. I mean, say you're just, just
standin' at the bus stop, you an' Sigmund Freud, the bus comes

along y' say to him, 'Does this bus go to Fazakerley,' he nods an says to y', 'Yes, this is one of the buses that goes to Fazakerley.' Well you'd get on the bus wouldn't y'? But I'll tell y' what – you'd be bloody lucky if y' ever reached Fazakerley. 'Cos Freud, y' see, he gave out the wrong information. There's only one bus that goes to Fazakerley. The clitoris bus. The other bus doesn't go anywhere near Fazakerley. But y' see everyone believed him an' they've been givin' out the wrong information for years, y' know like they did with spinach. It's marvellous isn't it – tellin' people there's two kinds of orgasm. It's like tellin' people there's two Mount Everests – some people stumble onto the real mountain while the rest of us are all runnin' up this little hillock an' wonderin' why the view's not very good when we get to the top. Well when I first read about all this I was fascinated, wasn't I wall? But y' know when you read a word for the first time an' you've never heard it spoken, you can get it wrong can't y'? Y' know pronounce it wrong. Like, when I was little there was a kid in our street called Gooey. Honest. Gooey. His mother used to go 'Gooey. Y' tea's ready Gooey. Come on in Gooey.' Well y' see when she'd been lookin' for a name for him she'd been readin' this American magazine an' she saw this name, G.U.Y. Guy. But she thought it was pronounced Gooey. So that's what she christened him. Gooey McFadden he was called. Well I was the same with the clitoris. When I first read the word I thought it was pronounced clit*or*is. I still think it sounds nicer that way actually. Clit*or*is. That even sounds like it could be a name doesn't it? Clit*or*is. 'And now the 10 O'Clock News with Clit*or*is Smith.'

She thinks about it.

Oh shut up wall, I think it sounds nice. Why not? There's plenty of men walkin' around called 'Dick'. Well, anyway, that's how I thought it was pronounced when I first mentioned it to Joe. We were sittin' in the front room an' I said, 'Joey. Joe have you ever heard about the clit*or*is?' He didn't even look up from his paper. 'Yeh, he said, but it doesn't go as well as the Ford Cortina.' (*Pause.*) Wait till he finds he's gettin' chips an' egg for his tea tonight. Well it's Thursday isn't it? And on Thursday it has to be mince. It's the eleventh commandment isn't it? Moses declared it.

'Thou shalt give thy feller mince every Thursday and if thou
doesn't, thy feller will have one big gob on him all night long.'
What will he be like wall? What will he be like when he sees it's
only chips an' egg? An' I wouldn't mind, it's not even my bloody
fault about the mince. Well I gave it the dog y' see. This dog at the
place I work. Well it's a bloodhound y' see. But this couple I work
for – they are vegans, y' know the vegetarian lunatic fringe – 'The
Marmite Tendency' I call them. Well they've brought up this
bloodhound as a vegetarian. Well it's not natural is it? I mean if
God had wanted to create it as a vegetarian dog he wouldn't have
created it as a bloodhound would he? He would have made it as a
grapejuice hound. But this dog is a bloodhound. It needs meat.
Well it was just on impulse really. I'm there today, an' I looked at
this dog an' all's I could think about was the pound an' a half of
best mince that's in me bag. Well d' y' know, I think it was worth
what I'll have to put up with from 'him' tonight; just to see the look
on that dog's face as it tasted meat for the first time. Course I don't
think Joe'll quite see it that way. 'Y' did what? What did y' do? Y'
gave it to the dog? You've gone bloody mental woman. Is this it?
Have y' finally gone right round the pipe?' (*She adopts a rather
grand gesture and voice.*) 'Yes Joseph I rather think I have. I have
finally gone loop the facking loop. I have become crazy with joy,
because today Jane gave me the opportunity of getting away for a
fortnight. Joe! I am to travel to Greece with my companion. Our
departure is less than three weeks hence and we shall be
vacationing for some fourteen days. And now I must away, leaving
you to savour your chips and your chuckie egg whilst I supervise
the packing of my trunk.' (*She drops it.*) Our Brian was round
before. I showed him the tickets. Didn't I wall? An' what did he
say? 'Mother, just go. Forget about me Father, forget about
everythin', just get yourself on the plane an' go.' (*Laughs.*) Well
that's how he is, our Brian; you wanna do somethin'? You just do
it. Bugger the consequences. He's a nutcase. But he couldn't care
less. An' he's always been the same. He was like that when he was
a little kid, when he was at school. Hey, wall, remember the
Nativity play? Oh God. Our Brian was only about eight or nine an'
the school had given up with him. The teachers just said he was
loop the loop an' that was that. I agreed with them. But the

headmaster, the headmaster was fascinated by our Brian. He like, like studied him. He said to me, there's no malice in the child, no malice whatsoever but it would appear that Brian has no concept of consequences. I think what we have to do with Brian is to try and give him more responsibility and so I've decided to give him the star part in the nativity play this year. Well when Brian learned he'd got the part of Joseph he was made up with himself. Agh, God love him, he thought he'd been picked 'cos he was great at actin' an' I couldn't say anythin' because it was workin', y' see, this psychology. All the time he's rehearsin' this nativity play his behaviour is fantastic; the headmaster's made up with him. I'm made up with him, the teachers are made up with him. An' he's made up with himself. He's practisin' every night in his room – (*One note.*) 'We are weary travellers on our way to Bethlehem an' my wife is having a baby an' we need to rest at the Inn for the night.' Well the day of the show, I got down to the school, the play started an' it was lovely, y' know all the little angels came on an' they all have a sly wave to their Mams. Then it was our Brian's entrance; he comes on an' he's pullin' this donkey behind him – it's like this hobby horse on wheels. An' perched on top of it is this little girl, takin' the part of the Virgin Mary an' she's dressed beautiful, y' know her Mother's really dolled her up to be the part. An' she's givin' a little wave to her Mam. So Brian gives the donkey a bit of a tug because he's takin' it dead serious an' he doesn't believe they should be wavin' to their Mams. He's up there, he's actin' like he might win The Oscar – y' know he's mimin' givin' hay to the donkey an' he's pattin' it on the head. Well the headmaster turned round an' smiled at me. I think he was as proud of our Brian as I was. Well Brian gets to the door of the Inn and he goes knock knock knock an' the little Innkeeper appears. Our Brian starts 'We are weary travellers on our way to Bethlehem an' my wife is havin' a baby an' we need to rest for the night at the Inn.' So the little feller playin' the Innkeeper pipes up, 'You cannot stay at the Inn because the Inn is full up an' there is no room at the Inn.' An' then our Brian is supposed to say somethin' like: 'Well we must go an' find a lowly cattle shed an' stay in there.' Then he's supposed to go off pullin' the donkey, an' the Virgin Mary behind him. But he didn't. Well, I don't know if it's the Virgin Mary, gettin' up our Brian's nose, because she's spent the whole scene wavin' to her Mother or whether it was just that our Brian suddenly realized that the part of Joseph wasn't as big as it had been cracked up to be. But whatever it was, instead of goin' off pullin' the donkey, he suddenly turned to the little Innkeeper an' yelled at him – 'Full up? Full up? But we booked!' Well the poor little Innkeeper didn't know what day of the week it was. He's lookin' all round the hall for someone to rescue him an' his bottom lip's beginnin' to tremble an' our Brian's goin' – 'Full up? I've got the wife outside, waitin' with the donkey. She's expectin' a baby any minute now, there's snow everywhere in six foot drifts an' you're tryin' to tell me that you're full up?' Well the top brass on the front row are beginnin' to look a bit uncomfortable – they're beginnin' to turn an' look at the headmaster an' our Brian's givin' a perfect imitation of his father, on a bad day; he's beratin' anythin' that dares move. The little Innkeeper's lip is goin' ten to the dozen an' the Virgin Mary's in floods of tears on the donkey. Well the Innkeeper finally grasps that the script is well out of the window an' that he has to do somethin' about our Brian. So he steps forward an' he says, 'Listen Mate, listen! I was only jokin'. We have got room really. Y' can come in if y' want.' An' with that the three of them disappeared into the Inn. End of Nativity play an' the end of our Brian's actin' career. Me an' our Brian, we sometimes have a laugh about it now, but at the time I could have died of shame. It was all over the papers: 'Mary and Joseph Fail To Arrive In Bethlehem.' I was ashamed. (*Pause.*) It's no wonder really, that I've never travelled anywhere meself; it must be God punishin' me for raisin' a child who managed to prevent Mary an' Joseph reachin' their destination. An' there was me when I was a girl – the only thing I ever wanted to do was travel. I always wanted to be a, a courier. Or an air hostess. But it was only the clever ones who got to do things like that. When I got my final report from school, the headmistress had written at the bottom of it, 'I can confidently predict that Miss Valentine . . .', that was me maiden name, 'I confidently predict that Miss Valentine will not go far in life. I feel this is just as well for, given her marks in geography, she would surely get lost.' She was a mare that headmistress. She used to come into assembly sometimes an' ask like a spot question, an' whoever got it right

would get loads of housepoints, an' it was nearly always Marjorie
Majors who got it right – she took private elocution lessons an' she
left school with just under four billion housepoints. One day, we
were all standin' there in assembly an' this headmistress appeared;
'A question,' she said to everyone, 'a question: what was man's
most important invention?' Well every hand in the hall shot up.
'Me Miss,' 'I know Miss,' 'Miss, Miss, me Miss.' An' my hand was
up with the rest of them because for once I knew the answer. But
this headmistress, she took one look at me an' said, 'Oh put your
hand down Shirley, you won't know the answer,' an' she started
goin' round the hall, the grin on her face gettin' smugger an'
smugger as she got answers like, 'the sputnik', 'the cathode ray
tube,' 'the automatic washin' machine.' Even the clever ones were
gettin' it wrong – even Marjorie Majors. But I kept my arm up
there in the air because I knew I had the right answer. I'd got it
from me Dad an' he'd got it from the Encyclopaedia Britannica.
Agh, y' know me Dad, he was still goin' on about that
Encyclopaedia Britannica when he was on his death bed. 'How can
those kids of mine be so thick when I bought them the
Encyclopaedia Britannica?' He got a lot of pleasure out of it
though. He'd sit there for hours readin' it an' then he'd try to
impress us all with these dead odd facts. An' I'd remembered him
sayin' about man's most important invention because it was so
ordinary. So I'm stood there in assembly, me arm stuck up in the
air, an' I am like the cat with the cream because this headmistress
has done the length an' breadth of the hall an' still no-one's come
up with the right answer. Well I'm the only one left so she turns to
me an' she says, 'All right then Shirley, come on, you might as well
get it wrong along with everyone else. Do you remember the
question Shirley – what was man's most important invention?' Well
I paused, y' know savourin' the moment, knowin' I was on the
brink of receivin' at least forty three thousand housepoints an' a
blessin' from the Pope. But when I said, 'the wheel', it was like
this headmistress had been shot in the back. I thought maybe she
hadn't heard me squeaky little voice so I said it again, louder, 'The
wheel Miss, man's most important invention was . . .' But I never
got to finish because I was cut off by this scream from the
headmistress. 'YOU,' she yelled, 'You must have been told that

answer!' I just stood there, reelin' with shock. An' I tried to ask her,
to say, to say, how . . . how the bloody hell else I was supposed to
learn the right answer. But she wouldn't listen. She just ignored me
an' told the demented music teacher to get on with playin' the
hymn. An' all me housepoints, an' me blessin' from the Pope just
disappeared before me eyes as she led the hall into singin' 'Glad
That I Live Am I.' I was never really interested in school after that.
I became a rebel. I wore me school skirt so high y' would've
thought it was a serviette. I was marvellous. I used to have the
chewy goin' all day, like that (*Chewing.*) an' I'd just exude
boredom out of every pore. I hated everythin'. 'Oh I hate him', 'Oh
I hate her,' 'I hate this, I hate that.' 'It's garbage,' 'It's last,' 'It's
crap.' 'I hate it.' But I didn't hate anythin' y' know. The only thing I
hated was me. I didn't want to be a rebel. I wanted to be nice. I
wanted to be like Marjorie Majors. I used to pick on her somethin'
rotten an' I really wanted to be like her. Can't y' be evil when
you're a kid? I saw her a few weeks ago, Marjorie Majors. Didn't I
wall? I hadn' even heard of her for years. I'm in town, loaded down
with shoppin' an' what's the first thing that always happens when
y' in town loaded down with shoppin'? Right. The heavens opened.
An' it's funny the way all these things are linked but they are; once
you're in town, loaded with shoppin' bags, caught in a deluge – it
always follows that every bus ever made disappears off the face of
the earth. Well I'm standin' there, like a drowned rat, me hair's in
ruins an' I've got mascara lines runnin' from me face to me feet,
so I thought I might as well trudge up to the Adelphi an' get a
taxi. Course when I got there the taxis had gone into hidin' along
with the buses. Well I'm just rootin' in me bag, lookin' for
somethin' to slash me wrists with when this big white car pulls up
to the hotel an' of course I'm standin' right by a puddle an' as the
wheels go through it, half the puddle ends up over me an' the
other half in me shoppin' bags. Well all I wanted to do by this
time was scream. So I did. I just opened me mouth, standin' there
in front of the hotel an' let out this scream. I could've been
arrested but I didn't care. Well I was in mid-scream when I
noticed this woman get out the white car an' start comin' towards
me. An' she's dead elegant. Y' know she's walkin' through this
torrential rain an' I guarantee not one drop of it was landin' on her.

But the second she opened her mouth I knew who she was. I'd recognize those elocution lessons anywhere. 'Forgive me for asking,' she said, 'but didn't you used to be Shirley Valentine?' I just stood there, starin'. And drippin'. 'It is,' she said, 'it's Shirley,' an' the next thing, she's apologizin' for half drownin' me an' she's pullin' me into the hotel an' across the lobby an' into this lounge that's the size of two football pitches. Well, she's ordered tea an' I'm sittin' there, rain water drippin' down me neck an' plastic carrier bags round me feet an' I'm thinkin', 'Well Marjorie, you've waited a long time for your revenge but you've got me good style now, haven't y'? Well go on, spare me the torture, just put the knife in quick an' let's get it over with; come on tell me all about your bein' an air hostess on Concorde.' But she didn't say anythin'. She just sat there, lookin' at me, y' know really lookin' at me. I thought I'm not gonna let her milk it so I said, 'You're an' air hostess these days are y' Marjorie? Oh yes, I hear it's marvellous. You travel all over the world don't you?' But she still just kept lookin' at me. The waitress was just puttin' the tea an' cakes on the table in front of us. I said to her 'This is my friend Marjorie. We were at school together. Marjorie's an air hostess.' 'An air hostess?' Marjorie suddenly said, 'Darling whatever gave you that idea? I certainly travel widely but I'm not an air hostess. Shirley, I'm a hooker. A whore.' Marjorie Majors – a high class hooker! 'Oh really Marjorie,' I said, 'An' all that money your mother spent on elocution lessons.' By this time, the waitress was pourin' the tea into the cream buns! Well me an' Marjorie – God, we had a great afternoon together. She didn't come lordin' it over me at all. Y' know she told me about all the places she works – Bahrain, New York, Munich. An' d' y' know what she told me? When we were at school . . . She wanted to be like me. The two of us, sittin' there at the Adelphi, one's like somethin' out of Dynasty, one's like somethin' out of the bagwash an' we're havin' a great time confessin' that all those years ago, we each wanted to be the other. I was sad when I thought about it. Like the two of us could have been great mates – y' know real close. We didn't half get on well together, that afternoon, in the Adelphi. We were rememberin' all kinds. I could've sat there forever – neither of us wanted to leave. But then the time caught up with us an' Marjorie had to get her plane. An' y' know somethin' – she didn't want to go. Paris she had to go to, Paris France, an' she didn't want to. An' an' on the way out . . . d' y' know what she did? She leaned forward an' just kissed me – there on the cheek – an' there was real affection in that kiss. It was the sweetest kiss I'd known in years. An' then she, she held my shoulders an' looked at me and said, 'Goodbye Shirley. Goodbye, Shirley Valentine.' (*Pause.*) On the way home, on the bus, I was cryin'. I don't know why. I'm starin' out the window, tears trippin' down me cheeks. An' in me head there's this voice that keeps sayin', 'I used to be Shirley Valentine. I used to be Shirley Valentine . . . I used to be Shirley . . .' What happened? Who turned me into this? I don't want this. Do you remember her, wall? Remember Shirley Valentine? She got married to a boy called Joe an' one day she came to live here. An' an' even though her name was changed to Bradshaw she was still Shirley Valentine. For a while. She still . . . knew who she was. She used to . . . laugh. A lot. Didn't she? She used to laugh with Joe – when the pair of them did things together, when they made this kitchen together an' painted it together. Remember wall? Remember when they first painted you an' an' the silly buggers painted each other as well. Stood here, the pair of them, havin' a paint fight, coverin' each other from head to foot in yellow paint. An' then the two of them, thinkin' they're dead darin', gettin' in the bath – together. And the water was so yellow that he said it was like gettin' a bath in vanilla ice cream. And Shirley Valentine washed his hair . . . and kissed his wet head . . . and knew what happiness meant. What happened wall? What happened to the pair of them – to Joe, to Shirley Valentine. Did somethin' happen or was it just that nothin' happened? It would be . . . easier to understand if somethin' had happened, if I'd found him in bed with the milkman, if, if there was somethin' to blame. But there's nothin'. They got married, they made a home, they had kids and brought them up. And somewhere along the way the boy called Joe turned into 'him' and Shirley Valentine turned into this and what I can't remember is the day or the week or the month or the . . . when it happened. When it stopped bein' good. When Shirley Valentine disappeared, became just another name on the missin' persons list.

She makes a partially successful attempt to change gear.

He says he still loves me y' know. But he doesn't. It's just
somethin' he says. It's terrible – 'I love you,' isn't it? Like, like it's
supposed to make everythin' all right. You can be half dead, down
in the dumps and barely sane an' if you complain he'll say, he'll
say, 'what's wrong, y' know I love you.' 'I Love You'. They should
bottle it an' sell it. It cures everythin'. And d' y' know somethin'?
I've always wondered . . . why . . . is it that if somebody says – I
love you it seems to automatically give them the right . . . to treat
you worse . . . than people they only like, or people they don't like
at all, or people they couldn't care less about. See, see, if I wasn't
my feller's . . . wife. If I was just a next door neighbour or the man
in the paper shop – he'd talk to me nice. An' he doesn't say he
loves the next door neighbour or the feller in the paper shop – he
says he loves me! An' he doesn't talk nice to me. When he talks to
me at all. It's funny isn't it – 'I love you.'

Pause as she begins the final stage in the cooking of the meal.

An' I know what you're sayin'. You're sayin' what Jane always
says – why don't I leave? An' the fact of the matter is – I don't
know why. I don't know why anyone should put up with a situation
in which a forty-two-year-old woman has the opportunity of
fulfillin' a dream, of travellin', just a little bit, just two weeks of the
year, an' can't do it. I don't know why . . . I just know that if y'
described me to me, I'd say you were tellin' me a joke. I don't
know why I stay. I hate it. I hate the joke of it. I hate a life of
talkin' to the wall. But I've been talkin' to the wall for more years
than I care to remember now. An' I'm frightened. I'm frightened of
life beyond the wall. When I was a girl I used to jump off our roof.
For fun. Now I get vertigo just standin' up in high-heeled shoes.
I'm terrified if y' want to know. I'm terrified that if I left him, I'd
have nowhere to go, an' I'd find that there was no place for me in
the life beyond the wall – they'd kept a place reserved for me. For
a while. But when it seemed I wasn't comin' back they gave the
place to someone else – maybe someone younger, someone who
could still talk the language of the place beyond the wall. So I stay.
Here. An' . . . an' if I have to give up goin' to Greece – well . . . sod

it. I mean, after all, what's the Acropolis? It's only an old fashioned ruin, isn't it? It's like the DJ's say, isn't it? 'We're all scousers – there's nothin' wrong with us – we've always got a laugh an' a joke haven't we? They're not like us in London are they? Not like us in Greece are they? Greece? Y' know what Greece is, don't y' love? Greece is what y' cook his egg an' chips in. (*Laughs.*) (*Pause.*) An' anyway, another bottle of Riesling I'll be able to pretend this is Greece. Hey, wall . . . look. (*Goes to the window.*) Look at the sun an' the way it's shinin'. Look at the sea, the sea. Smell the honeysuckle. Can't you just taste those olives, those grapes. Look wall, look at that woman, that lovely woman – doesn't she look serene, sittin' beneath a parasol, at a table by the sea, drinking wine in a country where the grape is grown.

As she lays a plate on the table, the backdoor opens.

Blackout.

Scene Two

Three weeks later/the kitchen.

A suitcase stands in the kitchen. **Shirley** *enters. She is dressed in a fairly formal and attractive two-piece suit, wears high heels and carries a hat which she places on top of the suitcase, and a large leather handbag/shoulder bag which she places on top of one of the work surfaces. Throughout the scene she constantly double and even triple checks details of the kitchen, contents of cupboards, whereabouts of utensils. When first she enters she is in a state of nervous agitation.*

Shirley   Guess where I'm goin'? Jane's booked a taxi to take us to the airport. She's pickin' me up at four o'clock.

(*Suddenly.*) Four o'clock. (*Checking clock and her watch.*) Oh Jeez oh Jeez. Passport. Passport. (*Checks the contents of her handbag.*) Passport, tickets, money. Passport, tickets, money. Yeh. Oh God, oh God please say it will be all right. O I feel sick. Those travel sickness pills mustn't be workin' – I still feel sick

an' I've taken four already. An' I've only travelled up an' down
the stairs. Oh God, passport, tickets, money, passport. I got a full
one, a proper passport. Well you never know Shirley – it could
be the start of somethin' – this year Greece, next year . . . the
world.

Slaps the passport shut with a cry of strained anguish.

Ogh. I know I should have told him. I know it would have been
easier if I'd told him. It wouldn't though, would it wall. If I'd told
him he would have talked me out of it. He would have found a
way. He would have made me feel guilty. Guilty? As if I don't feel
guilty enough as it is. Three weeks, secretly gettin' all me things
ready. It's been like livin' in bleedin' Colditz with a tunnel beneath
the floorboards an' every soddin' sound y' think it's the SS, comin'
for y' – they've found out about the tunnel. (*She looks up.*) God.
God I know . . . I'm bein' cruel. I know I'll have to pay for it, when
I get back. But I don't mind payin' for it then. Just . . . just do me a
big favour God an' don't make me have to pay for it durin' this
fortnight. Don't let anythin' happen to our Millandra, our Brian.
An' keep Joe safe. Please. (*Pause.*) Three weeks secretly ironin' an'
packin' an' cookin' all his meals for this two weeks. They're all in
the freezer. Me Mother's gonna come in an' defrost them an' do his
cookin'. With a bit of luck 'he' won't even notice I'm not here. Oh
I'll have to leave him a note. 'Gone to Greece – Back in two
weeks.' Ogh, you should've told him. Y' should have Shirley.
Shirley, y' silly bitch. How could you have told him an' still been
able to go? I know, I know. An' look what happened over the chips
and egg. I know I know. (*Pause.*) Keep thinkin' about the chips an'
egg, keep thinkin' about the . . . It was that that decided me, wasn't
it wall? I'd cooked those chips lovely, hadn't I? In oil. An' they
were free range those eggs. I mean, all right, so he was expectin'
mince but . . . he sits down at that table, doesn't he, an' he looks at
this plate of egg an' chips. Just looks. Doesn't make any effort to
pick up his knife an' fork. He sits there, with this dead quizzical
look on his face, an' he's starin' at the plate, studyin' it, y' know as
though it contains the meanin' of life. Well I just ignored him
didn't I? I just sat there, at the other end of the table. Well,
eventually, he goes, 'What's this? What. Is. This?' I said to him, I

said, 'Well when I cooked it, it was egg an' chips, an' as neither of us is Paul Daniels I'm assumin' it still is egg an' chips.' Well he leaned back in his chair an' he said, 'I am not . . . eating shit,' honest to God, an' he pushed the plate the entire length of the table. Well I'm sittin' there then, aren't I? With a lap full of egg an' chips. I've got yolk, drippin' down me leg an' 'he' has started talkin' to the fridge; 'cos he does that, when he's narked, doesn't he wall. If he's in a real nark he always talks to the cooker or the fridge or the mantelpiece. 'I'm pullin' me tripe out from mornin' till night,' he's tellin' the fridge, 'An' what does she give me when I get home.' Well of course, the fridge never answers him so whenever he asks it a question, he always answers it himself. He always goes – 'I'll tell y' what she gives me. Chips an' egg, chips an' fuckin' egg she gives me.' Well I don't know what possessed me but while he was screamin' at the fridge, I picked meself up from the table, cleaned meself down as best I could, got hold of a pen an' wrote, across the wall, in big letters – GREECE. He didn't even notice, 'cos by this time he's givin' the cooker an' the fridge his impression of Ian Paisley deliverin' the Gettysburg Address. Well I just walked out. I got me coat an' went round to our Millandra's flat. But there was no-one in. I just walked round the block a few times. I was gonna phone Jane but all the phones were out of order. They always are aren't they? Well they are round here – even the vandals are complainin'. I must have walked round for about an hour. I wanted to go an' see someone, someone I could talk to. But there wasn't anyone. I never felt so alone in me whole life. I used to know so many people. Where does everyone go to? In the end I just came back here. He'd been to the Chinese take-away. 'What's that?' he said to me, pointin' at the wall. 'It's a place,' I said. 'It's a place I'm goin' to.' 'I'm not goin' to no Greece,' he said. 'If that's why I'm not gettin' fed properly, because you're savin' up for a foreign holiday, y' can forget it.' Well that's when I started laughin'. I ended up . . . I was hysterical . . . I ended up rollin' on the kitchen floor. He just stepped over me, walked out. But I couldn't stop laughin' because I knew then. I knew I was gonna do it. I knew I was gonna go to Greece. An' everythin' went marvellous didn't it? I made all the arrangements, got me passport. I was quite impressed with meself. So yesterday I thought I'd nip into town an'

get a few last minute things, know the way y' do? Well as I passed
Marks an' Spencers I looked in the window an' y' know they had
some lovely underwear on display, y' dead silky. A little bit Janet
Reger but only half the price. Well normally I'm a bit conservative –
next to the skin as it were – but I thought oh go on, give y'self a
treat, it's the sort of stuff that'd be nice and cool in a hot climate.
So I get into Marks, I bought a new bra, a couple of slips, a few
pairs of pants an' I'm standin' there waitin' for them to be wrapped.
Well who comes up to me but 'her' from next door. Gillian. Well
what's she like wall? What's Gillian like? I'm not sayin' she's a
bragger, but if you've been to Paradise, she's got a season ticket. Y'
know she's that type – if you've got a headache, she's got a brain
tumour. 'Oh hello Shirley,' she says, 'cos that's how she talks,
know she begrudges y' the breath. 'Hello Shirley, oh they're nice,'
she said, spottin' me little garments. 'It's marvellous what they can
do with man-made fibres these days isn't it?' An' she's pickin' up
one of me slips y' know, havin' a really good gawp at it. 'You'd
almost think it was silk. If you weren't familiar with the real thing.'
I said to meself, 'Keep your mouth shut Shirley.' Because y' can't
win with her. Well she dropped the slip back on the counter an'
then she said, 'But I suppose they will look quite nice on your
Millandra.' Well I know I should've kep me mouth shut but that got
me really riled an' I suddenly heard meself sayin', 'Oh no Gillian
these aren't for Millandra, I'm buyin' these for meself. Of course, I
shan't be wearin' them for meself, I shall be wearin' them for my
lover.' Well her jaw dropped into her handbag. For once she
couldn't top it an' I got a bit carried away then. I heard meself
sayin', 'Yes Gillian, we fly out tomorrow, my lover and I, for a
fortnight in the Greek Islands – just two weeks of sun, sand,
taramasalata an' whatever else takes our fancy. Well I must be goin'
Gillian – I've still got a few things to buy. I don't suppose you've
noticed which counter the suspender belts are on? Oh well never
mind, I'll find them. Tarar Gillian,' an' I was off. Course, all the
way home on the bus I'm thinkin', 'Oh you silly bitch. Why did
you say that? What happens if she calls round tonight – while 'he's'
in? What happens if she just lets it slip?' 'Cos she's like that
Gillian, y' know she's got more news than Channel Four. But when
I got home I forgot all about Gillian. When I got home, what was

waitin' for me? Our Millandra, with all her bags an' cases. 'I hate
that Sharron-Louise,' she said. 'She's a mare. Mother, I've come
back to live with you.' Well I'm stood here lookin' at her, me jaw's
dropped halfway to Australia. 'Mother,' she says, 'Will y' make me
some Horlicks an' toast – like y' used to?' Then she was off. Up the
stairs to her old room. Well I made her the toast an' the Horlicks –
took it up to her. She's got herself into bed, sittin' there propped up
with two pillows, readin' her old Beano annuals. 'I love you
Mother,' she said, 'I don't know why I went to live with that cow
in the first place, Mother y' haven't put enough sugar in this
Horlicks will y' get us another spoon?' Well I go down, get the
sugar, bring it back, stir it up for her an' she's sayin' 'We'll go
down town on Saturday shall we Mother? We'll do a bit of
shoppin' eh Mother, just you an' me.' An' the thing is, I was
noddin'. She hadn't been back ten minutes an' I'd gone straight
into bein' 'Auto-Mother'. She's got me struttin' round like R2
bleedin' D2. Well it was when she asked me to bring the telly
upstairs for her that me head cleared. Instead of goin' downstairs
again I sat on the edge of the bed an' I said, 'Millandra, I'm really
pleased you've come back home because I've missed y'. I mean,
I've never said that or whinged an' whined because I believe that
kids have to have their own lives. But there's many a time y' know,
many a time that I would have loved to sit down with y' an' talk, go
to town with y', have a meal with y', share a laugh, just, like not as
your mother but as another human bein'. But I couldn't because
you had your own life, your own friends, your own interests – none
of it to do with me.' 'Well we'll be able to do all that now,' she
said, 'because I've come back home.' 'And that's fantastic,' I said.
'An' you couldn't have picked a better time – it'll be a great help
havin' you here to look after your father.' Well this look came on
her face, 'What's wrong with him?' she said. 'Oh there's nothin'
wrong with him,' I assured her, 'But y' know with me not bein'
here, with me an' Jane goin' to Greece tomorrow.' Well, d' y' know,
it was like her hot water bottle had sprung a leak. 'What?' she
yelled. 'Yeh,' I said, 'I'm goin' to Greece for a fortnight.' 'You,'
she said, 'You, goin' to Greece, what for?' 'For two weeks,' I said.
Well she flounces out of the bed, 'That Jane one, an' you,' she's
goin', 'In Greece. An' what's me Father had to say about that?'

Well when I said I hadn't told him, she went mental. She started gettin' dressed, 'I think it's a disgrace,' she's goin', 'Two middle aged women goin' on their own to Greece – I think it's disgustin'.' An' she's straight down the stairs an' on the phone, tellin' Sharron-Louise that she's comin' back to the flat. Well I'm sittin' there upstairs an' then it suddenly struck me – her sayin' I was disgustin'. I mean she's jumpin' to the same conclusions as her Father would. She thinks I'm just goin' off on a grab a granny fortnight. Well I started to get narked then. The more I thought about it, the more riled I got. I was gonna go down an' give her a piece of me mind but I heard the front door slam. I went to the window an' she's loadin' her things into a taxi. Well I flung the window open an' I shouted, 'Yes, that's right Millandra – I'm goin' to Greece for the sex; sex for breakfast, sex for dinner, sex for tea an' sex for supper.' Well she just ignored me but this little cab driver leans out an' pipes up, 'That sounds like a marvellous diet love.' 'It is,' I shouted down, 'Have y' never heard of it? It's called the 'F' Plan.' Well our Millandra slammed the taxi door an' off they went down the street. I just sat there in our Millandra's bedroom. I was livid at first but when I calmed down I just felt . . . felt like a real fool. All I could think about was Millandra sayin' 'What for. You goin' to Greece – what for?' Kids – they can't half destroy your confidence can't they? I'd spent three weeks tellin' meself I could do it, that I'd be all right, be able to go, be able to enjoy meself. I'd even convinced meself that I wasn't really that old, that me hips weren't really as big as I thought they were, that me belly was quite flat for a woman who's had two kids. That me stretch marks wouldn't really be noticeable to anyone but me. I'd even let that salesgirl at C&A sell me a bikini. But sittin' there on our Millandra's bed, after she'd said that – I suddenly had thighs that were thicker than the pillars in the Parthenon. Me stretch marks were as big as tyre marks on the M6 an' instead of goin' to Greece I should be applyin' for membership of the pensioners' club. I'm sittin' there thinkin', maybe our Millandra's right. 'You goin' to Greece. What for?' Maybe she's right, maybe it is pathetic. What am I goin' for? I mean, it might be easier not to go, to stay here. Where I'm safe. Where there's no risk. For three weeks I'd been buildin' up this marvellous picture of what it would be like, how I was goin' to feel with the sun on me an' the ocean everywhere. But after she'd said that I couldn't . . . couldn't get the picture back, into me mind. I couldn't bring back the feelin' I'd had. I just sat there thinkin', 'Shirley you are one silly bitch. Just another stupid woman who thinks she can have an adventure, when the time for adventures is over.' 'What for?' I kept askin' meself. I thought about the bikini I'd bought an' I felt ashamed. I felt embarrassed at me own stupidity, at lettin' meself think it was possible. 'What for?' 'What am I goin' for?' An' of course the truth of the matter was that I was goin' for the excitement of not knowing; not knowing where I was goin', not knowing what would happen, not knowing what the place would be like or look like, not knowin' just how hot the sun would feel, not knowin' the foreign language I'd hear, not knowin', for the first time since before I could remember, exactly what the days would hold for me. It was the excitement of somethin' that was foreign, to me. The excitement of jumpin' off our roof. An' when our Millandra had said that; it was like, like she'd caught me, on the roof, just as I was about to jump an' she'd said, ' 'Ey, you'll break your bloody neck. Get down off there an' don't be so stupid.' An' I hesitated, an' in that moment I saw how big the drop was, an' how hard the ground was an' how fragile me bones were. An' I realized that I was too old for jumpin' off the roof. I went downstairs, to phone Jane, to phone me mother an' tell her she needn't bother comin' in for the fortnight. I'd even picked up the phone. But the doorbell went an' I put the phone down an' went to the door. Gillian was stood there. 'Oh hello Shirley,' she said, 'Is Joe at home?' Well I just laughed. 'No Joe's not in Gillian. But listen, if you've come to spill the beans, y' might as well . . .' But she just pushed past me, came into the house. 'I don't want to spill any beans, Shirley,' she said, 'I just wanted to check that Joe wasn't in before I gave you this,' an' she handed me this beautifully wrapped package. 'I want you to have this Shirley. It's never been worn. You see,' she said, 'I was never . . . brave enough. Oh Shirley,' she said, 'How I wish I had. How I wish I'd had your . . . bravery.' With that she went to the door. Just as she was goin' out she said to me – 'You're brave Shirley. I just want you to know, I think you're marvellous,' an' she was gone. I opened up the package. (*Shirley opens the case.*) It was this. (*Produces a superb silk robe.*) Silk. Gillian was right – there's nothin' like the real thing. It must have been bought years an' years ago. It's got the original label – 'Liberty of London'. I didn't even dare try it on at first. I felt awful, about what I'd said to Gillian, about taking a lover. I mean, I didn't think she'd really believe me. But she had. Completely believed me. Gillian believed that it was perfectly possible for me to be some marvellous, brave, living woman. I got me mirror out an' looked at meself, an' tried to see the woman that Gillian had seen in me. In Gillian's eyes I was no longer Shirley the neighbour, Shirley the middle-aged mother, Shirley Bradshaw. I had become Shirley The Sensational, Shirley The Brave, Shirley Valentine. An' even if I couldn't see it in the mirror, even if none of it was true about me takin' a lover an' all that rubbish – the point is that Gillian had believed it. Believed it was possible of me. I tried the robe on. It was perfect. It was beautiful. An' in that moment . . . so was I. In that moment our roof wouldn't have been high enough for me. I could have jumped off a skyscraper. An' now the day's here. An' I'm goin'. I'm goin' to the land beyond the wall. I'm gonna sit an' eat olives on a Greek seafront. An' I don't even like olives. But I might like them in Greece. They eat squid y' know. An' octopus – they do. An' I'm gonna eat it too. I don't care. I'm gonna do everythin'. I'm gonna try anything. Like I used to. Unafraid. Without fear of anythin' new. I'll be Shirley The Brave. Course, I'm terrified really. But I'm not gonna let it show. I'm not gonna let it stop me from enjoyin' things. I don't mean I'm gonna be a girl again – because you can never be that; but instead of sayin' 'Christ, I'm forty-two.' I'm gonna say – 'Shirley, you're only forty-two, isn't that marvellous.' (*She looks at herself in the mirror.*) Not bad, not bad. Oh hold on, hold on.

She places the hat on her head and examines the effect in the mirror.

What do you think wall? Oh shut up wall, I'm not talkin' to you. (*She smiles at herself in the mirror.*) Well, that's it Shirley – all dolled up an' ready to go. Case packed? Case packed. Passport, tickets, money? Passport, tickets, money.

She closes her handbag and sits with it, on the suitcase. She takes a last glance at the kitchen to see if everything has been left in order. It has.

Four o'clock Jane's pickin' me up. (*She looks at her watch.*) Twenty past two.

Blackout

Act Two

Scene One

A secluded section of shore, dotted with rocks and baked by the Mediterranean sun. It is an underdeveloped corner of the bay, a place not yet appropriated by tourists. In the background we can see a hint of the village and the taverna. The deep blue of the sky dominates. A white table with parasol and some chairs has been placed in this spot. When we open, the parasol is still folded. There is a piece of rush matting laid out for sun-bathing. **Shirley** *enters. She has bare feet and wears* **Gillian***'s robe.*

Shirley   I'll bet y' didn't recognize me did y'? I hardly recognize meself these days. D' y' like me tan?

She opens the robe to display a deep tan. She wears only cut down denims and a bikini top.

It's marvellous isn't it? I love it here – don't I rock? (*Points to rock.*) That's rock. We met the first day I got here, didn't we? Well I didn't want to go down onto the beach y' see. I thought I'd get a bit of a tan before I ventured onto the beach because – let's face it – I was so white. If I'd walked onto that beach when I first got here, they would have thought I'd just had a fresh coat of white emulsion. When I first arrived there was more glare comin' off me than there was off the sun. So what I did, was I found this little place – I found you, didn't I rock? I talked to you. Rock. He's got his name written all the way through him. Course, I talk to rock – but he doesn't talk back to me. Well he can't can he? It's a Greek rock. It doesn't understand a bleedin' word I'm sayin'. I might have risked the beach if I'd been with Jane. But on me own I felt a bit . . . y' know conspicuous. Jane met a feller didn't she? Not here – on the plane – honest to God. An' the state of him. I wouldn't give y' tuppence a ton. Sporty type – y' know all groin an' Adidas labels. OOOgh. Designer teeth he had. An' bloodshot eyes. Y'

know when he smiled with these blazin' white teeth an' the
bloodshot eyes, I said to Jane, 'Oh he must be a Liverpool
supporter.' She didn't like that. But I didn't care. I'd got past carin'
to tell y' the truth. I mean, we were gonna do everythin' together.
We hadn't even landed an' she's got herself fixed up. She only
went to the loo. When she got back she said to me, 'Erm, I've just
been invited out to dinner. Tonight.' Well I looked at her, 'Pardon,'
I said. 'Yeh,' she said, 'I've just met this chap, sittin' up at the
back. He's stayin' at a villa on the other side of the Island an' he's
invited me over for dinner. Tonight. Oh Shirley you don't mind do
you?' Well I didn't say anythin'. There was nothin' I could say was
there? I just stared out the window of the plane an' I thought, 'D' y'
know, if I had a parachute, I'd get off now.' I even considered
gettin' off without a parachute actually. Course she was sayin' to
me – 'It's only for tonight. We'll still do all the things we planned
Shirley.' But I knew. Me instinct told me I'd hardly see her again
after that. An' I didn't want her to be spendin' time with me when
she'd rather be elsewhere. I didn't want her pityin' me. 'Listen
Jane,' I said, 'I think you've probably blown the feminist of the
year award – so will y' just leave it out, right? Obviously,' I said,
'It's been a difficult time for you since your feller ran off with the
milkman and now that you've got this opportunity I don't want y'
to give even a thought to me. You just go off to his villa an' enjoy
yourself an' give his olives a good pressing.' D' y' know what she
said to me? 'Thanks for bein' so understandin'.' An' she never
came back that night y' know. Or the next mornin'. She never came
back for the first four days. They must've been marvellous olives. I
was just left on me own. I was alone. But I wasn't lonely. Well I'm
an expert at it really. But what I found was – if you're a woman,
alone, it doesn't half seem to upset people; like whenever I walked
into the dinin' room at the hotel it was like everyone was lookin' at
me. I've got this little table to meself, an' it's lovely. I just love
sittin' there, in the evenin'. But on the third day, I'm sat there at me
table. I've been sunbathin' all day, I'm glowin' like a lobster an'
feelin' dead content an' quiet. I was in such a trance I hadn't even
noticed this woman come across. She was talkin' to me before I
realized she was there. 'We couldn't help notice you were alone
dear,' she says to me, 'Would y' like to come an' join us at our

table? There is a spare place.' Well I was shattered. I didn't want to join anyone. I didn't wanna talk. I wanted to be quiet. But she's standin' there, waitin' for me to say somethin'. An' then I notice that the whole of the restaurant's waitin' as well. All of them lookin', waitin' to see what would happen to the woman on her own. Well, of course, I couldn't say no, could I? I mean the woman was only bein' kind wasn't she? But inside I was cursin'. Well d' y' know, as I sat down at their table, with her an' her husband, it was like the whole of the restaurant let out this great sigh of relief, as if me bein' on me own had been like a great problem for everyone, an' now it had been solved, everyone could relax, everyone could talk louder an' laugh; I thought the waiters were gonna break into applause 'cos I'd been rescued from me loneliness by Jeanette an' Dougie. Jeanette an' Dougie Walsh – from Manchester. Well, I know the exact dimensions of her kitchen, the price of the new extension, the colour of the microwave an' the contents of the Hoover, an' we hadn't even started on the first course; it's a good job it wasn't soup – I would've put me head in it an' drowned meself. It wasn't until we got to the main course that they even acknowledged we were in Greece. And then I wish they hadn't bothered. Everything was wrong – the sun was too hot for them, the sea was too wet for them, Greece too Greek for them. They were that type, y' know, if they'd been at the last supper they would have asked for chips. An' I wouldn't mind but the family on the next table joined in as well an' started complainin' about everythin'. An' I'm sittin' there dead embarrassed out of me mind because there's this poor Greek waiter tryin' to serve our main course an' he's got to listen to this lot goin' about his country as though it's in the Fourth World. This feller on the table next to us is sayin' to Dougie, ' 'Ave y' not seent bloody fishin' boats they've got out theer int bay? 'Ave y' not seen em, 'ave y' not? Bloody hell, what they like love?' he says to his wife, 'What did I say to you when I saw them boats int bay. I said to her, I did, I said them boats, if y' look at the side of 'em ant find name of boatbuilder I'll bet y' a pound to a penny it says Noah. Din't I? I bloody did. Aye.' An' they're all roarin' with laughter. Well I was so ashamed I couldn't keep me mouth shut any longer. 'Excuse me,' I said to the feller on the next table, 'Excuse me. You do watch the Olympic games I take it? And y' do know I suppose that it was the Greeks who invented the Olympic games?' Well they were all lookin' at me. 'Oh yes,' I said, 'they invented a lot of things, the Greeks. In fact,' I said, 'It was the Greeks who were responsible for the most important invention of all – the wheel.' Course I didn't know if it had been invented by the Greeks, the Irish or the Cavemen but I didn't care. Once I'd opened me mouth there was no stoppin' me. 'The English,' I'm goin', 'The English? Don't talk to me about the English, because whilst the Greeks were buildin' roads an' cities an' temples, what were the English doin'? I'll tell y' what the English were doin', they were runnin' round in loin cloths an' ploughin' up the earth with the arse bone of a giraffe.' Well I hadn't meant to get so carried away like that. I suddenly realized how loud I'd been shoutin'. Everyone's lookin' at me – the feller an' his family on the next table have turned away an' Dougie an' Jeanette are sittin' there wonderin' why they asked this lunatic to join them. Well Dougie obviously decides to use diversionary tactics an' he says to the waiter who's just walkin' away. 'Hey mate. What is this?' An' he points to his plate. The waiter says to him, 'Et ees calamares Sir.' 'Yeh but what I'm askin' y',' Dougie says, 'What I'm askin' y', is what is it?' 'Erm . . . eet's calamares, sir, eet's er a type of er . . . feesh.' Well Dougie looks at his plate an' he's not convinced. 'It don't look much like fish to me,' he says. 'My wife's got a very delicate stomach. She's very particular about what she eats. Are you sure this is fish?' 'Sir, I can . . . promees you,' says the waiter, 'eet ees feesh. Eet ees feesh . . . was pulled from the sea thees morning, by my own father. In a boat called 'Noah'.' Well, the silence at our table is deafenin'. We're all sittin' there eatin' an' no-one's sayin' a word. I'm feelin' like a right heel because I've upset them all an' I'm tryin' to think of somethin' to say that'll make it all right. Well y' know what it's like when . . . when there's one of those silences an' you've got to force yourself to find somethin' to say – you always come out with the wrong thing, don't y'? Well what I said was, 'The squid's very nice, isn't it?' The pair of them stopped eatin' an' looked at me. 'Pardon me?' Jeanette said. 'The squid,' I said, pointin' to her plate, 'The squid, the octopus, it's quite nice really isn' . . .' Well it was funny the way Jeanette fainted. They didn't eat in the hotel after that.

Apparently they found this restaurant at the back of the hotel that
does proper Greek food – doner kebabs. After dinner, whilst
everyone else was makin' their way to the bar, I went up to me
room an' grabbed me light coat an' I walked out of the hotel an'
into this lovely night outside. (*Pause as she remembers it.*) Well
that's when I met him. Y' know . . . Christopher Columbus. That's
not his real name. His real name's Costas. But I call him
Christopher. Christopher Columbus. I'll bet y' don't know why I
call him that? It's because he's got a boat. Well it's his brother's
actually. And because it's er, he, we . . . discovered it. The clitoris.
I'm terrible aren't I? I suppose y' think I'm scandalous – a married
woman, forty-two, got grown up kids. I suppose y' think I'm
wicked. Jane does. 'Shirley,' she said, 'You're acting like a stupid
teenager. I suppose the next thing you're going to tell me is that the
earth trembled?' 'Trembled,' I said, 'Jane, I thought there'd been
an earthquake. It was at least point nine on the Richter Scale.' 'Oh
spare me the details,' she's goin', 'Spare me the details.' Well she
wasn't half jealous. But y' see, it wasn't my fault; if she hadn't
gone off, with the walkin' groin in the first place – I never would
have met Christopher Columbus. (*Pause.*) He kissed me stretch
marks y' know. He did. He said . . . he said they were lovely . . .
because they were a part of me . . . an' I was lovely. He said . . . he
said, stretch marks weren't to be hidden away – they were to be
displayed . . . to be proud of. He said my stretch marks showed that
I was alive, that I'd survived . . . that they were marks of life.
(*Pause.*) Aren't men full of shit? I mean, can you imagine him, the
mornin' after he's given me this speech – he wakes up an' he finds
his belly has got all these lines runnin' across it? I mean, can y' see
him? Rushin' to the mirror an' goin' 'Fantastic. Fuckin' fantastic.
I've got stretch marks. At last!' But the thing about him, the thing
about Costas was, when he gave y' a load of guff – *he* believed it.
What was marvellous about him was, he never made y' feel at all
threatened. An' he understood how to talk with a woman. That's
the first thing I noticed about him. 'Cos y' know most men, really,
they're no good at talkin' with women. They don't know how to
listen or they feel that they have to take over the conversation. Like
. . . like most fellers, if you said somethin' like . . . like, 'My
favourite season is autumn.' Well most fellers'd go, 'Is it? My

favourite season's spring. See what I like about spring is that in spring . . .' Then y' get ten minutes of why he likes spring. An' you weren't talkin' about spring – you were talkin' about autumn. So what d' y' do. You end up talkin' about what he wants to talk about. Or you don't talk at all. Or you wind up talkin' to y'self. An' whichever way it works out it always ends up that there's no talkin' goin' on. It just becomes words. Words without meanin'. Words that get spoken . . . but die . . . because they have nowhere to go. But it wasn't like that with Costas. When I came out of the hotel that night I just walked down the little esplanade. There was hardly a soul about, but I noticed the light was on in The Taverna an' outside the front of it there's these tables, with white parasols. Well I'm sittin' there an' he came out to serve me. 'Erm, excuse me,' I said to him, 'I know this sounds a bit soft but would you mind . . . I mean would you object if I moved this table an' chair, over there, by the edge of the sea?' Well he looked at me for a minute. 'You want,' he said, 'You want move table and chair to the sea? What for? You don't like here at my bar?' 'Oh yeh,' I said, 'yeh, it's a lovely bar but, but I've just got this soft little dream about sittin' at a table by the sea.' 'Agh,' he said, an' he smiled. 'A dream, a dream. We move this table to the edge of the sea, it make your dream come true?' 'Erm, yeh,' I said. 'I think so.' 'Then, is no problem. I move the table for you. And tonight when I serve in my bar, I say to customer – tonight, tonight I make someone's dream come true.' Well I thought for a second he was bein' sarcastic – 'cos in England it would have been. But no, he carries the table an' chair over here an' he brings me out this glass of wine I've ordered. Well I paid him an' thanked him but he said to me 'No, I thank you. Enjoy your dream,' then he gave a little bow an' he was gone, back to the taverna, leavin' me alone with the sea an' the sky an' me soft little dream. Well it's funny isn't it, but y' know if you've pictured somethin', you know if you've imagined how somethin's gonna be, made a picture of it in your mind, well it never works out does it? I mean for weeks I'd had this picture of meself, sittin' here, sittin' here, drinkin' wine by the sea; I even knew exactly how I was gonna feel. But when it got to it, it wasn't a bit like that. Because when it got to it I didn't feel at all lovely an' serene. I felt pretty daft actually. A bit stupid an' an' awfully, awfully old. What

I kept thinkin' about was how I'd lived such a little life. An' one way or another even that would be over pretty soon. I thought to meself, my life has been a crime really – a crime against God, because . . . I didn't live it fully. I'd allowed myself to live this little life when inside me there was so much. So much more that I could have lived a bigger life with – but it had all gone unused, an' now it never would be. Why . . . why do y' get . . . all this life, when it can't be used? Why . . . why do y' get . . . all these . . . feelin's an' dreams an' hopes if they can't ever be used? That's where Shirley Valentine disappeared to. She got lost in all this unused life. An' that's what I was thinkin', sittin' there on me own, starin' out at the sea, me eyes open wide an' big tears splashin' down from them. I must've sat there for ages because the noise from the hotel bar had died away an' even the feller from the taverna was lockin' up for the night. He came to collect me glass. It was still full. I hadn't even taken a sip. He saw that I was cryin' but he didn't say anythin'. He just sat down there, on the sand and stared out at the sea. An' when I'd got over it, when it was all right to talk, he said, 'Dreams are never in the places we expect them to be.' I just smiled at him. 'Come,' he said, 'I escort you back to your hotel.' An' he did. An' he told me his name was Costas an' I told him my name was Shirley. An' when we got to the front door of the hotel he said to me, 'Tomorrow, you want, to come with me? I take my brother's boat. We go all round the island?' I just shook me head, 'No,' I said, 'It's all right. You've been dead kind as it is. Thank you.' 'Is no problem, I come for you, early.' 'No,' I'm goin', 'Thanks but . . .' 'You afraid?' he suddenly said, 'No,' I said 'but . . .' 'You afraid,' he said, nodding, 'You afraid I make try to foak with you.' I didn't know where to put meself, but he just laughed. 'Of course I like to foak with you. You are lovely woman. Any man be crazy not to want to foak with you. But I don't ask to foak. I ask you want to come my brother's boat – is different thing. Foak is foak, boat is boat. I come fetch you tomorrow. I bring wine, I bring food and we go. Tomorrow, I just make you happy. No need to be sad, no need be afraid. I give my word of honour I don't make try to foak with you.' Well what could I say? 'Well I'll erm, I'll see y' in the mornin' then.' Course, the next mornin' I've just got dressed. I'm sittin' in me room, there's this knockin' on the

door, I thought, 'Oh Christ, he's come up to me room.' Well I
opened the door, an' guess what? Jane's back! 'Shirley, please
forgive me. I know I shouldn't have left you. Shirley, I know I've
been awful but please, please forgive me. I'll make it up to you.
Come on, it's still early, let's go and hire a car and drive out around
the island.' Well what could I do? I mean she had paid for me to be
there. If it hadn't been for Jane I would never have been in Greece
in the first place. She keeps askin' me if I forgive her. 'Of course I
forgive y',' I said, an' she threw her arms round me then. 'Come
on,' she said, 'Let's put it all behind us now. Let's make today the
real start of our holiday. I know you've had an awful time and
Shirley I'm sorry. Have you just been sitting here in your room the
past few days? I know you. Without me being here I suppose
you've just been sitting here talking to the wall, haven't you?' Well
I thought to meself, 'How does she see me? Does she think I'm an
old-age pensioner or a five-year-old child?' 'I'll only be a few
minutes,' she's sayin', 'I'll just pick up a few things from my
room.' Well it was just as she got to the door that there was a knock
on it. She pulled it open an' Costas was there. She took one look at
him an' said – 'What is it, room service? Did you order anything
Shirley?' But Costas just walked straight past her an' into the room.
'Shirley, Shirley, you come, you come. You late. I wait for you on
the quay. I already put the wine, the food on the boat. I stand I wait
an' then I think, 'Ah, Shirley and me, we get to bed so late last
night, Shirley she must have oversleep.' Well the look on Jane's
face could've turned the milk. 'Quickly now you get ready. Don't
bring much clothing. I wait on quay for you. Hurry.' An' as he
passes Jane he just goes, 'Apology for interrupting you. Now you
continue cleaning the room.' Well if Jane had kept her mouth shut,
if she hadn't tried to treat me like a child, I might have run after
Costas an' said I couldn't go, or could me friend come as well. But
she said, 'Shirley. What do you think you're playing at?' I didn't
say a word. I just looked at her. She was goin' on about how I'd
never been abroad before. When she got to the bit about 'men like
that, these Greek islanders who are just waiting for bored middle-
aged women to fall into their . . .', I just stormed straight past her
an' out. I steered the boat y' know. See me on that bridge – natural.
I mean, I knew I wasn't the first woman on that boat an' I certainly

woı ldn't be the last. But I knew I was with a good man. I knew
that whatever happened he wouldn't take anythin' from me. We
sailed for miles an' miles. An' we talked. Properly. An' we didn't
half laugh. We liked each other. An' isn't it funny, but if you're
with someone who likes y', who sort of, approves of y' – well y'
like, like start to grow again. Y' move in the right way, say the
right thing at the right time. An' you're not eighteen or forty-two or
sixty-four. You're just alive. An' I know if I could have seen myself
that day I would have said, 'Look at that lovely woman – riding on
the sea. Look at that lovely woman, swimming.' Well I know I'd
left me swimmin' costume in the hotel. So what? We'd parked the
boat an' was lookin' over the side. I said, 'How deep do you think
it is here Costas?' 'Mm. Maybe a thousand metres – maybe ten
thousand metres, who knows. Maybe so deep it goes on forever.'
An' when I stood there, on the edge of the boat, naked as the day I
was born, about to jump into this water that was as deep as forever
I felt as strong an' as excited an' as bloody mad as I did when I
jumped off our roof. The two of us just splashed an' laughed an'
swam in the water an' I knew Costas would keep his promise but I
didn't want him to because it was the most natural thing in the
world. So I swam up to him. An' I put me arms around him an'
kissed him. An' that's when I nicknamed him Christopher
Columbus. Mind you, I could just as easily have named him André
Previn – I don't know where this orchestra came from. Later on,
just lyin' there on the boat, with the sun beginnin' to dip towards
the evenin', that's when the thought came to me. I tried to like,
push it out of me head at first. Because it was too shocking. I kept
tryin' to think of other things, to make this thought go away. But it
wouldn't. It was just there in me head. An' this thought was 'If . . .
somehow . . . if . . . for . . . some . . . reason . . . I . . . didn't . . . go
. . . back . . . home . . . who would really care? Would it cause
anyone any real suffering? Would it damage anyone? Who would
miss – me? Why should I go back? Why should I go back an'
become that woman again when, when that woman isn't needed
anymore. Her job's done. She's brought up her kids. I mean, they'd
say it was awful, it was terrible to have a mother who went on
holiday an' never came back. I hadn't gone round the pipe. I
hadn't. I hadn't fallen in love with Costas. It had been sweet. It had

been lovely. It had been a day full of kindness. But I hadn't fallen
in love with him. I'd fallen in love with the idea of livin'. An'
every day when I woke up, when I came down here with Jane,
when we went an' had a coffee or a drink at Costas's taverna, when
I was lyin' in me bed, just droppin' off to sleep, it was always there
in me head – this shocking thought – 'I'm not goin' back.' 'I'm not
goin' back.' (*Pause.*) An' of course – all the time I knew really. I
knew I'd have to go back in the end. I knew that I was just one of
millions an' millions before me who'd gone on a holiday an' had
such a good time that they didn't want to go home. Because we
don't do what we want to do. We do what we have to do. An'
pretend it's what we want to do. An' what I wanted to do was to
stay here and be Shirley Valentine. And what I had to do was to go
back there, back to bein' St Joan Of The Fitted Units. An' all
through the days, an' when I said goodbye to Costas, an' on the
way to the airport, an' in the long queue for the check-in desk I
didn't know if I'd do what I wanted to do, or what I had to do. We
were standin' there, in this queue, me an' Jane an' all the others
who had to go back. An' I remembered this question I was gonna
ask Jane. So I said to her, 'Jane, Jane why is it that there's all this
unused life?' She just said it was because of men, it was all the
fault of men, an' went back to readin' her magazine. An' I thought
about it an' I thought, 'That's rubbish . . . It's not just men who do
it to women. Because I've looked at Joe, an' I know it's the same
for him. He had more life in him than he could use. An' so he
carries all this . . . waste around with him. It's the same for
everyone. I know it. When I'm out when I'm in the shops, when I
see people I grew up with, standin' there in the shop buyin'
vegetables. An' we say how are y' we all say fine an' we pretend
we are because the vegetables are fresh an' we haven't had a cold
this year an' our kids grew up with their limbs intact an' never got
in trouble with the police. We say we're fine. An' we carry on an'
on an' on until we die. An' most of us die . . . long before we're
dead. An' what kills us is the terrible weight of all this unused life
that we carry round.' We'd got to the check-in desk. Me suitcase
was on the conveyor belt with a tag on it, for England, for home. I
stood there, just watchin' it as it moved away, along the conveyor
belt an' through these flaps an' disappeared into this dark hole. An'

I knew then. I knew I couldn't go with it . . . Jane just called out at
first, as she saw me walkin' away. Then she realized, she knew an'
she screamed at me, to come back, to come back. All the people in
the queue were lookin' at me. An' I knew they all wanted me to
'come back, come back.' But I just kept walkin', across the
concourse. All I had left was me handbag, the clothes I stood in,
Gillian's robe, me passport an' a few drachmas. An' after I'd paid
me bus fare, even the drachmas had gone. (*Pause.*) When I walked
up to the taverna Costas was talkin' to this woman, sittin' on a bar
stool. As I walked in I heard him sayin' to her: 'You afraid? You
afraid I want make try you . . .' The poor feller, he nearly dropped
his olives when he saw me. 'Don't worry Costas,' I said, 'I haven't
come back for you. I've come back for the job. The job in your
taverna.' Nearly three weeks I've been workin' there now. I get on
well with the customers. Even the 'Dougies an' Jeanettes', we get a
pair of them every week y' know. They come in, order a drink an'
look all dead nervous at the menu. I always say to them, 'Would
you like me to do y' chips an' egg?' An' they're made up then. Bein'
a part of it here, a proper part of it – it's much better than bein' on
holiday. (*She moves to the table and puts up the parasol.*) I have
most of the days to meself an' just work the nights. I've got the
night off tonight though. Well Joe's arrivin' tonight. The first time
he phoned, y' know after Jane had got back, he screamed at me. He
said I must have finally gone mad. He said I was a disgrace – to the
kids, to him, to the EEC! It was the easiest thing in the world to
just put the phone down on him. The second time he phoned he
said you can't run away from life. I said I agreed with him an' now
I'd found some life I had no intention of runnin' away from it. He
started to scream an' shout again then; he said he knew all about
me 'holiday romance', an' how I'd made a fool of meself but, but
if I stopped all this arsin' round, if I got meself home, where I
belonged, he said, he said he'd promise never to mention it. I said
. . . said . . . 'The only holiday romance I've had, is with meself
Joe. An' . . . an' I think . . . I've come to like meself, really.' I said
to him, I said, 'I think I'm all right Joe. I think that if . . . if I saw
me, I'd say, that woman's O.K. . . . . She's alive. She's not
remarkable, she's not gonna . . . gonna be there in the history
books. But she's . . . she's there in the time she's livin' in. An'

certainly she's got her wounds . . . an' her battle scars but maybe, maybe . . . a little bit of the bullshit is true an' an' the wounds shouldn't be hidden away – because, because even the wounds an' the scars are about bein' alive.' There was a long pause. I thought he'd gone off the phone. An' then I heard this voice, 'I knew it,' he was sayin', 'I knew it, it's the bleedin' change of life isn't it?' 'That's right Joe,' I said, 'That's right, it's a change of life. An' that's why you're wastin' your money phonin' me to try an' get me back. I'm not comin' back.' The last time he phoned he said our Brian had been arrested – buskin' without a licence. An' our Millandra was frettin' for me. An' that he loved me an' the only thing he wanted in the world was for me to come back. I explained to him that it was impossible because the woman he wanted to go back didn't exist anymore. An' then I got his letter sayin' he was comin' to get me. To take me back home. Agh God love him, he must've been watchin' Rambo. He'll be here soon. I hope he stays for a while. *He* needs a holiday. *He* needs to feel the sun on his skin an' to be in water that's as deep as forever, an' to have his wet head kissed. He needs to stare out to sea. And to understand. (*Pause.*) I asked Costas if he'd put the table out for me again. He said to me, 'You look for you dream again?' 'No, Costas,' I said. 'No dream. But I'm gonna sit here an' watch for Joe an' as he walks down the esplanade, an' keeps walkin', because he doesn't recognize me anymore, I'll call out to him. An' as he walks back, an' looks at me, all puzzled an' quizzical, I'll say to him – 'Hello. I used to be the mother. I used to be your wife. But now, I'm Shirley Valentine again. Would you like to join me for a drink?'

Blackout

John, Paul, George, Ringo . . . and Bert

John, Paul, George, Ringo . . . and Bert was first performed at the Everyman Theatre, Liverpool, on 21 May, 1974, with the following cast:

Bert	George Costigan
John Lennon	Bernard Hill
Paul McCartney	Trevor Eve
George Harrison	Phillip Joseph
Ringo Starr	Antony Sher
Brian Epstein	Robin Hooper
Porter, Hitler & others	Nick Stringer
Linda McCartney & others	Helen Brammer
Bob Dylan & others	Terry Canning
Reporter, Photographer & others	Cengiz Saner
Titular 1 & others	Val Lilley
Titular 2 & others	Elizabeth Estensen
Titular 3 & others	Linda Becket
Singer and Pianist	Barbara Dickson
Musicians	Robert Ash
	Terry Canning

Directed by Alan Dossor
Designed by Graham Barkworth

John, Paul, George, Ringo . . . and Bert was subsequently presented by Robert Stigwood and Michael Codron, by arrangement with Liverpool Everyman, at the Lyric Theatre, London, on 15 August 1974, with the following cast:

Bert	George Costigan
John Lennon	Bernard Hill
Paul McCartney	Trevor Eve
George Harrison	Philip Joseph
Ringo Starr	Anthony Sher
Brian Epstein	Robin Hooper
Porter, Hitler & others	Nick Stringer
Teddy Boy & others	Barry Woolgar
Teddy Boy & others	Dick Haydon
Teddy Boy & others	Ian Jentle
Tiny Tina	Luan Peters
Titular1 & others	Elizabeth Estensen
Titular2 & others	Linda Beckett
Titular3 & others	Valerie Lilley
Singer and Pianist	Barbara Dickson
Musicians	Robert Ash
	Terry Canning

Directed by Alan Dossor
Designed by Graham Barkworth

Act One

*(Weather permitting, the show should begin in the street outside
the theatre, about twenty minutes before the show on stage begins.
The band and* **Bert** *(the Narrator) dressed as Sgt. Pepper's Lonely
Hearts Club Band, busk in the street.*

*The busking should be done with traditional busking instruments –
guitar, banjo, kazoo, big bass drum, etc. – the songs should be a
selection of Beatles songs arranged for busk. As the hour of starting
draws near, the band (still busking) should make its way inside the
theatre and up onto the stage. As the house lights go down, all the
members of the band – except* **Bert** *– tail off in the middle of a song.*
Bert, *oblivious that the others are no longer playing, still bashes
away at the guitar. Suddenly he realizes that he is alone. (On screen
an exterior shot of the Philharmonic Hall.)*

Bert   Come on, come on. Keep goin'. Y' can't just stop in the
middle of a medley. This is buskin' an' y' don't stop for nott'n.

Musician 1   But there's no queue to busk, Bert.

Bert   Well obviously the word hasn't got out yet. But when it
does. . . . There'll be millions in these streets soon.

Musician 2   What does it say on the posters? 'Wings' it
says. . . .

Bert   Well, y' soft tart, they're not gonna advertise it are they?
Wings? That's just the cover up. But I'm tellin' you la; The Beatles
are definitely playing the Phil tonight.

*Starts up again. But instead of joining in, the others begin to drift
off.*

Hey. Where y' goin'? Come back.

But it is hopeless.

Go on then . . . piss off. See if I care . . . Go'n play y' Donny
Osmond records. . . . I wouldn't have you in my backin' group. I'm
not missing it. I'm stopping right here.

(*Turns to audience.*)

You're in the right place, y'know. Who'd have thought eh? Who
would have thought that the great reunion would take place here
in Liverpool? But they (i.e. the buskers/band) don't realize you
see. I mean, people have been talking about this for so long now
that they don't believe you when you tell 'em it's really happening
(points to the Philharmonic Hall) That's where it's gonna happen.
. . . inside there, the Philharmonic Hall, home of the Royal
Liverpool Philharmonic Orchestra. Mind you . . . they sometimes
have good groups on as well. Anyway I'm not gonna miss it even
if I have to wait all day, I mean it's worth it, isn't it, for the greatest
event in the history of music.

*On sound we hear the applause from the Bangla Desh album as
band begin 'Your Mother Should Know'.*

  Throughout which we move backstage and see **Paul
McCartney** *dressed in an overcoat, enter the dressing
room/green room. He looks around and sees a coffin in the
centre of the room. He takes off his coat, produces a key from
his pocket and opens the coffin from which he takes out a
guitar.*

  *He smiles and puts it back. He goes across to a tea/coffee
machine and looks for a coin. He does not notice* **Lennon** *who
enters. As* **McCartney** *fumbles around looking for a coin,*
Lennon *watches him and finally speaks. They are both slightly
embarrassed.*

John   Hia. . . . 'Fab' Paul.

Paul (*turns*)   Hello John. (*There is an awkward silence*) Have, er,
have y' got a two p coin? Coffee.

John   I never carry money . . . I can sign y' a cheque.

Paul (*indicates the machine*)   It only takes coins . . . cheques not
accepted.

John   Another bloody conspiracy against the rich. I'll go see the porter if y' like. . . . see if he's got change. . . .

Paul (*stopping him*)   No. . . . don't. We don't want him to recognize you. It's okay if they recognize me . . . they'll think it's because of Wings. . . . but if they see you!. . . . Forget the coffee.

John (*coming into the room and putting down a travelling bag which he opens*)   Anyway, don't you think it should be something stronger than coffee. (*Produces a bottle of whiskey.*) I mean, after all, Paul. . . . (*taking a rise out of himself*) It's been a long old lonely time . . . (*grabs a couple of glasses and pours the drink*).

Paul   You're gonna do it then?

John   I'm here aren't I? Y' don't think I've come all this way just to listen to you and that crappy Wings outfit do y'?

Paul   *Hesitating for a moment, not knowing if it is a serious jab or a playful slap.* **Lennon** *smiles,* **Paul** *laughs.*

Paul   Everyone said you'd changed a lot.

John   Yeah?

Paul   Yeah. But you've not.

John   No?

Paul   No, you're still the same cunt you always were.

John   I'll drink to that. (*Pause.*) Whose idea was it anyway, gettin' together?

Paul   Ritchie. He just phoned up an' said he had this good idea about us turnin' up instead of Wings one night. He said if he could get you an' George to agree, would I play the gig.

John   An' why Liverpool like?

Paul   It just turned out that way.

John   When I heard it was to be Liverpool I thought, 'That's a Paul idea that is, a McCartney idea, ironic, just like his songs.'

Paul (*touchy*)   Why did you agree to turn up then?

John   I dunno. . . . Maybe I like McCartney songs.

Paul   Oh Christ. . . . Yeah. So I read in the papers. Escapist shit, that's what you said my music was. Trivial muzak, that's what you said in the papers.

John   Jesus, you haven't spent four years sittin' round readin' what I've said about you, have y'?

Paul   I couldn't help but read it. Every music paper I open is full of Lennon's Confessions, tellin' the world that he hated everythin' I was into.

John   I wasn't tryin' to hurt you. I just wanted to smash out at The Beatles. . . . After all that, all that Beatle scene. Why didn't you phone me up an' talk? I mightn't have said it all then.

Paul   Why didn't you phone me?

John   My dad's bigger than your dad. . . . Look, can't we just forget all the hassles. I mean, if this is really it, if we're really gonna play together again, there's no point in diggin' up the muck, is there?

Paul   Okay. We forget it. Let's have a toast.

John   Let's go mad an' have a plate full.

Paul   Here's to the return, of The Beatles. . . . .

John   No. Not that. No more Beatles. No more Apples or Beatles. . . . no Fab Four or Yeh Yeh Yeh.

Paul   Alright, alright. (*Pause.*) But what do you think *they'll* be thinkin', when we get out on that stage tonight? *They'll* all be thinkin' Beatles.

John   Let them think what they want. Just as long as *we* don't start thinkin' Beatles again. (*Beat*) Have y' thought about how we're gonna work it?

Paul (*shrug*)   We just go out there and play.

John   Yeah but, you go out first – they'll be expectin' to see you anyway, because of . . . 'Wings'. But don't mention Beatles. Just here's George Harrison, Richard Starkey an' John Lennon.

Paul   Okay. No Beatles.

John   'Cos, as all the Fab Listeners know, I don't believe in Beatles anymore.

Paul   Okay. Set list? Do we know what songs we want to do?

John   All mine.

Paul   Oh yeah?

John   Yeah! Yours are all 'escapist shit'.

Paul   Hey – why don't we go out an' do a night of just George's songs. That'd be different, eh.

John   Oh yeah, all's we'd need is Cliff Richard an' we could have a right fuckin' gospel rally. No, what we should do is send out for some white suits an' go on as The Osmonds. That'd really freak them out.

There's a knock on the dressing room door. A **Porter** *appears.*

Porter   Is one of you gentlemen Mr. McCartney?

Paul   Yeah, what's wrong?

Porter   I thought I better check with y' pal. There's two fellers out here . . . they say they're with your group. I thought I better check with y' son. I know the tricks these fans can get up to. They're bloody mad y' know, these young girls. They take 'em off y' know. Drop 'em . . . When there's a group on here they call it the Bare Arse Palladium. Anyway, sir, I thought I better check with y'. Would y' like to come an' identify these young fellers? They wouldn't tell me their names, security reasons they said.

Paul   These two? (*looks round the door*)

Porter   They are with your group then?

Paul   No . . . not them . . . throw them out.

Ringo   Hey Paul . . . come on, stop messin'.

George   Come on Paul, he won't let us in.

Porter   Right, out y' go boys. . . . Come on now.

Paul   No. . . . it's alright Jim. . . . I'm only messin'.

Porter   Well look Pal, either they are with you or they aren't.

Paul   Yeah, it's okay, they're with us.

Porter   Alright. . . . Go on in. You do understand though. . . .
I had to check. We can't have anyone wanderin' round the
Philharmonic Hall. It's not the bloody Empire y' know. . . . (*Off.*)

Ringo *and* **George** *enter.*

Ringo   Arsin' round. He's had us standin' out there for ten minutes.

Paul   You should have told him who you were.

George   I thought you said it was a strict secret.

Paul   He wouldn't have twigged on.

Ringo   He says to me, 'What d'you play then?' 'I'm the
drummer' I said. He picks up two sticks an' says, prove it. I'm
stood out there, like a right prick, drummin' all over the walls.

John   That's the price y' pay for not bein' famous anymore. I
walked up here, all the way from Lime Street Station. An' not a
soul recognized me.

Ringo (*to* **George**)   Who is he anyway?

George   Hey do you think there'll be any kind of hassle? I
mean. . . . It's a long time since we did something like this. They
might have forgotten us.

Paul   I wouldn't count on that.

Ringo   They might have done though.

John   No chance. They still remember Jesus don't they?

Ringo   Can I quote you on that Mr. Lennon?

John (*into bottle neck*)   I didn't mean it . . . . .

Paul   Well it looks like we all got here anyway.

George   Who chose the Philharmonic Hall for this historic occasion? Did we have to make our return in a mausoleum?

Paul   Pardon me. I would have got the Cavern if I'd known.

John   The Cavern? From what I've heard it's worse than this place isn't it?

George   Last time I was in Liverpool I crept in there. Man there's nothin' left.

John   They changed it all?

George   They've chipped the sweat off the walls an' turned it into a night club . . . . oh, an' they've moved it next door as well.

John   They're waitin' till we're dead. Then they'll reconstruct it, brick by sweaty brick.

Ringo   Our own little shrine.

Paul   What?

Ringo   Shrine. Y'know. (*He sings*) 'Oh when you're shrinin'/ When you're shrinin' (*The others join in*) The whole world shrines with you . . . .'

Ringo   Yeh.

There is a long silence.

Paul   Well. . . . This looks like it folks. It looks as though we made it safely back home.

Bangla Desh applause is heard again as lights fade on dressing room and we rejoin **Bert** *outside the hall. On slide a press photo of The Beatles.*

Bert   The Beatles. . . . Remember them do y'? Everyone knew them once. Ten years ago in Liverpool there were three quarters of a million people, and everyone of them had a brother or sister who'd been to school with one of the Beatles. And at the last count there were 4,692 families who claimed to have lived in the maisonette above the McCartneys. I wouldn't mind but the McCartneys lived in a bungalow. Terrible isn' it eh, the claims people make. Mind you, y' won't hear me goin' round makin' claims like that, you'll never hear me sayin' that I had a sister whose teacher's brother's milkman was once bitten by a dog that had puppies by a mongrel that lived next door to a woman who'd served in a sweet shop that once sold a lolly ice to Ringo Starr. Won't hear me makin' claims like that. I mean, I don't need to, me bein an ex-member of The Beatles. Alright, alright . . . you might doubt it, but there's proof. And there it is! See.

Bert (*cont'd*)   That's us in the early days. Beatles Mark 1. See me there can y'? That's me at the back. Heh! I'll tell you what I'll do. While I'm waiting for them to arrive, I'll give you my story. I mean everyone's got their story about The Beatles haven't they, but I'll just give you my story – how I saw it. Well, once upon a time when I was fourteen, I joined a group that was to become The Beatles. The first time I ever played in public with them was at a fete in Hunts Cross. I'll never forget it, 'cos two very important things happened to me that day. As well as makin' me debut with Johnny an' the Moondogs, as we were in those days, I spent the interval in a tent with Betty Barnston.

Beatles *packing their gear away. Bert goes into scene.* **Beatles** *all turn and look at him. They start jeering and shouting. . . . .*

John   Where've you been litte Bert . . .

Paul   Dirty Berty's been with Betty Barnston. . . . (*Sounds of total disgust.*)

Bert   I haven't . . . honest . . . Swear on me mother an' cross me heart I never went near her.

George   Oh yes y' did . . . 'cos we saw y' goin' into the tent with her.

John   An' anyone who goes with Betty Barnston . . . gets the mange.

Bert   Ah hey . . . What'll happen to me?

Paul   Depends how far y' went.

Bert   I didn't go *that* far.

John   Did y' touch her knockers?

Bert (*panic stricken*)   Yeah . . . why?

Paul   Which hand?

Bert (*Near to tears, holds out the offending limb. He walks forward with it*)   This one . . . .

They scatter, trying to get away from the 'infected hand'.

John   Keep that away from me.

Paul   Don't come near.

George   You're soiled you are.

John   Dirty Berty . . . unclean . . . unclean.

Bert   What'll happen . . . what'll happen to me?

Paul   There's only one thing to do if you wanna avoid the worst.

John   Only one way to wipe out the curse of Betty Barnston.

Bert   How? Tell me an' I'll do it.

John   You've gorra do everything we say though . . . everything.

George   Or else your hand'll drop off.

John   It's your only chance.

Bert   Just tell me what I've gorra do.

John   When y' go to be tonight, you'll have to cover that arm in treacle . . . .

Paul   An' keep it held up in the air like that all night . . . .

Bert   But I won't be able to go to sleep like that.

George   Do you want the curse of Betty Barnston to be with you for life?

Paul   An' y've got to keep recitin' the 23rd Psalm backwards.

Bert   Okay. (*Comes forward.*) Me mam wasn't half suspicious when she saw me takin' a tin of treacle to bed. I lay there all night with me treacled arm stuck in the air. I must have fell asleep though . . . cos when I woke up in the mornin' the sheets were covered in treacle. (*Pause*) I'll tell y' what though (*holds out hand.*) See . . . it did the trick. (*Goes to* **Beatles**, *Shows them his hand*) Look, look. . . . It's alright me hand's okay. I can still play the guitar.

Paul   Yeah . . . well y' better go'n find another group t' play with.

John   Y' not playin' with us again. . . . Kid.

Bert   Not playing . . . Why?

George (*on way out*)   Cos last week you did something far worse than getting the mange from Betty Barnston . . . something unforgiveable.

Bert   What?

John   Hasn't anybody ever told you you don't play an A minor chord when you're supposed to be playing G7th.

Bert   An' that was it. Me destiny in the space between A minor an' G7th. I couldn't complain though; knowin' three chords, I was obviously musically inferior. Lennon knew four chords. An' George Harrison, he could even play the chord of B Flat. In them days bein' able t' play B Flat meant that y' were a genius. You've gorra stretch y' fingers t' get B Flat . . . But it was worth it if y' made the effort. I've seen fellers, little runts whose lives have been transformed overnight cos they could play B Flat. One day they'd be shrunken, insignificant runts – an' the next day, you'd see them walkin' down the road, proud an' manly like Big John Wayne. You'd step aside, move into the shadow of the gutter; you'd even give a little bow out of respect for the feller who'd mastered the bastard B Flat. (*Pause.*) And that's how a single chord lost me the chance of fame an' fortune. Anyway, I don't think I was capable of the perseverance that was gonna be needed. See, this was in the old days, the late fifties, when the music scene was firmly clenched in London's jewelled grip. London was one big production line, stampin' out instant stars; stars like the fabulous, the very wonderful, the latest teen sensation – Ladies and Gentlemen, *Tiny Tina and The Titular Three* . . .

Tiny Tina and her Group appear. They are three identical looking chicks dressed in fifties gear. They go straight into their song, which should be a good impression of that fifties sound.

Chorus   Ooee boppa ooee boppa
Shang a lang a wah wah . . .

Ooee boppa ooee boppa
Shang a lang a wah wah . . .

It was at the high school dance that
Tony gave me my big chance
He wanted to take me home
But all I could do was moan

(*Spoken*)
Well I love you Tony
But Mommy an' Daddy say,
You're a wild boy,
From the wrong side of town.

Chorus (*cont'd*)   Ooee boppa ooee boppa
Shang a lang a wah wah . . .

Ooee boppa ooee boppa
Shang a lang a wah wah . . . .

(*Sung*)
So Tony rushed out into the night
And jumped upon his motorbike
Before I could stop him he was gone
Roaring up the old M1.

Ooee boppa ooee boppa
Shang a lang a wah wah . . .

Ooee boppa ooee boppa
Shang a lang a wah wah . . .

(*With soft chorus background, the middle section is spoken*)
       Oh Tony! He wouldn't listen,
       His heart was full of pain
       As he drove like a madman into the night
       Which was starting now for to rain,
       He didn't see the frozen food lorry
       As it rolled on down the hill
       Carrying ten ton of fish fingers,
       Bound for a shop in Bexhill . . . .

Chorus   Ooee boppa ooee boppa
       Shang a lang a wah wah . . . .

       Ooee boppa ooee boppa
       Shang a lang a wah wah . . . .

       That lorry, it hit my Tony
       It killed my high school dish,

       (*Spoken*)
       He died on the roadway with his heart full of pain,
       And his face full of Bird's Eye fish . . . .

       (*Sung*)
       Ooee boppa ooee boppa
       Shang a lang a wah wah . . .

       Ooee boppa ooee boppa
       Shang a lang a wah wah . . . .

Bert   Not exactly the sort of music that could inspire an' excite an' give voice to the feelin's of a bright-eyed rockin' youth, as I was in those days. But I didn't have to get my music via London. It was 1959, an' up here in Liverpool, a slight breeze had started to blow; the clubs were openin'. I'd begun workin' by this time – stackin' stockin's in the warehouse of Coggins an' Co. – an' after a day of fillin' boxes, an' stackin' boxes, when it came to the night time, I wanted to be where the action was . . . where the music was strong an' raw.

Behind **Bert** *we see* **Alice** *enter. He goes and joins her.*

Bert (*cont'd*)   Come on . . . let's go.

Alice   Where we goin'? Eh? Where?

Bert   Come on, or we'll be late.

Alice   Where we goin' though?

Bert   Penny Lane Bus Depot.

Alice   What for?

Bert   The Social Club there, there's a group I wanna see.

Alice   What group?

Bert   For Christ's sake; a group called the Silver Beatles.

Alice   OOer: I'm not gonna see them.

Bert   An' why not?

Alice   They're scruffs they are. Real Buckos, the lot of them. Arr Maureen went to see them an' she says they're always sayin' dirty rude things when they're on stage.

Bert   I'm not goin' t'look at them. They play good music.

Alice   They can' even play proper.

Bert   An' how the bloody hell d'you know?

Alice   Arr Maureen says. She says they get all the notes wrong.

Bert   An' how the hell does your Maureen know so much about it?

Alice   She goes t' musical college, that's how. She's very musical arr Maureen is.

Bert   What does she play?

Alice   The organ.

Bert (*looks to the audience*)   There's no answer to that, is there? Now come on . . .

Alice   Why can't we go to the Empire, Bert?

Bert   Because the Silver Beatles aren't on at the Empire.

Alice   Ah . . . . but The Shadows are.

Bert (*insulted*)   The Shadows, The Shadows? If they were playing in our backyard I'd pull the curtains.

Alice   But they do that lovely dance Bert . . . . with their feet . . .

She hums a passage from a Shadows tune and does a bit of the Shadows dance routine.

Bert (*to the audience*)   That was it. The second she started that stupid foot routine I knew arr romance was not destined t' last. (*Back to* **Alice**.) Here. Here's y' bus fare home. . . . I'm off.

Alice   Bert!

Bert (*to the audience*)   It was obvious that my great love affair was gonna be with the music. I left her prattin' about on the pavement an' shot off t' Penny Lane Bus Depot. (*Begins to go off*) Mind you . . . I needn't have worried about gettin' there in time – I arrived before the group did. Their means of transport was what y' might call primitive. (*Off*)

Band begin to play 'Penny Lane'. **Beatles** *straggle on. The character who was playing* **Ringo** *now plays the Stuart Sutcliffe part. They carry battered amps, instruments, microphones etc. and are seen to be hitching.*

Hitching routine which should be a bit of a shambles. Fade song. **Group** *arrive at gig. Cheap and nasty ballroom – effects.*

John   Jesus Christ! (looking around) The sweet smell of success.

Paul   This is the pinnacle.

George   Sunday Night at Penny Lane Bus Depot. I wonder where the dressin' rooms are.

Ringo   Wow! This is really cool isn't it?

John   Who are you?

Ringo (*to audience, lifts his dark glasses*)   I'm Ringo.

John   What do you mean Ringo? It's only 1959. Ringo's not been invented yet.

Ringo   I know that, but 1962 doesn't come round for years and I'm fed up sitting around waiting, so for this section I'm playing the part of Stuart Sutcliffe. I'm your bass player, aren't I?

Paul   Y' can't play though.

Ringo   Well. Neither could he. I'll turn me back on 'em like he did.

George   Look, you know what you want to do. You should flog that guitar and get a set of drums. 'Cos we need a drummer more than a bass player . . .

Bert *enters, approaches* **Beatles**.

Bert   Hia lads . . . alright? You got here then. What time y' startin'?

John   Christ we've been playin' for two years an' we can't even keep a regular drummer. We're getting nowhere.

Bert   Hey . . . I'll sit in on drums if y' like.

John   You . . . on drums.

George   He wouldn't know a drum roll from a cheese roll.

Paul   Hey listen Bert . . . if you wanna do somethin' really useful we've got a job for y'.

Bert   What?

Paul (*handing him a tin hat*)   Put this on an' y' can be arr personal bouncer. They mob us when we start playin'.

Bert (*putting on hat and addressing audience*)   What he means is . . . they're all crappin' themselves in case any of the teds jump on the stage an' stick one on them. (*Pause*) So am I! (*gets into bouncer position*).

John   He's right . . . we're only half a group. Playin' in dumps like this . . . obsolete plug sockets an' a stage made out of orange boxes. We deserve better than this.

Paul   Stop complainin' John. Y've got t' suffer if y' gonna make it really big.

John   I know I should've been blind.

George   What?

John   All the best musicians are blind . . . or crippled.

Paul   Get lost. You're a nutter.

John   Django Reinhart . . . look at the stuff he can play. Shit hot guitarist an' he's only got two fingers on his left hand. When I heard about that I went into the kitchen an' got the carvin' knife out. I couldn't do it though.

They begin to set up.

Bert   It really was a bloody shambles in those days. All the other groups laughed at them 'cos they could never get themselves organized. They even had to make an announcement before every gig they played, to ask if anyone in the audience could lend them three plectrums.

John (*to audience*)   Anyone got three plex?

Bert   They didn't give a monkeys for anyone. They just got up on stage an' did what they wanted.

John (*to audience*)   This one is for all the teddy lads here tonight. It's called, 'Don't put y' hand up me drainpipes Nelly, you'll tickle me nine inch cosh.'

Paul   Yeah . . . an' if y' don't like it . . . don't come here again.

George   We're not comin' again an' we do like it.

Voice 1   Get on with it.

Voice 2   Or get off.

John   I'm tempted to come down there an' stick one on whoever said that. But instead I'll retort with a cuttin' piece of sarcasm. . . . Fuck off.

*And straight into a heavy Beatle rocker. Raw and earthy. During the song **Bert** is stood at front of stage as bouncer, a fight breaks* *out. The fight should extend to the auditorium. It should be like those big ballroom carve-ups from the old days (50s and 60s),* **Beatles** *playing throughout,* **Bert** *is trampled into the ground. Suddenly the music stops, someone has switched off the power,* **Beatles** *look round in amazement as* **Bert** *tidies himself up.* **Ballroom Manager** *enters.*

Manager   Here . . . there's your money. Now pack y' gear an' bugger off.

Paul (*counting the money*)   Hey . . . hold on mister. There's only three quid here.

Manager   So what. . . . Y' didn't play your full spot.

John   Only cos you switched the power off.

Manager   I should bloody think I did an' all. I've never seen owt like it. You're a bloody disgrace the lot of y'. In all my years in show business I've never seen anythin' like it – swearin', smokin' eatin' while y' up on the stage . . . incitin' a bloody riot. By the hell, where d' y' think I would have got to if I'd behaved like that when I was front vocalist in Jimmy Johnstone's band?

John   Where did y' get to, Mister?

Manager   A bloody sight further than you lot'll go. (*Pause.*) D' y' want a bit of good advice? Will y' bloody listen if I tell y' summat?

John   Give us your pearls of wisdom Mr. Manager. . . . We're all ears.

Paul   John, shurrup an' let's listen to him.

Manager   I'm tellin' y' – I've seen some of the best in this business, I know real talent when I come across it. An' I can tell y' one thing . . . you lot haven't got what it takes . . .

Paul   Well what do you suggest we do? What changes would y' suggest?

Manager   Sell y' gear an' get y'self a proper job. You'll only crucify yourselves if y' try an' make it in this business . . . cos y've not got what it takes lads. It might be harsh . . . but it's true.

He goes off. The others sit around, really dejected.

George (*after a long pause*)   I wonder if I could get me old job back.

Bert   Hey . . . if you want, I'll have a word with the Foreman at arr place . . . see if I can get y' in with me.

Paul   Me dad said he could get me in at the cotton exchange, what d' y' think John?

John   About what? Getting' ordinary jobs? On y' bike. D' y' wanna end up like him, like that manager? If you lot wanna get up an' trudge out t' some poxy job every day go 'n do it . . . But don't take me with y' – I'm not stickin' round here . . . I'm goin' places I am; Lennon's not gonna let them tie a lousy job an' a shitty house round his neck. What's wrong with y'? Take no notice of that manager. Him? He's only tryin' to make us jack it in cos he knows we're good . . . an' he never was. Don't listen. We're good, y' know we are. We're good, an we're gonna make it to the top.

They quickly go into a bit of a 'made it' fantasy.

Paul   Yesterday, the Empire Theatre Liverpool was the scene of an incredible display when hundreds of teenage fans queued for tickets to see a show by The Beatles . . .

John   Where are we goin' fellers?

Others   To the top Johnny.

John   Which top fellers?

Others   To the toppermost of the tops Johnny.

Beatles *exit.*

Bert (*calling after them*)   I'd go up there with y' lads but there's a lot of overtime at arr place this week. (*Addresses audience.*) I never saw them to speak to after that. I followed them, I stood an' watched them everywhere . . . but they'd gone miles away from me. They were told that if they could get themselves a drummer they could do some bookin's in Germany. Hamburg, it was, the

city of vice and sin . . . the only place in Europe where the Nuns
carry steel-tipped rosary beads. Corruption blooms on every
pavement in Hamburg. Gangsters, violence, drugs an' sex.

An' while they went off to Germany, I felt the first pangs of envy
begin t' gnaw me plectrum hand, a young lad called Pete Best got
the drummer's job an' the four of them marched forward to take
Hamburg by storm . . .

And we see the **Group** *led by* **Lennon** *who leads them in a
goose-step.*

John   Achtung: right turn.

They all stop and line up and **Lennon** *inspects them.*

Vell, herr comrades, vere are we going to?

Others   To z top, herr kommandant.

Lennon   To vitch top, herr comrades . . .

Others   To z toppermost of z top herr kommandant.

Lennon (*stepping forward and taking a close look at* **Ringo**)   Ah,
so, who is zis leetle fellow vit z ugly nose and eyes like z piss
holes in z snow?

Ringo   It is me, Ringo, Herr Kommandant. But as Ringo . . .

Lennon   Do not tell me; as Ringo has not been invented you are
playing z part of z drummer Best Peter? Yah?

Ringo (*back to ordinary voice*)   Yeah. I wouldn't normally do it
but I need the money.

George   Money, money, money, loads of German marks for us.

Lennon   Germany look out, here we come.

Paul   Wine, women and booze.

George   Lots of lovely money . . .

Pete   Let's go an' grab it.

*They all shout and begin to run off. They are stopped by the
appearance of a 'Hitler'-like immigration officer.*

Hitler   Stop! Not so fast, English Peedles.

George   Hey, look who's there.

Paul   Oh yeah . . . it's er, Christ, what's his name?

George   Yeah . . . that's him. You know him don't y' John, thingyo, that Austrian painter.

John   Beethoven?

Paul   No . . . what's his name?

George   Yeah, that's what I said.

Paul   Hitler!

John   Oh yeah. Hey, I wonder if it's true.

Paul   What?

John   Y' know. (*Whispers*) Go on, ask him.

Pete (*goes up to* **Hitler**)   Hey mister . . . is it true, what my mates say, about you only havin' one thingy? Y' know, like in the song . . .

They all sing, 'Hitler, He's only got one ball, the other is in St George's Hall'.

Hitler (*shrieks*)   Be quiet. It iz you who vill have z loss of z bollocks. You think you are going to sweep z table clean here in vonderful, vonderful Germany. However, Peedles, zat vill not be so.

George   Y've got the name wrong mate. We're the Beatles, not the Peedles . . .

Hitler (*laughing*)   But no, here in Germany you are z Peedles; and do you know what Peedle means in z German language? (*laughs*) It means z male sexual organ, and zat is very right because you look like a real shower of pricks (*laughs*) zat is good, yah? (*laughing*) Peedles . . . pricks (*laughs*). Now pay attention. You might be under z impression zat Germany will provide you vit lots of fame and fortune. Zat is not so. Vile you are in zis country you vill do exactly as ordered . . . zere vill be no fame for you, but zere vill be lots and lots of hard work.

George (*stepping forward*)   No . . . it's not gonna be like that, cos we've come here t' be made famous so that . . .

Hitler   Be quiet!

George   Me mum can get this gold plated bath that she's always wanted . . . see, we're gonna . . .

Hitler (*shrieking*)   Be quiet! From zis place you vill be taken to z Indra club vere you vill play every night for eight hours, vere you vill play until your fingers bleed, your vocal chords vill swell up and your eyes will close up because of z lack of sleep. For a dressing room, ve have provided you vit vat I think you call, z bog. For a hotel room ve have managed to secure z local cinema . . . but you von't be able to sleep zere because z films never stop running . . . (*laughs*) Goot, goot, yah? You vill work until z blood in your veins dries up. You vill slog and slave z whole day long . . . (*becoming very shrieky*) Zere vill be no sleeping like z log, you vill be tired as a dog. (*Shrieking at the top point . . . he reaches the climax with*) IT VILL BE A HARD DAY'S NIGHT.

On sound the roar of Zieg Heil.

Yes, Peedles, you vill wish zat you never had set your foots in z Fatherland . . . you vill be verked into z ground until your balls drop off vit z pain. And zen, oh, zen it vill be my turn to sing.

He sings as he is going off:

> 'Z Peedles, zey have got no balls,
> Zey lost zem,
> In German music halls'

Pretty damn goot yah? (*going off.*) If only z svines voot let me go in for z European Songing Contest . . . (*off*).

George   Pretty bloody far out him, isn't he? I like his haircut though.

Paul   Hey, we could try that on us . . .

John (*producing a comb*)   Adolph's hair style . . .

*He combs his hair down into what we recognize as the Beatle cut. The others, apart from **Pete**, follow suit.*

Pete   Y' can't go around with an haircut like that?

John   Why not?

Pete   'Cos mine won't go like that . . .

Paul   Why not?

Pete   Well it's cos me . . . me follicles are bent . . .

The others, laughing.

John (*jeering*)   He ate too many crusts.

Paul   An' now his bollicles are bent . . .

Pete   Follicles . . . in me head . . . .

John   In his head . . . that's why they call him bollock brain . . .

Pete   Piss off . . . (*he goes out*).

The others follow him, still jeering and taking the piss.

Bert   Old Hitler, he hadn't been jokin'. They were flogged in Germany. But it paid off. When they came back to Liverpool they had more than new hairstyles – havin' to pump out the music night after night had given them a sound that y' could break someone's skull with, it was rock n' roll so thick an' heavy y' could chew it. The first bookin' they played when they got back was the Cavern. I was workin' overtime that night, but as soon as I'd clocked me card, I was on me way, jumped a bus to Dale Street an' didn't stop leggin' it till I reached the top of Mathew Street.

On sound we hear in the background the recording of 'Long Tall Sally'.

And then I heard it. I couldn't move. There was just me and the bouncer . . . an' this other feller, this posh feller (**Bert** *is joined by man in suit and cravat*). An' this wall of sound driftin' up from beneath the street . . . the smell of rotten fruit waftin' out from the warehouses an' this sound, as harsh, as raw as a pneumatic drill cuttin' its way out of the cellar. This wasn't just music, this was history. I knew it, an' he knew it. And he . . . was Brian Epstein.

Bouncer appears at the doorway of the club.

Bouncer   Sorry lads no chance. We're full up.

Bert   Well, well, er . . .

Epstein   Excuse me . . . I'm erm . . . I'm Brian Epstein, from Nems. I'm a record retailer and I'd like to see the er, The Beatles.

Bouncer   Come on in Mr Epstein . . . sorry, I didn't realize it was you there . . . watch the steps now . . . that's right.

Bert   Excuse me, I'm erm . . . Bert McGhee, from Coggins, I'm a stockin' stacker an' I'd like to see the, er, The Beatles as well.

Bouncer (*leaning over him*)   Piss off! We're full.

Bert *shrugs at audience. On sound 'Long Tall Sally', crashes to full volume as we move into* **Epstein**'s *office. As* **Brian** *sits at his desk the sound fades.*

Brian *in his office addresses audience.*

Brian   I went . . . inside the club, and watched them, stood at the back and just watched them. I couldn't take my eyes away from them. You see . . . I hadn't been exactly, well, fed up of life up to this point. But it hadn't been as exciting as I'd hoped. I ran the family record business and I was efficient, I had a few good friends, I was quite well off. I'd always supposed I was as happy and as sad, as contented and as lonely as everybody else. It was certainly bearable . . . life. But it was also a disappointment. I found art much more exciting than life itself.

I'd look at a lovely painting, or listen to music, I'd close my eyes and then it would become exciting, alive, vital; I'd sink into this music, immerse myself in it, live inside it . . . really live. But then, the music would be over, it would always end.

And then, when the music was past, there was only . . . well, life really! And it never lived up to the promise of the music, or the painting. And then, then I saw the boys. And the boys, they were life . . . but not ordinary life, they were life, like the paintings and the music promised. I knew nothing about managing beat groups. But, we had a meeting.

George, **Pete** *and* **John** *enter the office.*

George (*looking around the office*)   Is this your office then, Mr. Epstein?

Brian   Yes.

George   Good, isn't it John?

Brian   You like it then?

George   No, it's rotten.

Brian   Oh.

John   Take no notice of him. We're not used to offices, that's all.

Brian   . . .Yes. Well . . . don't you think we should get started?

Pete   We can't . . . Paul's not here.

Brian   Well where is he? I said two o'clock. Why isn't he here?

George   He said he had to have a bath . . .

Brian   A bath?

George   No a bath.

Brian   But he'll be late!

George   Late . . . but very clean.

Paul *enters, hurried.*

Here he is. Have a good bath, Paul?

Brian   Can we start now please? Thank you . . . thank you. Well, to begin with . . . let me say that if I am to manage you then I'm not going to be a ten percent man . . .

Paul   Great, a manager, for free . . .

Brian   I'll be taking twenty per cent . . .

Protests – Y' what? Jeez! Bloody hell. Let's go etc.

But look, look . . . the percentage isn't the point I'm trying
to make. If I am to join you as a manager then I must become,
in effect, the fifth member of the group. I am not interested
in sitting at a telephone and creaming ten per cent off four people
I never see.

John   Well y' not gonna be able t' come on stage with us . . .
Can't play the telephone, can he?

Brian   I don't mean that . . . but the part I'll be playing backstage
must be as valid as the contributions you will be making out front.
Your talent is your own . . . I think it is something of an
exceptional talent . . . I don't have that talent, but I have a faith, a
faith as strong as iron. I will dedicate myself totally to trying to
make others aware of the talent I recognize.

The four boys go into a huddle.

George   I think he likes us.

John   Listen. No one's ever said anythin' like that about us. I
know we arse around a lot all the time, pretendin' we don't wanna
be taken seriously, but we do . . . I do.

Pete   He sounds like he means what he says. I like him.

Paul   But do you think he's the manager type John?

George   He's posh. What he's got . . . I think they call it class.

John   Alright, he's posh . . . an' he mightn't know much about
managin' groups, but he's serious . . . about us. We need him.
(*Nods*) Yeah?

They turn back to **Brian**.

Paul   Mr. Epstein, you are offerin' to manage us then?

Brian   Yes . . . if you accept certain conditions, conditions which
I think are necessary if you are to become acceptable to a national
public.

Scene freezes. **Bert** *comes forward.*

Bert   The now famous Epstein declaration: no smokin' eatin' or swearin' on stage, no more ad libs till they learn to do them well, no more takin' the piss out the audience, no more scruffy dressin', no more disorganization. And the funny thing was . . .

Back to scene.

Pause as the **Group** *look at each other, before* **John** *turns.*

John   Right, you manage us Brian.

Bert   An' whenever y' saw them after that, y' knew that it wouldn't be long . . . y' knew that you were livin' through an era that was gonna end one day. Brian didn't change their music, he knew that wasn't his territory. But, like he said, if y' wanna go t' the Celebration Ball, y' can't walk in with shit on y' shoes.

Back to scene.

Brian *holds a number of 'Beatle jackets'.*

Brian   Right boys . . . new gear.

They line up. **Pete** *is at the back.* **Brian** *is helping each one into a new jacket.*

Pete   Oh . . . great, look at that for gear. This is it eh lads? We'll go places with Brian . . . No stoppin' us now. John, Paul, George, an' Pete are on the road. Watch out London, America, The World.

The others have put on their jackets. They get out of the way, standing at the back while **Pete** *puts on his jacket.*

Hey . . . what's this . . . (*looks inside*) . . . Hey . . . hey what's this? It says, Ringo Starr.

Brian   Pete . . . the boys have asked me to have a word with you.

Pete   What? Can't they speak t' me themselves?

Brian   Pete . . . they want you out . . . and Ringo in . . . (*pause*) I'm sorry Pete.

Pete   But they can't do this now. . . . They can't throw me out now, now that we're gonna make it . . . I've been through all the shit with them . . . I can't be thrown out now that we're gonna make it.

Brian   I could get you into another group . . . I'd even be prepared to form a group around you Pete . . .

Pete   I don't wanna nother group . . . The Beatles, that's my group.

The band play a very plaintive version of 'With a Little Help From My Friends'. We see **Bert** *turn and approach the others. They turn away, guilty, embarrassed.*

As the song ends, and **Pete** *goes off,* **Bert** *addresses the Audience.*

Bert   That was the only time The Beatles came near to losin' their number one admirer. I couldn't figure out why they'd given him the hatchet; he'd become a good drummer an' he never let them down on a gig. I think his biggest faults were his hair, he couldn't comb it forward, and his popularity. There's nothin' like a bit of good old down to earth jealousy, nothin' like it at all – if y' wanna create a few casualties. Yeah . . . that was the only time they came near to losin' the attention of Bert Mcghee. But, in the end, I had to agree that the new feller they got seemed to fit in well.

Short routine as **Ringo** *finds his place in the* **Group**.

Scene changes to The Punch and Judy Café near Lime Street Station.

So while Brian took their music to the big city, London, they waited. Just waited for the posh feller's triumphant return.

Café music – boredom.

Brian *enters quietly. The* **Beatles** *leap up.*

Paul   When do we go Bri? I'm all packed an' ready.

George   Can I have a sub from me royalties Bri?

Brian   I'm sorry they wouldn't listen.

Ringo   Why?

John   They have t' listen . . . it's their bloody job t' listen.

Brian   You misunderstand John. They listened to the tapes . . . oh they did that. But they couldn't . . . or wouldn't recognize it. I think it's because they've never heard anything like it before. Your sound is new to them . . . they can't cope with originality.

Paul   Did you play all the stuff? Did you play the songs we wrote?

Brian   Everything. I told them that they were experiencing something unique in popular music.

George   An' what did they say?

Brian   They said that if you could manage to spend six months coming up with something like the sound of The Shadows, they might be able to use you as a backing group for one of their solo singers . . .

John   The fuckin' wooden headed bastards!

Brian   John! Language.

John   Well, that's what they are . . . stupid bastards; they just wanna make us into someone else . . . they can piss off.

Paul   Did they all say no, Bri?

Brian   Everyone.

Paul   Well, where do we go next? Haven't we got any other companies t' go to?

Brian   Well that's the one bit of good news . . . I've arranged a meeting with Parlophone.

Paul   Good news? I've never heard of them.

George   I have. That's the label that records those Peter Sellers comedy records . . . an' Jimmy Shand an' His Band.

Ringo   Another well known comedy record.

John   That's just us isn't it? That'll suit us fine. Bunched t'gether with all the freaks.

Brian   Well . . . I admit, it is something of a specialist label.

George   Wasn't it Parlophone who did that L.P. of a vicar from Huyton singin' hymns from under ten feet of water?

Ringo   No, that was H.M.V.

George   His Master's Voice?

Ringo   No, Huyton's Mad Vicar.

Brian   We can't hold out much hope for Parlophone anyway. A friend in the city tells me that there's every chance of the company being bankrupt in twelve months' time. (*pause*) It's just that there's very little left. (*pause*) Do you want me to carry on?

John   Course we do. We're not narked at you. It's just them thick bastards in London Bri. You get down there t' Parlophone.

Ringo   An' if they won't listen, give us a ring an' we'll come down an' duff them up for y'.

Brian   I'll see you all tomorrow. Keep your fingers crossed, but don't order any champagne.

They say tarar to him and all sit down, dejected.

John   I knew I should have been a footballer. It's easier to get out if you're a footballer.

The **Band** *sing the verse of the carol 'In the Bleak Midwinter' as a washer-up methodically clears the café table. Then the carol changes naturally into 'Good Day Sunshine'. We see* **Brian** *enter, with a contract.*

The others run towards him. They throw their arms around and jump up and down. Scene develops into a party in the café, and girls chase the Beatles. This should be a chase that hints of the Beatlemania scenes. The first taste of being 'mobbed'.

Bert   The changes that came about were incredible. See, Liverpool had suddenly become the place t' be – *the* cultural centre of the universe. On the day that the third Beatle record in a row got to number one, every stationers in London sold out of its stock of ordnance survey maps for the North West of England. Liverpool was swamped by an army of contract wavin' record producers. Every street had one. They were everywhere. An' they only had to hear a window cleaner whistlin' Nellie Dean an' they'd have him down the ladder, whip his chamois leather out of his hand an' hundle him into the recordin' studio. Liverpool in 1963, the golden age, it was New Orleans, all over again, it was the Kondike and the Texas Oil Boom all rolled into one.

Announcer (*Voice over*)   Ladies and gentlemen – The Beatles.

Straight into a straight and perfect mime of The Beatles. In order to make this as authentic as possible we must lay screaming over the top of it so that it is the screaming and not the singing, which is at the forefront. This coupled with a studied impression of the Group's characteristics in performance, should give us the impression that it really is The Beatles up there. 'She Loves You' plays.

Enter **Alice** *in full* **Beatle** *gear.*

Alice (*screaming*)   Ooh the Beatles, the Beatles. The Beatles are ace.

Bert   Remember her do you? Alice Flynn. Her who fancied the Shadows.

Alice   The Shadows? Shadows? If they were playing in my back yard I'd pull the curtains.

Bert   And that was it! I asked her back to the flat . . . for coffee! And while she was makin' it she spoke to me . . .

Alice (*she talks fast and very Scouse*)   An' y' know my mate Linda from work ah, well she had this party, her twenty first it was an' Paul McCartney come to it an', I nearly had an' orgasm when she told me that bit, an' while he was there she offered him this piece of chicken but he only took one bite and left it. But Linda kept the piece of chicken an' put it on the dressin' table in her room, y' know as a souvenir like, an' after a week it began t' smell a bit, an' after two weeks it began t' smell a lot, an' after three weeks it stunk the whole house out, the smell of chicken flesh, slowly rottin, an' soon the whole road was smellin' of it, so her dad said he was gonna throw it away, but my mate Linda locked herself in the bedroom – just her an' the stinkin' chicken – an she wouldn't come out or open the door t' no-one an' after a week her dad couldn't get no answer from her so he called the police in an' they broke the door down an' guess what they found?

Bert (*with poetic conviction*)   What?

Alice   Linda . . . lyin' there dead, breast to breast with Paul McCartney's chicken . . . I thought it was dead poetic, that bit. Here's yer coffee . . . Hey; you haven't said you liked me gear yet.

Bert   What?

Alice   The gear I'm wearin' . . . me Beatle Boots, me Beatle Skirt, me Fab Ringo lipstick . . . me Beatle ba . . . an' me Beatle coat.

Bert *feels her Beatle skirt.*

Alice   Y' wouldn't be tryin' to seduce me would y'?

Bert   Depends.

Alice   On what?

Bert   Me chances of success.

Alice   An' what d' y' reckon those are?

Bert   I dunno. I haven't tried to find out yet.

Alice   Well y' better get a move on hadn't y'.

Bert (*to audience*)   An' that was it . . . in no time at all we were making music in me little Beatle bed.

We hear 'She Loves You' on record.

She did love me an' all . . . head over heels she was. But me? My mind was on other things. You see once upon a time there'd only been two ways of escape from this city – go t' sea or get signed by a football team. But now another lifeline had been thrown . . . music. It suddenly hit me. I was on me way t' work one mornin' an I stopped, an' thought for a minute. Gerry and the Pacemakers, The

Searchers, The Big Three, The Fourmost, The Swinging Blue Jeans
– there was everyone else making it while I was still stackin' boxes
of stockin's for Coggins and Co. The Pied Piper had come an' here
was me hobblin' about like the kid on crutches. I stopped outside
this record shop in Whitmore Street, I looked up an' saw the whole
window display had been given over to a ten foot picture of The
Beatles.

We see this on screen.

I stood an' looked at them, ten foot high an' bathed in colour, the
lads I used to play with an' I thought this is it Bert, if you don't
move now you're buggered. Hey I might have done it an' all if
Alice hadn't paid me a visit one morning.

Alice (*anxious*)   Bert . . . Bert . . . I've got t' talk to y'.

Bert   But I'm late for work love.

Alice   Can't y' spare a minute?

Bert   What is it?

Alice   I'm pregnant.

Bert (*as the picture of the* **Beatles** *slowly fades*)   How d' y' know?

Alice   A man on a flamin' pie appeared at the window and said
from this day forward you are pregnant . . . with a capital P.

Bert   Yeah, I know the one, he came to my window an' said
you're knackered with a capital F. (*To audience*) An' so, for me,
that was it. The songs that had always been in me head just started
t' crumble n' fall t' bits, the notes seized up an' the tunes wouldn't
play. I suppose I could have tried to con me way out of it – but the
only words that came out were (*to* **Alice**) we better get married
then.

Alice   Thank you Bert.

Alice *exits.*

An' we did. The gravy train had come an' gone, an' I'd been left
standin' at the platform with me luggage all around me. I settled

down with Alice an' a Coronation Street that ran from one end of arr road to the far side of infinity. An' sometimes I'd open a paper or switch on the telly an' they'd be there, John, Paul, George and Ringo. An' I'd say 'Go on there lads, give us a song, let's have a good one just for Bert.'

Band play 'Long and Winding Road.'

End of Act One.

Act Two

*The Dressing Room. Band sing a cut down version of 'Carry That Weight/You Never Give Me Your Money'. We see a young freaky Journalist (**Platt**) enter the dressing room. He looks around, finds a glass and pours himself a glass of whisky, sits down. Song fades.*
Beatles *burst into the room, they are excited, exhilarated because their rehearsal is going well. They should be talking as they enter, ad lib on theme, 'yeah, great, really tight sound, an' you've got t' keep that bass goin' right hard until the end, thud, thud, thud . . .'*
Platt *jumps up.*

Paul   Sorry no-one allowed.

Platt   Jesus . . . I knew it, I knew I was right.

Paul   I don't know who let you in, but no-one's allowed this side of the dressing room door.

Platt   Wow . . . your actual Beatle reunion . . .

George   Look, I don't know if you've got the picture yet . . .

Ringo   Out . . . go on, split will y'?

Platt   Ah, come on . . . Jesus, I've spent two days tryin' to track down this event.

John   Well now y've found it fuck off.

Platt (*holding up his hands*)   Okay, okay . . . I get the picture, no need to be like that. I'm going, I've got my story . . .

Makes for the door. **Paul** *stops him, stands in his way.*

Paul   You from the papers?

Platt   *Orchid.* The People's Paper.

George   Trust the honest underground to poke its head through the door.

Ringo   Christ. I was worried for a minute there. But if it's underground we're okay. It takes 'em six months t' set up a page of type. No danger.

Platt   Christ almighty, you don't think I'm keepin' this for me own paper, this is news, it'll be on the streets by this evening.

John (*getting angry. Moves across to him, slightly threatening*) Look . . . I don't know how much of this you've managed to suss out but get it straight, we are playin' a concert tonight, just a quiet concert an' no hustler from a second rate students' gossip column is gonna screw it up. No one gets to know about this gig till we've played it an' gone. Right?

Platt (*undeterred*)   Wrong.

John (*beginning to go for him,* **Paul** *stepping in*)   What d' y' mean wrong?

Ringo   Ask him how much it'll cost t' keep his mouth shut.

Paul   Well?

Platt   Yeah?

Paul   How much?

Platt (*laughs*)   Is that the usual procedure, buying people off? (*laughs*) Jesus, I'll bet you bought a lot of silence in your time.

Paul   Look, we don't wanna make a big thing of this do we? Tonight we wanna do a concert, just a small thing with us and an audience. We don't want press an' camera . . . right?

George   An' we don't mind payin' a little bit t' protect ourselves from all the hassle, so how much?

John   What about a nice holiday in the sun? Or a lovely little motor car, it's your lucky day sonny.

Platt   You think you can patronize anyone don't you?

John   Listen, I don't give a fuck what you think. This is a business arrangement. Tell who you like after we've played the gig, it won't matter to us then.

Platt   And what about all the people?

John   The what?

Platt   People have a right to see you lot. You owe it to the people . . .

Ringo   Owe them what for Christ's sake?

Platt (*becoming just a little angry himself*)   The right to see you, to read about you, to switch on the TV and look at you. This should be the biggest event of a decade; what right have you got to keep it away from the people who made you?

John (*in despair*)   Oh sweet Jesus. Get him out, get rid of him. I've had enough of peoples' champions.

Platt   Look, Lennon, I was one of the millions who made you, I was one of those who ran around buyin' Beatle records an' Beatle boots, my pennies went towards makin' you millionaires. And okay, nobody minded that, nobody minded you bastards making your fortunes; but you've got to pay for all that. We made you. Just who do you think you are, trying to play a concert to a handful of people? We should all know about this, the whole world and I am going to tell them. You are public property.

Pause.

Ringo   I think we should duff him up.

Pause.

Paul   Look, what's your name?

Platt   Platt, Sam Platt.

Paul   Well look Sam . . .

John   For Christ's sake Paul. Bugger it. Okay, we won't play the gig. That'd make a good story for him wouldn't it?

Paul   No, hold on John, will you? Listen, Sam. You want everyone to hear about this?

Platt   Okay that's fair enough. We'll let them hear about it. We'll give you an interview, an exclusive, here and now . . .

John   Oh Jesus.

Paul   . . . as long as you agree to hold the story till after the gig. Does that suit you?

Platt   An interview isn't news.

Paul   It might not be news but it would make you into news.

Platt   Meaning what?

Paul   Well look. Just think what you could do with an exclusive interview with The Beatles – they'll pay a fortune for it in the States, syndicate it from coast to coast. And you'll be the man who interviewed The Beatles.

Pause.

Platt   Would you sign a declaration saying it was an authentic interview?

Paul   Of course.

Platt   You'll answer all my questions?

Paul   Anything you want to know.

Platt   ALRIGHT . . . I'LL AGREE.

John (*quietly*)   They all have a price.

Paul   Are we all agreed on that then?

George   If we wanna play we'll have to be, won't we?

Paul   John, what do you think?

John   I think it's turning shitty again.

Platt (*getting his cassette fixed up*)   I haven't got a brief so we'll just have to work it as it comes. Okay, okay. Let's start.

John   Fire away Beaverbrook.

Platt   Let's erm . . . let's start with this one: why did The Beatles break up? (*The* **Group** *look at each other. Long pause.*)

Ringo   It was an accident – someone dropped them.

Band play one chorus of 'Carry That Weight'.

Bert   Been having a drink 'av y'? Been down the interval bar? They're very good, very good to me they are. They send me a pint round you know. Mind you – terrible pint. This is the Guinness. Anyway here I am back in Liverpool. No sign of them yet but I'm keeping me eyes open just in case, and while I'm waiting this kid comes up to me.

Kid   Hey mister can you play that banjo eh, can y' eh?

Bert   What?

Kid   I thought y' couldn't.

Bert   Go 'n find a car t' rob.

Kid   Just a poser aren't y'?

Bert   Beat it will y'. Go 'n play with a few of y' dad's razor blades.

Kid   I'll bet y' can't play 'Rocket' on it, or 'Remember Me This Way' by Gary Glitter.

Bert   Gary Glitter, shurrup. You're turnin' me ale sour. (*To audience*) That's what's wrong with the kids t'day, they're all sufferin' from musical malnutrition. Forget Gary Glitter kid.

Kid   He's ace!

Bert   Ace? Y' don't know what y' talkin' about. Ten years ago in this city there was a group goin' that were ace. We knew the real meanin' of the word ace when they were here.

Kid   What group was that then?

Bert   What group? You're jokin', I'm talkin' about The Beatles lad, The Beatles.

Kid   I think I've heard me dad talk about them.

Bert *splutters out half his ale.*

He played a record of theirs once . . . they copy David Cassidy don't they?

Bert   David Cassidy? Go on . . . get lost before I kick y' up the arse.

Goes to run at him so that the **Kid** *moves off some distance.*

Kid   I told y' y.' couldn't play it. You wouldn't know a crochet from a bloody hatchet.

He goes off singing whatever song is most popular with the teenage/ juvenile market during the show's run. **Bert** *comes back in front on.*

Bert   Try an' talk music t' kids today, they don't know what y' on about. See, what they don't realize these days is that comparisons are hopeless. The Beatles conquered everywhere, there wasn't a house, a town, a country that wasn't in some way affected by The Beatles. It was so bloody vast you can't compare it with nothing can you? The Beatles made the world go crazy.

And we should go into a scene which bears out **Bert***'s words. It should be a college scene, a manufactured blitz on the mind of the audience in order to let them experience some of the chaotic madness which was caused by and which surrounded The Beatles. Words alone are not enough. The scene should be put together so that it contains the same sort of crazy circus/nightmare quality of some of the songs. A medley of the tunes from early Beatle hits. The endless 'Number 9, Number 9, Number 9' chant from the white album should be at the fore. On the screen we should see Beatlemania newsreel – run it backwards, forwards, slow, fast, distort it, anything to add to the sense of madness. In the middle of this we should see The Beatles, smiling as cameras flash, like Pavlov's Dogs. On top of it we hear the straight facts, as follows:*

FACT: There are a quarter of a million orders for the next Beatle single – it is not yet written. 'She Loves You' has advance orders totalling half a million. Fifteen million viewers watch Palladium show starring, The Beatles. In one week a pop group hits the front page of every national newspaper in Britain – The Beatles. In September, 1963, the top selling E.P., L.P. and single by The Beatles. The highest advance ever for an L.P. record – it is by The Beatles. Throughout the country, young teenage boys are refused permission to enter schools because they wear hairstyles like the Beatles. In Plymouth, police turn on hoses to control fans of The

Beatles. In one week there are seven singles in the top twenty, by
The Beatles. One hundred thousand people buy tickets for a
Christmas show by The Beatles. Queen's plane is delayed at airport
due to reception to welcome The Beatles. Viscount Montgomery
wants to meet The Beatles. G.P.O. says it deals with twelve and a
half thousand letters a day for The Beatles. Royal Variety
Performance – members of Royal Family and twenty-six million
TV viewers to watch The Beatles. The Beatles. The Beatles.

Bert   An' when it got to be as big as that, there was no stoppin'
them . . . there was no stopping any of them. Suddenly everyone
had a link with Liverpool, all the top families hired butlers with
Liverpool accents, a slave trade started, dealing in authentic
Liverpool dockers. Even groups who'd been around for years
suddenly claimed they'd been born and bred on the banks of
the Mersey. It was disgustin'. I mean would y' take a look at this
lot. Ladies and Gentlemen . . . introducing the very fabulous,
the truly gear . . . the super scouse tones of Bootle Betty and the
Big Tits.

*The GIRLS come on, they are recognizable as the GIRLS who
were once Tiny Tina and her group, but now they wear 'Beatled'
black wigs etc. They should exaggerate the accent to the point
of grossness.*

Ooee whacker ooee whacker scouse a louse a Mersey

Chorus   Ooee whacker ooee whacker scouse a louse a Mersey
Ooee whacker ooee whacker scouse a louse a Mersey

It was at dis fazakerly dance
Dat I met Tommy Vance
He wanted t' take me outside
Just for a little ride . . . (so I said)
(*Spoken*) Well I think y' ace and gear Tommy

But me Mum an' Dad say
Y' nottn but a soddin' layabout
Of the wrong denomination at that!

Ooee whacker ooee whacker scouse a louse a Mersey

Bert (*dispersing them*)   Go on . . . get off. Y' should be locked up, the lot of y's. Beat it. (*to audience*) An' while the parasites were suckin' an' bitin' the lads themselves just kept goin' an' every step got bigger and bigger. They couldn't play the clubs anymore, they weren't large enough to hold the hundreds of thousands of besotted Beatlemaniacs. It was the theatres now, up and down the country theatres all the time, the flash of bulbs an' the one minute call, the tinglin' nerves, the joy of it all . . . God! It must have been great!

Dressing room. Slide showing London.
Beatles *preparing for a performance.*
Brian *enters.*

Brian   Everything okay Boys? (*general 'yes's' from* **Beatles**) Right boys . . . I'm goin' out front now, and remember, this is London. The press will be watching you like hawks. If you must do any ad libbing, think about it first. Don't say anything which they might be able to turn against us. Okay John?

John   Don't worry. I'm not gonna insult anyone. I promise I'll be a good little Beatle.

Brian   Thanks. (*Smiles.*) Well . . . good luck.

George   I suppose I better go an' tune my guitar. (*Exit.*)

Ringo   I suppose I better go an' tune my sticks. (*Exit.*)

Paul (*getting up*)   You coming John?

John   I'm gonna have another few drinks.

Paul   Hey, take it easy will you? We're not playing at Litherland Town Hall now y' know. Like Brian said, this is London.

John   An' for God's sake, what difference does that make?

Paul   Oh . . . don't start that. You're famous man. Didn't you realize it's make a difference.

John   I'm famous . . . oh yeah, Mother I'm famous. Look at me now. I'm free Mother. I'm free an' that means I can't go out (the fans might crush me), now I can't even get pissed. Oh yeah, it's great bein famous all over the place isn't it?

Paul   You go on that stage pissed and by tomorrow afternoon you'll be free alright. People won't even give you a second look if you play this one wrong.

John   Why is everyone worryin' about me for fuck's sake? Don't worry Pauly . . . bad John's not gonna let y' little Beatles down. I mean, if I'm an embarrassment to y', get someone else to . . .

Paul   Don't be fuckin' stupid. (*Pause.*) Look . . . look I'm sorry John . . . it's just y' know . . .

John   I know. I'm crappin' meself as well. I dunno why, as soon as the screamin' starts that's it, no-one hears us anyway. We might just as well go out and sing shit.

Paul   Let's go on and try it for a laugh. (**John** *and* **Paul** *sing: 'She loves you shit shit shit, she loves you . . . '*)

Ringo *enters.*

Ringo   Hey.

Paul/John   What?

Ringo   Have y' seen the corridor?

John   No. What's the matter?

Ringo   It's full of . . . there's loads of . . . wheelchairs, people in wheelchairs out there.

John   Doin' what?

Ringo   Waitin' for us.

Paul   What for?

Ringo   They wanna meet us.

John   The bloody dressin' room's supposed t' be kept clear before a show. (*Becoming angry*) Does Brian know about this?

Ringo   There's this blind feller in there talkin' t' George, tellin' him that he'd been t' Lourdes an' that hadn't done no good . . .

Theatre **Manager** *enters.*

Manager   Everything okay boys?

John   No, it's not. Just come here, will y'?

Manager (*coming in*)   What's the matter?

John   Whose idea was it to put a pile of cripples in our dressing room?

Ringo   An' someone says we're supposed t' be photographed with them.

Manager   That's right. I was approached by some people and so I thought it would be, well, alright.

John   Well it's not.

Manager   And whyever not? God, what harm will it do? It's not asking a great deal of your time.

Ringo   Listen man, there's one of them in there talking about Lourdes an' us in the same breath.

Manager   I know that, what's wrong with that? Some of them do think that you might be able to, well . . . affect them.

John (*disgusted*)   Cure them?

Manager   Yes. And personally I think you could at least give them the benefit of trying . . . surely it's not . . .

Paul (*incredulous*)   For Christ's sake man, we're just four fellers in a group.

John   Get out there an' get rid of them.

Manager   Look, I know it sounds ludicrous but they think . . .

John   Get out there an' tell them t' stop thinkin'.

Manager   Now listen to me. What harm is it going to do? They asked to be brought here – they're not going to blame you if it doesn't work. (*Pause*) Now come on boys – you've not been in this business long – you probably fail to see the publicity potential of something like this.

John (*moves threateningly to him*)   I could really fuckin' hit you mister.

Manager (*backing away*)   Don't you dare come near me . . .

Paul (*getting in quick*)   Look . . . We've got nothing against handicapped people – we're sorry man, we are sorry. But we're just four fellers . . . we're not goin' through a masquerade like that.

John   Publicity potential? I wanna spew.

During the above, **Brian** *enters with* **George**.

Brian   What in the hell's going on? Why are all those people in the corridor?

Manager   Ah, Mr Epstein, I was just . . .

Brian   Look at the time boys, you're not even ready yet. Come on.

Manager   Mr Epstein . . . I've been trying to explain . . . There are some people in the corridor, they want to meet The Beatles – doesn't everyone – and I said that one or two press photographers could . . .

Brian   You had no right to do that . . .

Manager   But . . .

Brian   No right whatsoever. (*Pause.*)

Manager   It might have slipped your notice but I am the manager of this theatre.

Brian   But you are *not* the manager of this group. I am. And I will not tolerate anything being done without my consent. In thirty minutes' time this group is going out on stage to play a very important engagement. They need rest before an engagement of this nature.

Manager   But can't they. . . .?

Brian   Absolutely not.

Pause.

Manager   Alright. Alright Mr Epstein, have it your own way. But I have invited the press to come along and a headline which reads 'Beatles snub handicapped people' might not read too well for you. Good luck. (*Off*.)

John   I don't care what the papers say.

Ringo   Interferin' bastard.

Paul   What do we do though?

Pause.

Brian   I'm terribly sorry about this . . . but I'm afraid he has got us in a spot.

Paul   I know he has.

Ringo   Come on . . . let's go say hello to the people.

George   Oh Ritchie.

John   I'm not doin' it.

Paul   Look John, none of us want to do it, but Brian's right – we're cornered.

Brian   You three go out to them, please. I'll talk to John.

They go off.

John   I don't care what y' say Bri.

Pause.

Brian   John . . . we've been outmanoeuvred. It's my fault, I'm totally responsible for having allowed you to be forced into this position.

John   But did you hear what he was saying Bri? They expect us t' cure them. They're waitin' for Gods to walk through the door, Gods to come in an' make miracles happen. For Christ's sake how are those poor bastards gonna feel when they just see four ordinary fellers who can't cure anythin'?

Brian   I do understand John . . . But the public do think of you as four gods. (*Pause.*) Have you thought about what happens if you won't go in. It's just the thing the papers have been waiting for; it's their chance to crush us. Remember how they ignored us in the early days – we weren't from London, they didn't want to know. They'll rip us to pieces if we give them this one. (*Pause*) It's entirely up to you John; I won't try and force you, I never have and I never will do that. But you've got to decide whether you want to wake up as a Beatle or as John Lennon in the morning. If you want to go on, you've got to walk through this door.

The Band play 'Help', a version slowed down to begin with as Brian exits and John takes a long drink of whiskey. As the drums break in John slams down his drink and exits.

On screen newsreel of departure for America. Thousands of waving fans. 'Help' gradually over and with screams more and more. During all this the group and Brian enter carrying travelling bags. They wave to the fans. Screaming drops in level as we hear a radio announcer.

Announcer   This is station W.C.M. Beatle, reporting live from Kennedy International Beatle airport which at present resembles a packed baseball arena: over ten thousand fans have invaded the airport to await the arrival of the boys themselves, The Beatles (cheers from inside the plane) At the moment it's six thirty Beatle time, the temperature is 32 Beatle degrees and a slight touch of Beatle snow is beginning to fall. It is now only a matter of minutes before the Beatles plane touches down on the Beatle runway. America waits . . .

Slide changes to British Embassy in U.S. On sound Boston Pops version of 'And I Love Her'. Over this we hear the **Ambassador** *and* **Wife** *at breakfast, on tape.*

Ambassador   Darling we're having a reception at the Embassy this evening.

Wife   Oh . . . good. Who for?

Ambassador   Ahm . . . the ahm . . . what are they called now? Let me see that paper . . . Ah, yes, The Beatles.

Wife   The who?

Ambassador   No . . . The Beatles.

Wife (*putting her toast down*)   And what may I ask, are The Beatles?

Ambassador   A pop group darling.

Wife   Oh no. This really is the very end!

Ambassador   Yes. I know.

Wife   You don't mean . . . surely you can't be serious a pop group . . . at the Embassy.

Ambassador   I'm afraid so.

Wife   But it's preposterous. Why in the name of heaven should there be a reception to honour a pop group?

Ambassador   Because darling, for this group the merchandising contracts alone amount to (*very slowly spelling it out for her*), one hundred and twenty five million dollars.

Wife   I'll order the champagne.

Guests *at party. Very cocktail. An* **Aide** *announces:*

Aide   Ladies and Gentlemen. The Beatles.

Wife (*conducting*)   Ready guests, one, two, three . . .

And the **Guests** *break into song:*

Guests   'Let us all clap and cheer
            Because The Beatles are here
            And we'd just like to say
            We think you are gear.'

All the **Guests** *stand expectantly looking towards the* **Group**.
Waiting for a reaction. The **Group** *just smile back at them.*

John (*under his breath, still smiling*)   Fuck this, I'm goin' back to the hotel.

Paul (*claps*)   Very good that. (*To the* **Guests**.)

And suddenly the party springs into 'LIFE'.

Ambassador   Do come and take a drink. (*He whisks off three and leaves* **John** *who is immediately cornered by a woman.*)

Woman   Aren't you having a drink? Oh deary dear, I did say to the Ambassador that he should have ordered some beer. I said you wouldn't like any of the cocktails. That's what is so incredibly boring about working class people, they're so damn conservative, don't you think? (*No answer.*) Oh, really? Which one are you?

John   The one with the big cock.

Woman   Pardon?

John   The one with the big clock.

Woman   Is that a joke?

John   It's not to the women who've seen it.

Woman   Your clock?

John   No, me cock.

Woman   I'm sure I don't know what you're talking about at all.

John   You're not likely t' find out either.

Ambassador's **Wife** *approaches* **Ringo**.

Wife   I'm so pleased you could come. Aren't you the percussionist in the combo?

Ringo   Me? No. I'm just the drummer in the group.

She laughs, not because of anything she has heard but because she's been told that this mob are supposed to be entertainingly comical.

Wife   That's what I do like about working class humour, it's so primitive in presentation. Almost a verbal reconstruction of the paintings by the Primitives; don't you think?

Ringo   That depends on whether you subscribe to the theory that the form of humour under discussion is a humour rooted essentially in an oral rather than literary tradition. The basic an' fundamental essence of workin' class humour is its brutal disregard of pretension as displayed by its great reliance upon deflation even when it's required to be self-effacing. (*Pause*) Don y' think?

Wife (*moving away*)   Yes . . . well if you'll just erm . . . yes.

She goes off and **Ringo** *smiles to himself sort of. 'That's one up the nose for you,' type of gesture.*

Paul *signing. A sexy deb chick has cornered* **George**.

Deb   Would you like to drive me home? Now?

George   Nah. The ale's not run out yet has it? Anyway, I didn't bring me car.

Deb   I've got the Aston Martin outside.

George   I thought y' would have.

Deb   Why don't you get the keys?

George   To tell the truth, I don't know where they are love.

The **Deb** *takes out keys and drops them down her cleavage.*
George *looks down as though he's looking down a well.*

(*Looking back up at her*) D' you suffer from nose bleeds? Your mum should have told y'. Y've got to put them down y' back, the keys. It doesn't stop the bleedin' if y' put them down the front.

Deb   Why don't we go next door? It's quiet . . . you can retrieve them for me.

George   I used to have terrible nosebleeds meself. I tried everythin' to stop them but nothing'd work.

Deb   I said to Marilyn – I said they must get tired of all these little sluts. I wonder what one of them could do with a real woman?

George   Keys down me back, ice packs on me head, pinchin' the bridge of me nose . . .

Deb   A real woman, who could appreciate and savour the rough, callous, common hands.

George   But me mum come up with this idea of whittlin' down two corks an' shovin' one up each nostril, an' it worked . . .

Deb   Take me home . . . be my gamekeeper, do things to me . . .

George   It meant that all the thick globs of blood kept slidin' down me throat . . . but it did the trick.

George   You can do it to me . . . we can even do it with the lights off . . . you'll like that won't you?

George (*pause*)   Listen love. We've got a very busy day tomorrer an' our manager he doesn't like it if we . . . y' know?

Deb   What?

George   Y' know. I mean I hate refusin' an' . . .

Deb   Refusing? Refusing what?

George   Well, t' take you home.

Deb   Take me home? You must be out of your mind love. How dare you make such suggestions to me (*going off*). Darling. . . . Just wait till I tell you. . . .

A man, an **Aide**, *goes over and grabs* **John**'*s arm.*

Aide   Come over here.

John (*quietly*)   Get off.

Aide (*trying to pull him*)   Come over here!

John (*shaking free*)   Take your hands off me.

Aide   Look, will you come here? Somebody wants to speak to you.

From another part of the room we hear **Ringo** *shouting.*

Ringo   Gerrof will y'?

Deb 2   I've got it . . . I've got it. Look, a piece of his hair.

She has taken a pair of scissors and cut a piece of hair off **Ringo**. *She holds it for all to see. They applaud.*

John (*springs across, grabs the scissors and throws them down*)
You mindless bitch! Cow!

Ringo   You could have had me ear there.

Ambassador   . . . I say.

John   An' you. The lot of you. We've not come here to be treated
like shit.

Wife   Charming. I'm quite aware that they're supposed to be
show business people and all that, but surely that's slightly beyond
the bounds of decency.

Ambasssdor (*to his* **Wife**)   My God, even that little poet chappy
from Wales was never as bad as that. (*Trying to deflate the
situation*) Now chaps – is this really the way to behave when
you're invited . . .

Paul   Invited? The only reason we were 'invited' is because we're
famous. You didn't invite four people – you expected performin'
chimpanzees.

George   You just brought us here because it's good publicity for
your British Bloody Embassy.

John   Well, I'm not puttin' up with it. I'm goin'. I'm not standin'
round here waitin' t' be insulted by a shower of jumped up middle
class bitches an' bastards who wouldn't give us the air to breathe if
it was left up to them.

Ambassador   Oh dear . . .

John   Come on, we're going.

Beatles *storm out.*

Ambassador   Let me show you the buffet.

The party dissolves.

The **Beatles** *re-appear.*

Ringo   What do we do if they tell the papers?

John   We'll do nothin'.

Pause.

Ringo   Yeah. I suppose I'd be glad . . . in a way. It might be a good thing if they finished us off.

George   I'm pissed off with it all anyway. It's all turned out crappy. Y' can't even enjoy it when y' get out on stage; nobody can hear y' playin' an' y' crappin' y'self in case some maniac takes a pot shot at y'.

Ringo   Sod them. If the papers destroy us, they might be doin' us a favour.

John   The papers won't touch us.

Paul   If the Embassy told every reporter on the tour about it, it still wouldn't matter.

John   Right. If they'd have wanted to kill The Beatles off they could have done it by now – we've given them enough opportunity. But who's gonna mention the bribes, the orgies, the dealin' an' all the hype? For Christ's sake, if there's no Beatles then there's no more Beatle piss ups, no more Beatle hand outs, no Beatle Whores. Man, when we hit town they love it – it's Rome. We can screw women, we can drop pills, we can piss in the middle of the street an' they'll still turn it into a nice clean time with The Fab Four. They don't wanna see us, they just wanna see the myth. They don't even wanna hear the music when we get out there. (*Pause*) We were the best live band ever to walk out on a stage.

Paul   We still are. When we put it together we can knock the leaves off the trees.

George   In a recordin' studio yeah. But what about on the stage?

Ringo   All we ever play is a twenty-five minute session, the same songs every night. We used t' blast away for hours on end. Why doesn't someone have a go at us an' say that the live music we're playin' now is crap . . . 'cos it is.

John   But they won't say anythin', they want us t' go on forever. There's sweet pickin's for everyone when you're as popular as Jesus Christ.

On **Lennon***'s line about Jesus we hear a very ominous sustained chord from the guitar.*

Ambassador   Really put your foot in it now eh. Chaps?

We hear the following voices on sound.

Redneck   Now we gonna give you big headed Limey bastards one helluva good ol' whuppin', yes sir.

Man   I said t' my kids. I said get them filthy records outta this house. And my kids said don't worry poppa, we're gonna burn them on a bonfire.

Hysterical Woman   You would not make light of my Jesus if you had borne the cross that my Jesus had to bear.

Businessman   Y' stooped gooks Beatles. What d' y' wanna go say a thing like that for? For Chrissakes, we had another ten million to make outta youse guys.

The **Band** *sing just the two opening lines of 'Golden Slumbers', unaccompanied.*

Brian's *voice (On tape)*   Boys, you don't have to tolerate this. Do you want to go on being Beatles?

John   What else is there for me if I'm not a Beatle. It's humiliation. It's degrading. But there's not much left if you're not a Beatle. What should I do Brian?

Distorted ominous feedback effects laid over the above.

The **Band** *again sing the two opening lines of 'Golden Slumbers', unaccompanied.*

Brian's *voice.*

If you want to go on, you must say you didn't mean what you said about Jesus.

The **Band** *now sing the chorus line as follows, repetitive, building in power and meaning.*

Band   Boy you've got to carry that weight
　　Carry that weight a long time

Boy you've got to carry that weight
Carry that weight a long time
Carry that weight a long time.

This is broken by **Lennon** *shouting.*

John   I didn't mean it.

*Suddenly immediately the entire scene changes, lights full up,
people rushing on waving flags, throwing ticker tape and singing
'We Love You Beatles' by The Carefrees.*

Cheers and shouts, The **Beatles** *are covered in streamers and
bunting. As the singing fades,* **Bert** *enters.*

Bert   I mean, it was okay for me – I'd never been anywhere
anyway – when I looked up at the sky, the stars still twinkled and
shone – but them – they'd been up there to the top of the universe
and they found that the stars were made of tinsel and the moon was
made of sand. I was in work one day an' I picked up a paper – 'No
more tourin' for The Beatles' – it knocked me back a bit that; I'd
always hoped that I might see them again one day.

Lights have faded on The **Beatles** *by now as* **Brian** *reappears.*

But no – that side of it was over. I knew it – and the Posh feller
knew it as well.

Brian   I knew they were right to give up touring. The only
records left to break were ones which they had created. In the past
there had been many first times to keep them going on. The first
times were exciting; the first time you are trapped in a hotel
besieged by thousands of fans is a joyous, dizzy moment. The first
time you have a member of the aristocracy crying over the phone,
pleading with you to attend her party is touching, elevating. The
first time you make a million pounds is worth celebrating. (*Pause*)
But first times are pinnacles . . . endings, not beginnings. Nobody
could expect them to continue pitching themselves into madness. I
knew they were right, but I also knew that I did not want to lose
my Beatles. (*Pause*) I had a large empire I had that . . . but I didn't
want it. I wanted, most of all, to be with them – arranging the tour,
slotting times and dates into place, balancing engagements, caring

for them, protecting them. Brian they'd say, Brian come and sort this one out. Hey Brian, like this suit Bri? Will it be alright Brian? Get us out of this one Brian, come and help us with this Bri, will it be alright Bri? (*Pause*) No more. No Beatles to look after now . . . No Paul or John, or George or Ringo.

Pause.

You see . . . the Sergeant had appeared.

The character **Sergeant** *appears on slide.*

And I knew that after five glorious years of wearing the stripes I was suddenly a private again. I went back to the office – the office that ticked over nicely whether I was there or not – and the Sergeant told them what to wear. The Sergeant suggested the words in the song. The Sergeant lifted his finger . . . and pointed out the way to go.

Brian *off.*

The **Band** *play 'Lucy in the Sky with Diamonds'. During it* **Beatles** *enter in Pepper Gear, with droopy moustaches.*

During the above, they stand in a row, spaced out, transfixed, hallucinated. The music continues through the scene.

Ringo   Hey . . . is this what y' call 'turnin' on'?

John   That's it Ringo.

Ringo (*stops. The others turn and look at him*)   Hey . . . hey I dunno if I fancy that.

Paul   Why?

Ringo   Me mum said if y' do that it makes y' blind.

George   No, that's wankin' that does that.

Ringo   Oh.

Paul   So you'll be alright.

Ringo   Apart from one thing . . .

John   What's that?

Rin␣o (*stumbling blindly after them*)   I can't see a bloody thing . . .

Paul   Pretty freaky . . . this . . . I'm flyin'.

Ringo   I think I'm . . . havin' . . . a bad trip . . . man . . . er, men!

George   Wow . . . that's really . . . cool man, cool . . .

Ringo   I know . . . I keep . . . thinkin' I'm a fridge . . .

John   I had this mate . . . once . . . It was at a . . . party. An' an' he was trippin', he went . . . into this kitchen . . . an' there was this gas cooker there . . . (*begins quietly to laugh*). An' he starts switchin' on all the . . . gas taps. (*laughs a bit more. The others begin to join in*) An' he kept sayin' . . . he said . . . how d' y' get this record player t' work? (*laughing uncontrolled by now. They're all falling about*) He turned on every gas knob . . . tryin' to make the cooker play records . . . (*shrieks of laughter*) He killed himself . . . waitin' for the records to come on the cooker . . . (*they roll about the floor, laughing helplessly*). What a gas . . .

As The **Beatles** *fall about, the* **Band** *play one more chorus of 'Lucy in the Sky'.*

Bert *comes on.*

Bert   Sergeant Pepper! Saved my life. Without noticing it, I'd become a juvenile geriatric, a pensioner in my teens until the Sergeant came along and taught me to say peace instead of hia. Love and peace to all my far out friends. (*This, to audience*) Love and peace, peace and love. Mind you my new found freedom had to be fought for.

Alice *on – very fast and Liverpool, frantic.*

Alice   Just look at you Bert. Just look at the state on you. Oh me mother she said, she said 'Marry him and you'll have a dog's life', and I have an' all. A blooming mongrel's life I've had with you. Beads in your hair. Well I'm up to here wi' it Bert. Look at you with y' poems an' y' flowers. Ye nothin' but a big soft tart. A man. You a man. Well I'm not puttin' up with it. I'm already under the doctor with me nerves. And me mother said, an' arr Maureen, she told me what you'd turned into . . . a hippy. Well I've 'ad enough. I tell you what. You've burnt your last joss stick with me Bert

McGhee. Other wives don't have to put up with it. I don't see why I should. I'm leaving you, Bert. It's over. It's finished. I'm off.

Bert   What. You mean you won't be back at all?

Alice   If you want me back you know what you can do. (*Off*.)

Bert   I couldn't believe me luck. Want her back? No chance. She'd only got past the front gate and I was on the blower to me mates telling them that I was starting Liverpool's first commune. It was great. We burnt joss sticks from morn to night. We played Pepper till the tracks were worn out. We even had a go at Yoga – till me mate Billy got cramp practising his full lotus. Don't laugh. He was stuck like that for three hours till the fire brigade came an' prised him apart. An' at night, you know, we'd go round the neighbours' gardens pinching flowers and giving them to anyone – the postman, the milkman. Arcadia Close became known as Little San Francisco. And Utopia! It might have gone on for ever – if I hadn't taken a flower to work for the foreman.

Foreman *enters. Big and boiler suited.* **Bert**, *flower in hand, approaches.*

Bert   These petals
    Over your mind I shower
    Turn in
    Turn on
    With flower power.

Foreman (*taking the flower he slowly rips off the petals*)
    Hickory
    Dickory
    Dickory dock
    Collect y' cards
    At five o'clock.

Foreman *off.* **Bert** *forward.*

Bert   With no more wages comin' into the house, me brothers an' sisters left Arcadia Close. Said they were goin' to another commune. But I know they all went back to work. (*Pause*) Slowly, the flowers started wiltin'. The joss sticks suddenly began to smell like smog.

An' for the first time in months I noticed that y' feet got wet . . . if y' wore sandals in the rain. '67 started to fall to bits for me . . . an' for them as well. In the middle of 1967 Brian Epstein was dead.

The **Band** *play 'Yesterday'.*

During the instrumental gap between penultimate and final verse, **Bert** *addresses the audience:*

Bert   Suddenly, they were alone in the world. He'd sheltered them, protected them and made good decisions on their behalf. In five years of the most phenomenal success ever known, the team had never put a foot wrong. In the eyes of the world they were invincible, in music an' business they always moved the right way, at the right time. But the team was five, the magic was five; and now, there were only four.

Complete the final verse of the song as The **Beatles** *enter. All sit except* **Paul** *who remains standing, looking at the other three.*

Bert   The rot had set in. (**Paul** *exits*). And slowly the greatest phenomenon in the history of music began to visibly decompose.

John   Nothing lasts. Everythin' comes down in the end. Y' grow up thinkin' Elvis is the King . . . an' when y' meet him he's just some feller . . . drugs are like that. They let y' down in the end . . .

George   Trips never last for ever.

Ringo   So what do we do now?

George *goes into a heavily breathing Lotus position which* **Ringo** *tries to copy, and fails.* **Paul** *enters, brisk, efficient.*

Paul   Right . . . let's go. Everything's booked, we're ready to start.

John   Start what?

Paul   The film.

John   Which film?

Paul   I told you . . . Magical Mystery Tour. Come on, everything's set up.

John   I'm not makin' no crappy film.

Paul   Listen . . . if you lot didn't sit around gettin' so bloody paranoid it wouldn't have to be a crappy film. We could produce somethin' that was as good as 'Pepper' was.

Ringo   Is there a good part in it for me . . . a good character part?

Paul   It's not that sort of film Ringo.

Ringo   Oh.

Paul   I've been reading loads of books about people like Bunnel an' Antonioni, Goddard . . . people like that. We're gonna do what they call an expressionist film.

Ringo   What, like them continental films, avant gardey like?

Paul   Yeah, right . . . now come on . . .

Ringo   I hate them films. Y' can never read the words at the bottom.

Paul   Look, I'm not askin' you to like it. Just make yourself available to work on it.

John   I thought we shared the decisions in this group.

Paul   Oh . . . Christ John. Since Brian died we haven't moved. What are we supposed to do? Fall to bits just because Brian isn't here anymore?

George   We could go and see the Maharishi again.

John   What for? He's like the rest of them, a goldhunter.

George   He's pretty bloody cosmic all the same.

John   As cosmic as my arse.

Paul   Look, do we make this film or not?

John   We'll think about it.

Paul (*pause*)   Right, right, well while you bastards are sittin' round thinkin' about it, I'm gonna get it started. (*Goes off.*)

Ringo   I wish Paul wouldn't try an' manage us now that Brian's gone.

George   He thinks he has to.

John   I'm not goin' through all them film hassles just to make the Paul McCartney Show.

Ringo   Like he wanted Sergeant Pepper to be. 'Here Ringo,' he says to me, 'move over, give me the sticks an' let me show you how to play this drum section.'

George   I can't complain. He did let me have my Indian song on the album.

Ringo   What's he wanna come up with one of these avant gardey films for? Why don't we just make a Western.

George   I think he's started to believe all those things that The Times an' those arty farty reviewers say about us.

John (*pause*)   I hardly ever talk to him now. (*Pause*) I don't want it t' be like that. We never write songs together anymore. We don't talk . . . we just stab at each other. I don't really want it to be like that . . . but that's how it's gone. I think we all must have grown up somewhere along the way.

Paul *re-enters.*

I thought you'd gone off to make a film.

Paul   Wait till you hear this. I've just seen Clive.

George   And?

Paul   He's finished goin' through the books . . . And if we don't move quickly we're going to be taken apart by the taxman.

Ringo   What do we do then?

Paul   Well, if you read this you'll see. We've got to spend and spend quickly. We've got to get rid of about two million dollars.

Ringo   I'll start smoking again.

Paul   He says we've got to invest so that eventually it will turn into profit. But at the moment we've got to be seen to be spending. Either that or a tax bill that could cripple us all. But it's okay. I've got this great idea for setting up a company, and I want to call it Apple.

They exit over this last line. **Klein** *enters. He is big, very ugly, and very Bronx. He should remind us all of our favourite gangster.*

Klein   My name is Alan Klein. There's a little sayin' of mine I thought y' should hear. It goes somethin' like this: 'Yea. Though I walk through the Valley of the shadow of Death I will fear no evil . . . for, I am the biggest bastard in the valley.' (*Pause as he surveys the scene.*) So no-one, but no-one puts one over on me . . . Right? (*Pause*) Now let me tell you something else . . . I always wanted The Beatles and with Epstein outta the way, all I had to do was wait . . . An' then I heard they was settin' up this Apple thing.

A large apple appears with a door cut out in it.

They must have been out of their heads when they came up with that one. Utopian business structure . . . I ask y'. I mean don't get me wrong, I got nott'n against Utopia, I've even bought a couple of records by Bobby Dylan, but what good's Utopia if it don't make a profit . . . That Apple was full of maggots right from the very start. To me, it was a prime case of . . . Apple Crumble (what do you want? – Shakespeare?) But was those Beatles worryin'? Huh, they didn't even notice what was happenin'. They was too busy playin' their games, too busy searchin' for somethin' to occupy themselves they didn't see they was bein' screwed. Remember that Julius Caesar? The guy who played with himself while Rome was boinin' down? Well it was the same with The Beatles. Johnny Lennon,

Lennon *enters with* **Yoko**

I found Johnny Lennon in a hotel in Amsterdam doin' somethin' called Bed Piece. Bed Piece, I ask y'?

Yoko   Bed Peace is saying peace and love to all the warring nations of the world. It is striving to bring joy and great happiness to the whole of mankind.

John   Yeh . . . that's it.

Klein   And Ringo . . . Ringo was gettin' it together on some film set.

Ringo *enters, dressed as Hamlet. He talks to an imaginary film director:*

Ringo   Hey Rodney . . . couldn't we get someone in to re-write this . . . as a Western, you know . . . No . . . Oh Jesus.

Klein (*helpless gesture*)   The world's gone nuts. Did you see it? Ringo Starr playing King Lear . . . Too much. And Paul . . . Paul was at home in Scotland . . . living with the sheep.

Linda *and* **Paul** *enter –* **Linda** *attempting to play a guitar.*

Paul   For Christ's sake, Linda, you've got to stretch your fingers to play B. Flat.

Linda   Your little wife is really trying, Pauly.

Klein   Ain't she just. Now George . . . George Harrison, he was spaced out on the banks of the Ganges (**George** *has entered with a sitar*) learnin', learnin' to play the sitar,

Beatles *and their wives exit.*

I had to see them, to talk to them. But every time I got on the phone all I ever heard was a bit of Shakespeare, four thousand moanin' sheep, the time in Indian dialect, or some screwy dame who kept tellin' me to put my finger up my arse for peace. I tell you. I was almost on the point of giving up, when at last The Beatles realized how rotten that Apple was.

Klein *off.* **Beatles** *revealed.*

John (*on the hoof*)   All I know is that the bastards aren't gonna make me bankrupt!

Ringo   It's not as bad as all that is it John?

George   It's worse Ritchie.

John   Twenty grand – twenty grand a week goin' out the back door. For Christ's sake, they think they can feed off the backs of The Beatles forever.

Paul (*to* **John**)   Maybe if there'd been a bit more work an' a little less Love and Peace you . . .

John (*barging in*)   You what? Don't you start. This (APPLE) was your idea. Utopia! Some bloody Utopia that loses four hundred thousand in its first year. And let's get that on record.

Paul (*angry*)   Listen! (*spelling it out*) It was an idea for all of us. What did you do to help it get off the ground? The only time you come runnin' is when we're goin' broke. Well, how are you gonna save us now Messiah? Are y' gonna get Yoko in to chant love an' peace. Oh yeh that'd bring the bank notes droppin' from the sky. That'd really turn on the Official Receiver. At least I came into the bloody office every day. I did try an' do somethin' for us.

Ringo   Look . . . can't we just . . .

George   Oh Sergeant McCartney's been doin' everythin' for us hasn' he? Remember, remember Pauly who let us play in his group with him?

John   Oh yeh. We all know how much kind Paul's been helpin' The Beatles. I mean, he thinks so much of us all that he's plannin' a solo record. That's how much Paul thinks of The Beatles.

Ringo   Oh come on John . . . . .

Paul   Okay. What did you expect me to do? Was I supposed to sit on me arse while you an' Yoko went off to liberate mankind? I wanna make music John. I'm not sittin' round waitin' for him (**Ringo**) to finish doin' his Marlon Brando. An' Christ knows why you're (**George**) complainin'. It was you who wouldn't tour when I wanted the band to get out on the road again. (*Pause*) I've got music to make . . . an' I'm gonna do it . . . Beatles or not!

John   Oh right . . . Pauly's got music to make!

Paul   Listen John . . . who are you tryin' to fool? Why the sudden interest in Beatles eh? Six months ago you were wantin' out of the group.

John   I stayed though.

Paul   Yeh. An' why? Because you were told about the adverse effect it could have on share prices if you left the group. Don't you start tryin' to lecture me. You stayed for one reason an' one reason only . . . money!

George   Listen . . . I'm goin' if y' don't mind. This was supposed to be a business meetin' . . . not a slangin' match.

John   Look George . . .

George (*firm*)   No – I've had enough of lookin', I've spent years lookin' an' listenin' to you two battlin' it out. Well thanks very much for lettin' me play in your band fellers. Give me a call if y' want me to play on anythin' . . . but otherwise, don't bother. There's a lot of songs I've got to get written. (*Pause as they watch him leave. He has sobered them slightly.*)

Paul (*sighs*)   Anyway . . . All that apart. I thought we came to talk about the money.

Ringo   An' as we all know, that's all The Beatles are nowadays.

He exits.

John   I don't need to talk about money. From now on Klein handles all my business.

Paul   Klein! Klein, what about the Eastmans?

John   What about them? They blew it! Klein'll do a better job. He'll straighten us out. From now on he handles all my stuff. George an' Ritchie agree with me.

Paul   Alright . . . (*nodding*) Okay. If that's the way it's gone . . .

John   Look, I know they're your in-laws an' all that . . .

Paul   . . . but I don't go with Klein. From now on, the Eastmans handle all *my* work.

John   Paul . . . Come on Paul, don't be an idiot. The money men are movin' in. We could end on the scrap heap after all. If we don't stick together we'll be eaten alive. Come on Paul . . . forget the in-laws. All's fair in love an' business.

Paul (*stubborn*)   From now on all my work is handled by the Eastmans.

John   Paul . . . .

Paul   No further comment.

Pause.

John   Are they handlin' your solo job an' all.

Paul   Yeh . . . yeh . . . why not?

John   Well . . . you'd better get them to put the release date back.

Paul   Pardon?

John   There's a group album ready . . . we can't let your solo effort go out just before it.

Paul (*incredulous*)   You can't . . . *you* can't . . . who can't?

John   Me, Ritchie an' George . . . the group . . . remember the group?

Paul   The group . . . yeh, the group, an' Klein an' Yoko Ono . . .

John   Look, if we let you release your solo before the group album it's . . .

Paul   It wouldn't matter a fart and you know it!

John   It'd kill sales on both albums.

Paul (*pointing, incensed*)   You lot . . . you've tried to fuck up my work once too often . . . Right. That's the game is it . . .

John   It's only the game you started.

Paul   An' it's the same game that I'll end.

They stare at each other.
Voice over:

Klein's voice   Listen. McCartney's out the group. So what are you worried for? I'm waiting for you, John.

Exit **Paul**, **Linda**, **John** *and* **Yoko**. **Band** *play 'We Can Work It Out'. Slides show headlines:*

1   'McCartney's Muzak Rubbish' by Lennon

2   *'Lennon Thinks He Is God' by McCartney*

3   *'Paul Always Thought He Was the Beatles' by Lennon.*

4   *'Lennon Was Always Jealous' by McCartney*

5   *'Other Beatles Delay Release of McCartney Solo Record'*

6   *'Paul McCartney Seeks Dissolution of Beatles Business Partnership'*

7   *'Beatles'*

8   *'Split'.*

At the end of the song, **Bert** *in.*

Bert   No-one was singing or whistling a Beatle tune when the deals were bein' made, when Triumph took over Nems, when Lew Grade an' ATV managed to get control of Northern. The Beatles had got caught up in the Power game. The Money game. And that – apart from one or two lawsuits an' lots of rumours – brings us to today. An' what's been happenin' today? Well, while I've been stood out here talkin' to you lot, there's been people driftin' in there, people with cameras, guys with contracts, fellers in Afghan coats an' training shoes. An' that makes me begin to suspect that the mob I'm waitin' for are already there, probably in the dressin' room while I'm stuck outside on the pavement with not even a ticket to see the show. Well, there's only one thing for it – there's a bog window around the back. If someone's forgotten to lock it, I'm in. See y'.

The dressing room which is now swarming with people. There should be lots of extras here bearing cameras, wearing headphones, carrying cables. Although the dialogue which follows has been printed separately, it should all happen at once, a very quick kaleidoscope scene. People surrounding The Beatles who look very weary. A television reporter is spot-lit.

Tv Man   This is Clive Kennedy speaking to you live from the Philharmonic Hall Liverpool where tonight The Beatles are to appear onstage. It's now twelve years since four young men turned the spotlight of the world onto this provincial backwater. As the news leaks out and crowds begin to form outside, the crowds, which are gathering to pay homage to this the superest supergroup of all, we are going inside the dressing room.

We will try to bring you an interview with one or all, of the group . . . let me see if I can get hold of one of them now.

An American film maker is trying to set up a deal.

Film Man   So will y' listen fellers . . . this ain't gonna be no bummer, I know y' hate the filmin' an' all that crap but I'm gonna give you guys a film that'll make you proud of yourselves . . .

Agent   We get control of your song rights, okay. They should never have gone in the first place. Now, in the States I reckon we should be able to screw about 25% royalty out of them on wholesale recording . . .

Film man   An' it'll make every other film you've ever done look like a home movie . . .

Man On Phone   Yeah, that's right, forty thousand tee shirts an' I want right across the front, 'The Beatles Are Back' in big bold lettering. I want them in the shops by tomorrow . . . well get your bloody finger out an' try . . .

Tv Man   Well things do seem to be a little chaotic here in Liverpool. But before I hand you back to the Nationwide studio, I'll just try once more to get a word with Ringo. Ringo . . . excuse me Ringo, would you like to say a word to the viewers?

Ringo   No I wouldn't.

Tv Man   Well, er apologies for that viewers . . . these things will happen in a live show. For the moment I'll just hand you back to the studio.

Promoter   We could easily make it a national tour . . . and then what about the States? I could get someone working on that right away. Perhaps a festival, open air so that we can get in as many as possible.

While this is going on we notice a figure climbing in through a window. It is **Bert**, *complete with guitar.*

George   Oh, for Chrissake. They've even started comin' in through the windows.

John   Just a quiet concert we said . . .

Film Man   I thought that was a really smart idea boys – tryin' to keep it quiet so that y' cause the maximum amount of interest.

Bert *comes forward and holds out his hand to* **George** *who walks right past him.*

George   Christ, even the hangers on are back with us . . .

Tv Man   Hey can I get in there to them, the studio is coming back to me in eight minutes and I've got to get something up . . .

Bert   Y' probably don't remember . . . (*holds out his hand to* **John** *but the* **Film Man** *just pushes him right out of the way*).

Film Man   Like, where George's Bangla Desh film fell outta the window was on the approach . . .

Agent   I'll provide you with personal management like you've never known before . . . I mean, look at the figures, now I guarantee I can get you those deals.

John *stands, moves free from a crowd,* **Bert** *goes up to him.*

Bert   Remember . . . in Hunt's Cross that time . . .

John (*shouting at everyone in the room*)   Shut up!

There is a silence. All we can hear is the sound which floats in through the window, sound which tells us people have begun to gather outside.

Are you all ready for a statement? Well start writin' now.

The reporters get their pencils ready.

Tv Man (*quietly*)   Studio, for Christ's sake, give me the studio . . .

John   When we came here today, it wasn't to make money. Not even to make history. We just wanted to make some music.

Paul *has started to pack the instruments into the coffin.*
We thought we could keep it quiet. We thought we could keep this
lot out. But it was a dream wasn't it? That's what you can tell the
fab listeners; tell them that we nearly got together again but this lot
wouldn't let us. It was just another stupid Beatle dream, like drugs
an' meditation, another dream which wouldn't work. Tell the fab
listeners we wanted to play but the music got lost in contracts an'
deals. You lot stay, have a drink, but forget about us, we're goin'
home.

The **Beatles** *pick up the coffin and march out. We hear the crowds
outside chanting 'We want The Beatles, we want The Beatles, we
want The Beatles' etc.* **Bert** *sits down in the corner and quietly
picks his guitar.*

Ringo returns for his drumsticks pursued by the media freaks.

Promoter   Come on Ringo . . . don't be stooped hey? Get the
'fabs' to come back here.

Agent   Look Ringo . . . why don't you stay? Forget the others.
We'll set it up as a solo concert for you.

Film Man   Hey, yeah . . . The Ringo Show. Whaddya say Ringo?

Promoter   Christ, come on Ringo. We've got to have someone
out there. We can't disappoint all those people.

Film Man   They're expectin' somethin' . . . we can't let them
down.

The **Film Man** *is tugging at* **Ringo**'s *sleeve.* **Ringo**, *through the
above dialogue, has been looking at* **Bert** *who is quietly playing
his guitar.* **Ringo** *pulls free. He walks across to* **Bert**. *They all
follow him.*

Ringo   Y' need someone t' play? Right?

Film Man   He's gonna do it . . . Ringo's gonna do it . . .

Tv Man   Studio . . . for God's sake, studio!

Ringo   There's your lad. (**Bert**) Hey pal, how would you like to
be a pop star?

Bert   Who, me? What . . . yeah.

Ringo   What's your name?

Bert   Bert.

Ringo   Not any more, Leroy.

Promoter   Leroy . . .

Film Man   Hey . . . Leroy Lover!

Bert   No . . . the name's er . . .

Ringo   There you go lads. He'll make a million for you.

Promoter   I can see it . . . I can see it.

Film Man   Jesus . . . yes indeed.

Ringo   He's all yours fellers . . . a present from The Beatles . . .

The **Band** *play a repetitive chorus line from 'Working Class Hero'. The Hustlers go to work on making* **Leroy Lover**.

As they finish off their work, **Ringo** *goes and stands by the door. They all stand back and admire their product.*

Ringo   Bloody marvellous.

Promoter   Do you really think so Ringo?

Ringo   Magic, magic. Go on . . . get him out there quick, get him out an' tell all the world that The Beatles came, an' The Beatles went, an' this is all they could manage to leave behind. (*Exits*.)

The Media Men take **Leroy** *off as we return to the* **Tv Interviewer**.

Tv Man   Welcome back to the Philharmonic Hall Liverpool where tonight we were to have brought you the return of the pop phenomenon of the Sixties, The Beatles. I say, were to have brought you, because tonight you can witness an incredible scene. Instead of the sixties phenomenon, we bring you the stamp of the Seventies, the man The Beatles chose to replace them . . . Leroy Lover.

Promoter   Ready . . . house lights are down . . . spots are going up . . . Leroy, you're on.

Pushes **Bert** *onto the stage. He is the complete 70's star. The screaming starts immediately. The* **Band** *play the intro to his song and he gyrates – screams. Phony American accent.*

Bert   This is one for all the girls . . . (*screams*) I love you all . . . but maybe, out there tonight . . . is the one girl . . . like the girl in my song . . . (*screams. Straight into the song*).

I Will Be Your Love

I will be your love
If you will be my love
If you will be my sweet little girl.

I'd love you forever
We could spend our lives together
We could defy the whole wide world . . .

What a romance we could have
You could be my sweet sixteen
What an affair we could live
Me an' my teenage dream . . .

I will be your love
If you will be my love
If you will be my sweet little girl

I'd love you forever
We could spend our lives together
We could defy the whole wide world . . .

For the song's instrumental break, **Bert** *goes into a big bum gyration. Suddenly the music changes and we hear the notes of 'Day in the Life' forcing their way in. Over the first two verses of the song we see the tableau from the Pepper Album being formed.*

Bert   That was it . . . I made it in the end. I made it but I knew that the sort of music I made was rubbish. I could never believe that anyone would buy me; but they did, they bought me by the million. I could have refused it, resisted it, but I didn't; it was easier to become a Working Class Hero than go on bein' a working class worker. So I went out on stage every night an' hated the muck

I fed to them. But that's the way things had turned out. The hole that The Beatles had left behind was plugged up with plastic men like me. An' every scream that came my way, every record I ever sold, every puerile date I played told me that my mates The Beatles were dead. An' eventually I began to wonder if they'd ever really been here at all.

Bert *moves back and takes his place in the tableau. The entire company sing the final two verses of 'Day in the Life'. It should be both a chilling lament, and a final celebration.*

Curtain

The End